RED CLOUD

The Oklahoma Western Biographies
Richard W. Etulain, General Editor

This photograph of Red Cloud taken sometime during his years of influence shows a confident leader, one who could be a formidable obstacle to the designs of the federal government. *(Photograph by J. E. Meddaugh, Nebraska State Historical Society)*

RED CLOUD

Warrior-Statesman of the Lakota Sioux

By Robert W. Larson

UNIVERSITY OF OKLAHOMA PRESS : NORMAN AND LONDON

Larson, Robert W., 1927–
    Red Cloud: warrior-statesman of the Lakota Sioux / by
Robert W. Larson.
        p.   cm. — (The Oklahoma western biographies; v. 13)
    Includes bibliographical references and index.
    ISBN 0-8061-2930-1 (alk. paper)
    1. Red Cloud, 1822–1909. 2. Oglala Indians—Kings and
rulers—Biography. 3. Oglala Indians—Wars. 4. Oglala
Indians—Government relations.   I. Title. II. Series.
E99.O3R374   1997
973'.04975'092—dc20
[B]   96-30793
                                                                            CIP

Red Cloud: Warrior-Statesman of the Lakota Sioux is Volume 13
in *The Oklahoma Western Biographies*.

The paper in this book meets the guidelines for permanence
and durability of the Committee on Production Guidelines for
Book Longevity of the Council on Library Resources, Inc. ⊗

        1   2   3   4   5   6   7   8   9   10

For my grandchildren,
so that they may know a great people.

Contents

Illustrations

Series Editor's Preface

STORIES of heroes and heroines have intrigued many generations of listeners and readers. Americans, too, have been captivated by the lives of military, political, and religious figures and of intrepid explorers, pioneers, and rebels.

The Oklahoma Western Biographies Series endeavors to build on this fascination with biography and to link it with another subject of abiding interest to Americans: the frontier of the American West. Although the series volumes carry no source notes, they are prepared by leading scholars, are soundly researched, and include a brief listing of sources used. Each volume is a lively synthesis based on thorough examination of pertinent primary and secondary sources.

Above all, the Oklahoma Western Biographies aim at two goals: to provide readable life stories of significant westerners and to show how their lives illuminate a notable topic, an influential movement, or a series of important events in the history and culture of the American West.

Robert Larson's new biography of the notable Indian leader Red Cloud accomplishes all these goals. Diligently researched, smoothly written, and impressively presented, Larson's study of Red Cloud will appeal to scholars and general readers alike. In the last generation or two many Americans have lionized warriors such as Sitting Bull and Crazy Horse, but, Larson implies, it is time that we see anew the central importance of Red Cloud, who helped shape events during those tumultuous years when the Sioux were driven from their free, nomadic existence on the plains to reservations, where they become increasingly dependent on government largesse.

Larson's account is neither one-sided nor simplistic. He admits that Red Cloud was sometimes brutal, particularly in his early years; eager beyond necessity to make his name; and sometimes duplicitous in his dealing with others, white and Native American alike. Larson also comments at length on Red Cloud's use of delaying tactics, obstructionism, and other combative methods to hold on to Sioux lands and thereby sustain tribal organization and cultural traditions. To his credit, the author demonstrates that what contemporaries often criticized as Red Cloud's treachery and double-mindedness were, in fact, revealing examples of the warrior-statesman's ability to stall off the inevitable, to hold on to Sioux rights and traditions as long as possible before they were trampled under the white juggernaut that he saw in Washington and had experienced firsthand on the Northern Plains.

Overall, Larson's biography smoothly blends traditional historical methods with the new social and environmental historiography so popular in the last generation. As he also shows here, Red Cloud, probably more than any other Sioux leader, was the central figure in the transitional period between the nomadic and reservation years. Altogether, Larson provides the first thorough life story of Red Cloud in more than thirty years.

RICHARD W. ETULAIN

University of New Mexico

Preface

NINETEEN ninety-seven is a good year to publish a biography of Red Cloud. A generation has passed since any major study of this remarkable Lakota leader has appeared, and attitudes toward Native Americans have changed significantly during that period. These changes in perception are a result, in part, of the revelations made in recent years about the valiant effort of nineteenth-century Plains tribes to preserve their traditional way of life. Red Cloud was in the forefront of the resistance, as both historians George E. Hyde and James C. Olson recognized in their earlier studies of the great Oglala chief. Yet neither of them was aware of the true value and nature of Red Cloud's 1893 autobiography; Hyde probably did not even know it existed. Indeed, Red Cloud's long-neglected autobiography was not authenticated until R. Eli Paul, senior research historian of the Nebraska State Historical Society, validated it in a 1994 article for *Montana: The Magazine of Western History*. Also contributing to these newer perspectives about the last stand of Native Americans against the encroaching tide of white settlement was a judicious reworking by other historians of such primary sources as the interviews conducted by Judge Eli S. Ricker during the early part of this century.

My own interest in Red Cloud goes back many years. It was part of a fascination I had with the Sioux while growing up in the West during the 1930s and 1940s. Although I loved the lofty Rockies to the west, it was the Plains country to the east of my Denver home that best retained the flavor of the Old West. This sometimes overlooked area included the rolling prairie lands extending from the Arkansas River valley to the south, northward along the South Platte River to the broken country encompassing such sites as Pawnee Buttes in northeastern Colorado and Scotts Bluff in western Nebraska, to the Black Hills of South Dakota, where the High Plains sprawled eastward to Wyoming's Powder River country and northward to the Little Bighorn country of southern Montana. These lands were once the hunting grounds of the Cheyenne, Arapaho, and Lakota tribes, whose turbulent histories had always enchanted me.

The Sioux, or the Lakotas, as they prefer to call themselves, were particularly intriguing to me, perhaps because their large numbers made them the most formidable of this region's early nomadic inhabitants. Sitting Bull, of course, was a household name, only rivaled by Geronimo as far as its ease of recognition was concerned. As the years passed and my knowledge of the Sioux grew, I, along with an increasing number of people, began to understand better the other great Lakota chiefs, such as the martyred Crazy Horse and the respected Red Cloud. Yet Red Cloud still remained a rather remote and misunderstood figure. In my own research, I could not understand why this imposing leader, one of the few Indian chiefs to make the federal government back down (as he did in the case of the ill-fated Powder River Road), continued to project such a blurred image, notwithstanding Olson's excellent study on his vital role in Sioux affairs during the post–Civil War years. It was with this puzzle in mind that I began my current research on Red Cloud six years ago.

It is difficult to know where to start in acknowledging the valuable assistance given me on this project. Surely R. Eli Paul was of inestimable help in authenticating Red Cloud's autobiography and making it available to me. He also directed me to the relevant Sioux collections at his Lincoln archive and made available to me some important materials he gathered from the South Dakota State Historical Society. Others associated with Paul who were helpful to me at the Nebraska State Historical Society include James Potter, editor of *Nebraska History*, and John Carter, Katherine Wyatt, and Marty Miller, who helped me acquire most of the photographs used in this book. Assistance in gathering other photographs and essential materials was provided by the staff of the Western History Department of the Denver Public Library under the direction of Eleanor Gheres; A. D. Mastrogiuseppe, the curator, proved particularly helpful. Palma E. Wilson, chief ranger at the Agate Fossil Beds National Monument in western Nebraska, was kind enough to photocopy a May 13, 1908, letter written in Red Cloud's behalf that provided the premise for my first chapter. Sources recommended by Herbert T. Hoover of the University of South Dakota were also crucial to that chapter.

Invaluable background information was also given me during my 1992 research trip to the Black Hills and the Pine Ridge Reservation in South Dakota. Through contacts largely arranged by J. Gilbert Hause, former president of Black Hills State College and a board member of the Crazy Horse Foundation, I was able to interview Jessie Sundstrom, recording secretary to the board of directors of the Crazy Horse Foundation, and Arthur W. Zimiga, vice-president of development and research at Oglala State College. During my visit to Pine Ridge, I also had profitable conversations with Brother C. M. Simon, director of the Heritage Center of the Red Cloud Indian School, and with William K. Powers, whose anthropological studies have greatly improved our understanding of the Lakota Sioux.

Other people to whom I owe much include David Fridtjof Halaas, chief historian of the Colorado Historical Society, who not only provided me with helpful information about Red Cloud's sturdy Cheyenne allies but also, during the society's 1993 tour of the major Indian battle sites, increased my appreciation and understanding of the bloody Sioux wars of the 1860s and 1870s. I gained additional insights during the 1994 Little Bighorn Legacy Symposium in Billings, where I was able to benefit from conversations with knowledgeable scholars and students of the American Indian such as Joseph Porter, Richard Williams, and Jerome A. Greene. Ideas of my former wife, Carole Larson, regarding the use of photo captions were also most useful, as were the ideas provided by several former colleagues at the University of Northern Colorado; these include several members of the History Department and retired professor Norman T. Oppelt, whose own work on Indian culture and education has been extensive. Jerry Keenan of Boulder was also helpful, giving me insights into such military matters as brevet ranks in the post–Civil War army.

Throughout the entire process I received the aid and cooperation of John M. Drayton and his efficient editorial staff at the University of Oklahoma Press. Of exceptional help was Richard W. Etulain of the University of New Mexico, General Editor of the Oklahoma Western Biographies; his editorial assistance undoubtedly improved the quality of this book. I am especially indebted to Noel Parsons, who edited my manuscript with both knowledge and good judgment, and to Associate Editor Sarah Iselin, who provided me with all the help I could possibly need. I also owe much to two of the manuscript's readers, Robert M. Utley and John H. Monnett; their constructive criticism did much to improve the final product.

Much of the essential momentum necessary to complete a project of this caliber was provided by my wife, Peggy, an honest and patient critic who typed the first draft of my study, and Patricia L. Reed, who typed the final draft. Words of encouragement were supplied by my sister and walking companion, Sally Cumine, and words of inspiration by my son and daughter and their families, including my grandchildren, to whom I have dedicated this book.

ROBERT W. LARSON

Denver, Colorado

RED CLOUD

CHAPTER I

The "Old Trails"

IN May of 1908 a half-blind old Sioux chief visited the ranch of one of his good friends, Captain James H. Cook. The chief and his party camped contentedly along the wooded banks of the Niobrara River, which flowed through Cook's spread near the now famous fossil beds of western Nebraska; the cool shade of the area was in sharp contrast to the treeless, wind-swept hills of the chief's home in Pine Ridge. This stooped and wrinkled man in his late eighties was Red Cloud, once among the most powerful and best known Indian leaders of the country. Forty years before, his name commanded instant recognition and respect from both whites and Indians. Indeed, for years the hills around Cook's ranch were part of a vast area widely known as Red Cloud country.

Red Cloud felt no resentment that Cook, who was among the thousands of intruders now living on once prized Indian lands, grazed cattle where the Sioux's beloved buffalo had roamed. Cook had been a true friend, a man whom Red Cloud once backed as Indian agent for the Pine Ridge Reservation in South Dakota, where Red Cloud's Oglalas, one of seven tribes of the once formidable Western Sioux confederation, had lived for almost a generation. As proof of his good will, Red Cloud put his mark on a May 13 letter written for him by his nephew Phillip Romero in which Red Cloud characterized Cook as not only a loyal friend but also one whose words should be respectfully heeded by all of Red Cloud's people.

The old chief urged Cook in this gracious letter to keep a portrait of the chief painted by one of his host's friends, Bessie Sandes Butler, a graduate of the Chicago Art Institute, during an earlier visit to the Cook ranch. His comments regarding this painting, made seventeen months before his death, also summed up Red Cloud's perception of where the Sioux were during this first decade of the twentieth century, which most of his people viewed as a period of decline. He urged Cook to keep the painting so that Red Cloud's children and Cook's children could "always Go and look at the face of one of the Last of the old Chiefs that Lived before the white men come [*sic*] to take over lands and turn us from the old trails we had followed for so many hundreds of years."

Red Cloud could not have known all the specifics, but the "old trails" he alluded to in his reminiscence included countless long and twisting ones taken by the Sioux during their tumultuous history. Most of those trails extended from the woodlands of Minnesota to the High Plains west of the hundredth meridian. They were the pathways of an epic migration that took more than two centuries, a migration that was largely obscured by the lost or hazy memories of Red Cloud's people. That part of the Sioux heritage that Red Cloud could recall most vividly, of course, was the one encompassed by his own life. It was a collection of the old chief's rich memories: the excitement of the buffalo hunt, the anticipation of a war party ready to count coup, the feeling of freedom afforded by a swift mount, and the knowledge that the tribe's hard-working women could break camp within minutes so that a wandering band could move to a new river bottom where game was plentiful. Indeed, Red Cloud's life probably spanned his people's most glorious years, when mounted Sioux warriors dominated Indian life from the Missouri River westward to Wyoming's isolated Bighorns and from the upper Republican River in the south to the Yellowstone River in the north.

Red Cloud's life also spanned the tragic decline of his people; in the late nineteenth century their golden age began to unravel, and they were forced to live on reservations that comprised only a modest part of their once grand domain. Red Cloud had been one of the most conspicuous leaders in resisting this bleak de-

cline and had reason to feel its consequences more than most
Sioux.

The aging Oglala would probably have appreciated the
tragedy suffered by his people even more if his knowledge of
their more remote past had not been based almost exclusively
on oral tradition. Written documentation would have provided
him with a more complete picture, but it too was scarce. Historian George E. Hyde, in his *Red Cloud's Folk*, noted that for
twenty years following the Sioux's crossing of the Missouri
River, about the time of the American Revolution, there was
practically no solid information about their activities except for
that provided by the winter counts.

The winter counts were the closest thing to a written language that the Sioux and some of the other Plains tribes had.
They were pictographs, drawn on deerskins or buffalo hides,
that pictured one major event in the life of the Sioux for each
year. Although some of these winter counts dated back to the
1700s, they were more commonplace during the nineteenth century. While collectively these pictographic records revealed the
kinds of experiences the Sioux regarded as important, their depiction of only one event per year obviously limited their value.
Nevertheless, each winter count provided at least a snapshot of
life during a given time. In 1857, for example, the Brulé Sioux
Iron Shell's count was called the Buffalo Bull Hunt because it
depicted the destruction of a herd of bison made up exclusively
of bulls. A Sioux warrior born in 1857, as a consequence, could
say he was born the year of the Buffalo Bull Hunt.

There were, of course, a few written sources which could have
improved Red Cloud's memory. These included the recorded
observations of French, English, Spanish, and American traders,
trappers, and explorers. Although as written records these
sources could have been helpful, they tended to reflect the values
and priorities of the European and American observers rather
than the values and priorities of the Sioux; thus, they, too,
were flawed.

Were the old Sioux chief alive today, his historical memory

could benefit from the archaeological findings made since his death in 1909. Curiously, though, his knowledge of the pre-Minnesota years of his people would not be substantially better. In fact, the only consensus that today's historians, ethnologists, anthropologists, and other scientists share about this earlier era is that the Sioux probably came to Minnesota from somewhere in the South. Because they belonged to the large and widely scattered Siouan linguistic family, numerically second only to the Algonquian language family among the Indians north of Mexico, some scholars have speculated that the ancestors of the modern Sioux (after they had presumably crossed the Bering Strait) might have come from the southeastern part of the United States. The Catawbas, for example, the principal tribe in the East to speak a Siouan dialect, lived in the Carolinas. Other students of these migrating people have located the early Sioux in the Ohio River valley, where they allegedly wandered for many years as hunters and food gatherers. About the time of Columbus, however, intense pressure from the powerful and feared Iroquois Confederacy pushed them north and west toward the headwaters of the Mississippi, where they began their lives in the Minnesota woodlands. Additional evidence about these "old trails," to use Red Cloud's own words, is not much more conclusive than that.

More revealing, as far as the Sioux's own perception of their historical origins, is that important institution they called the Seven Council Fires. According to tribal tradition, the Sioux evolved as an association of seven nomadic tribes. Their council fires provided the glue that held this loose confederation together. The council fires around which they were organized ultimately became the symbol of that loose confederation. The seven Sioux tribes were the Mdewakantons, Sissetons, Wahpekutes, Wahpetons, Yanktons, Yanktonais, and Tetons. The Santee Sioux, many of whom still live in Minnesota, trace their heritage back to those tribes that tended the first four of these seven council fires. The Tetons, or Western Sioux, Red Cloud's people, would become the most numerous of the

Sioux and would migrate the farthest west; in fact their name, when translated into English, means "Dwellers of the Plains." All of the tribes belonging to the Seven Council Fires spoke the Siouan language, and all called themselves by the same name, which when translated means "allies." The Santees pronounced the word Dakota, the Yanktons and Yanktonais pronounced it Nakota, and the Tetons, Lakota. In recent years the term *Lakota* has become increasingly popular in designating the Teton Sioux because it is the name they use and prefer.

The history of the Sioux after their arrival in northern Minnesota during the sixteenth century was dictated to a surprising degree by three European imports: the gun, the horse, and the devastating disease smallpox. Of these three causes for change, the gun had the most immediate impact. The introduction of European arms by the late 1600s had a particularly significant effect on the Sioux and was one of the major reasons for the Lakota migration westward; obviously, consideration of an adequate food supply, such as the availability of game, was also an important factor.

The gun altered the Sioux way of life in more ways than one. During their early years in the woodlands of the upper Mississippi, life was fairly simple. The Sioux, like most Indians in this region, were a forest people, hunting in the woods and gathering wild rice from the marshes. They may have grown some corn, but planting crops was not a major economic pursuit; the early Sioux were never known as an agricultural people like their stout allies of the nineteenth century, the Cheyennes. Much Sioux travel was by bark canoe, although Red Cloud's nomadic ancestors also blazed those winding forest trails that enlivened the old chief's imagination. Because they were aggressive as well as numerous, they did well in their bitter rivalry with the largely Algonquian-speaking tribes living near them, against whom they waged almost constant war.

But their growing mastery in this region was eventually challenged. For example, the arrival of the French and English in the interior of North America tended to push many tribes westward,

thus increasing the population of the vast woodlands adjacent
to the Great Lakes, including the area around that 132,000-
acre lake, Mille Lacs, in northern Minnesota, where most of
the early Sioux were concentrated. By the mid-seventeenth century the influence of these Europeans became more direct as
French traders entered the region in search of furs. In the long
run, though, the English would have a greater impact on the
lives of the woodland tribes. The colony of New France was
based on the fur trade; therefore, it was to the French advantage to keep intact the woodland habitat in which furbearing
animals thrived. The English from the more populous Thirteen
Colonies, however, were primarily agriculturalists, and when
they moved into the continent's hinterland in significant numbers, the very essence of the forest primeval was profoundly
threatened.

Even before these European intruders arrived in the Great
Lakes region in appreciable numbers, their influence was felt
through the trade patterns they had already established. The
French, for example, placing a high value on furs that could
be marketed in Europe, willingly traded for them the firearms,
liquor, trinkets, and household items the Indians coveted. The
English also traded arms for furs; the effects of their trade, always more lucrative because of Britain's substantial mercantile
base and superior merchant marine, was even more disruptive.
Armed with English weaponry, the Five Nations of the powerful Iroquois Confederacy were able to rampage through the
woodlands below the Great Lakes, forcing many tribes in that
region to move north with the Sioux or push farther west. Algonquian tribes, especially those in Canada, received the same
tempting trade package that the Iroquois had been offered. Although their traditional way of life was also jeopardized in ways
too subtle to realize at first, they, too, eagerly traded for the
European muskets which gave them a decided advantage over
such warlike rivals as the Sioux.

French accounts probably give the best evidence about the decisive advantages that early possession of European arms could
provide. They indicate that, before the arrival of the gun, Sioux

influence in the area west of the Great Lakes was both strong and expanding. In fact, the French trader Nicholas Perrot revealed that the Sioux, before 1650, conducted devastating raids on their hated rivals, the Crees, an Algonquian people living north of them. The introduction of European arms, however, changed the old balance of power significantly. In 1674, for example, a Cree party armed with guns boldly massacred a number of Sioux envoys at Sault Sainte Marie, their Sioux victims having only flint knives and other primitive weapons to defend themselves.

When the English reached the Great Lakes area, those tribes that had already been strengthened through trade with the French substantially improved their favorable position. In 1684, a large flotilla of Cree canoes sailed down the Hayes River to Hudson Bay to trade with the English; the Crees were especially interested in acquiring guns and ammunition in exchange for their furs. Because many of these weapons would be used against the Sioux, this new trade made the Sioux even more vulnerable.

The Crees were not the only Indians to gain from early contacts with European traders. The Chippewas, located east and north of the Sioux, near the base of Michigan's upper peninsula, also acquired arms that could be used against the troublesome Sioux. These Indians, also known as the Ojibwas, were being squeezed on one side by the Iroquois, whom they dubbed "the True Adders," and on the other side by the Sioux, whom they dubbed "the Lesser Adders." Because the Sioux were not armed with European guns, the Chippewas turned on them, forcing these hated rivals to retreat to the west and the south. The Chippewa word for Lesser Adder, incidentally, was Nadoweisiw, the last syllable of which was garbled by the French into the word Sioux, the term by which most Americans know Red Cloud's people today. Unfortunately, it is a negative word meaning "enemy."

Regardless of the pressures the Chippewas were able to put on the Sioux, the Crees and their closest allies, the Assiniboins, were probably most responsible for launching the great Sioux migration west to the plains. The Assiniboins, originally a Sioux people, were located between the Crees and Yanktonai Sioux. As these two neighbors were constantly at war, the Assiniboins became the object of fierce pressure from both sides. Because their survival was at stake, they ultimately felt compelled to trade with the Crees, especially when the Crees acquired guns. When the Yanktonais became aware of this trade, they retaliated against their Sioux brethren, especially when they heard that the Assiniboins and Crees were intermarrying. Put in such an impossible position, the Assiniboins joined the Crees, placing their security above factors of blood and custom. Eventually the Assiniboins became a separate people, who, armed with European guns and allied with the Crees, warred against the rest of the Sioux for perhaps a generation.

Because of this struggle the Sioux began a slow retreat southward toward the Minnesota River. The Yanktonais and the Yanktons gave ground first. The embattled Yanktonais, being geographically closest to the Crees, reluctantly abandoned their familiar hunting grounds between the headwaters of the Mississippi and spacious Red Lake. This migration left the Tetons or Lakotas, who had been living to their south, near present-day Sauk Rapids, Minnesota, in an exposed position.

Sometime after 1670 the migrating Yanktonais reached the prominent elbow bend of the Minnesota River near Swan Lake, a natural dividing point for all the westward-bound Sioux. There, a difficult choice had to be made. Should they follow the Minnesota River to its headwaters far to the west, or should they cross the river and move into the tall-grass prairie below? Following the wooded banks of the Minnesota River westward would keep them in a more familiar country, but heading southward also had its advantages. The region south of the river, for one thing, was home to large herds of buffalo, which at that time ranged as far east as the Appalachian Mountains. The value of these craggy beasts was almost immediately recognized; not only were they capable of providing an abundant food supply, but their hides were also an excellent source of clothing and shelter. Consequently, even though the Yanktonais and Yanktons were being forced southward by Crees and Assiniboins, teeming herds of buffalo were drawing them at the same time into the rich, largely unbroken prairie south of the Minnesota. Apparently, the Yanktonais, historically the older or parent group of the two, elected to follow the Minnesota River westward, while the Yanktons pushed across the river and headed south to occupy the land between the Blue Earth River, a tributary of the Minnesota, and the famous Pipestone Quarry in southwestern Minnesota.

The Lakotas took basically the same route. Although it is unclear whether they preceded or followed the Yanktonais and Yanktons in this migration, most evidence favors the latter assumption. The Lakotas, it appears, dwelt in the Sauk Rapids region along the Mississippi as late as 1680. It was not until about the year 1700 that they joined the Yanktonais and Yanktons in the new Sioux hunting lands far to the south. In fact, it was the Lakotas who ultimately blazed the legendary trails westward to the Dakota country, becoming the vanguard of the Sioux migration to the Great Plains. Other tribes of the Seven Council Fires were also being forced to evacuate their traditional hunting lands; by 1735, for example, many Santee Sioux, who had borne the brunt of Chippewa attacks, reached the elbow bend of the Minnesota River. They, too, divided; members of the more conservative parent group of these Eastern Sioux followed the river westward, while the rest crossed the river into the prairie country of southern Minnesota.

During this migration the individualism associated with the Sioux was boldly revealed. The Oglalas, one of the largest of the Lakota tribes, insisted on crossing the Minnesota River after they reached its elbow bend. These people, whom Red Cloud would lead many generations later, would scatter on the prairie below, seeking the shelter of woodlands along the Blue Earth River for their encampments. A French trader, who met them because they wintered near his stockade in 1780, referred to the Oglalas and their campsites as the Village Divided into Many Small Bands. This term was an appropriate one given the fact that *oglala* means "scattered" or "divided" in the Sioux language.

Joining the Oglalas in their trek across the river were the Burnt

Thighs or, as they later would become known, the Brulés. This Lakota tribe would stay in the south with the Oglalas, eventually pushing west with them. Ultimately, the Lakotas would break into seven distinct tribes, of which the Brulés and Oglalas would become the most adventurous, at least at this early date. The other five would follow the Minnesota River to its headwaters, cautiously paralleling the Brulés and the Oglalas in their bolder course westward.

These more conservative tribes which followed the Minnesota River probably comprised the parent group of those Lakotas who evacuated their homeland to the north because of Cree and Assiniboin attacks. The fact that they followed the more familiar woodland terrain along the river, where more traditional game such as deer abounded and where beaver could be trapped for the fur trade, is one important indication of their conservatism. Indeed, their more adventuresome kin, the Oglalas and the Brulés, eventually nicknamed them the Saones, meaning Shooters among the Trees. While this name also applied to the Yanktonais, who rarely strayed too far from the banks of the Minnesota, it was, until the late nineteenth century, the most familiar term for those Lakotas who stayed close to the river.

Although the Saones, or northern Lakotas, proceeded much more slowly to the west than did the Oglalas and Brulés, they eventually reached the head of the Minnesota River, camping for many years around Big Stone Lake before moving to the banks of the Missouri, where they congregated upriver from the Oglalas and Brulés. One of these five northern tribes was the Miniconjous, or Those Who Plant by the Stream, a group which, according to ethnologist Harry Anderson, was the largest of the Saones when Lewis and Clark reached the Upper Missouri in the early 1800s. Another Saone tribe was the Two Boilings or Two Kettle Sioux. When all the Lakotas finally crossed the Missouri to live on the Great Plains, the Miniconjous and the Two Kettles located just north of the Brulés, who were positioned southeast of the tribe with the greatest wanderlust of all, Red Cloud's Oglalas.

Other members of these migrating Saones included the Sihasapas, or Blackfeet Sioux, and the Itazipchos, or Without Bows (better known by their French name, Sans Arcs). The Lakotas of the fifth Saone tribe were called Hunkpapas, or Those Who Camp at the Entrance. This name was a prestigious one because the entrance was always an honored place in any circle-shaped Sioux encampment. Although the Hunkpapas later gained great renown for their role in the Battle of the Little Bighorn, Sitting Bull and Gall being Hunkpapa leaders, they were probably the last of the Lakotas to venture across the Missouri in search of a permanent home on the Northern Plains.

Expansion across the plains following the division of tribes at the Minnesota River's elbow bend was slow at first. There were, of course, bountiful herds of buffalo to hunt on the treeless lands south of the river. But without horses, killing these mobile beasts was not always easy. The men of the tribe, working in close cooperation, would often sneak up on the milling herds, concealing themselves with wolf skins over their backs until they could get close enough to strike. Many times they would coordinate their movements in order to panic the animals and drive them over cliffs or into steep ravines, where the women could butcher and skin their broken bodies. Travel from one camp to another was also slow and ponderous. Women and children were often used as beasts of burden, carrying heavy loads for miles upon miles. Dogs were regarded as work animals rather than pets. Equipment for travel would be loaded on their backs or tied to the poles of the heavy travois they dragged.

There were other reasons for the slow progress of the Sioux. The abundance of buffalo herds below the Minnesota River kept them fairly close to their old homes in the north. Trading fairs at the confluence of the Minnesota and Mississippi rivers also discouraged the Sioux from drifting too far west. By the early eighteenth century, these yearly fairs became increasingly significant to the Sioux, who began to acquire needed guns and ammunition from them. But their push westward, as slow as it was, would ultimately affect the entire region. By 1750, for example, many of these trade fairs were being held at the headwaters of the Minnesota River to attract the westering Sioux.

The acquisition of guns from these trade fairs emboldened the Oglalas and the Brulés to attack two rival Siouan-speaking tribes, the Iowas and the Otoes, who, as late as 1700, claimed the lands along the Blue Earth River. These two tribes were driven west to join the Omahas, another Siouan tribe, which was living along the banks of the Big Sioux River, where the present-day states of Iowa and South Dakota meet. The Omahas had already been driven out of the Pipestone Quarry district in southwestern Minnesota sometime after 1680. As the Yanktons were the aggressors in this case, further evidence is provided that the Yanktonais and Yanktons preceded even the Oglalas and the Brulés in the early Sioux push to the west. Eventually the Omahas, Iowas, and Otoes sought refuge in the Missouri River country. But their new homes further west did not make them immune from Sioux attacks; when the Oglalas and Brulés finally reached the Dakota country, they organized periodic expeditions against these and other Missouri tribes, their war parties often using the Big Sioux and Little Sioux rivers to canoe to their destinations.

The Lakota tribes did not reach the east bank of the Missouri River in appreciable numbers until about 1760. The impetus for this major step in their westward migration, which took the Oglalas and the Brulés even further from the still-important trading fairs along the Minnesota River, were the dwindling numbers of bison remaining on the plains adjacent to the Blue Earth River. Once plentiful, these herds were being rapidly depleted because many eastern or Santee Sioux were now hunting there. Consequently, the two Lakota groups felt compelled to migrate westward, bypassing the Yanktons, who were finding game plentiful enough near the head of the Des Moines River. Although the Oglalas and Brulés first moved into the James River valley east of the Missouri River, they finally left that home for a much more extensive one along the banks of the meandering Missouri.

When these two tribes of southern Lakotas reached the Missouri, they encountered one of their most formidable barriers, a Caddoan-speaking Plains tribe called the Arikaras. These Indians lived in well-fortified villages along the Missouri River, extending from Pierre, South Dakota, downstream to the mouth of Crow Creek. Unlike the Oglalas and Brulés, who became almost exclusively buffalo hunters, the Arikaras had developed what environmental historians such as William Cronon and Richard White call an ecological security net. They raised corn, squash, bean, and sunflower crops, but if their harvests failed, they could use hunting as a security net to cushion the disaster. Conversely, if hunting was poor, the crops would be a godsend. Like the Sioux, the Arikaras had become formidable buffalo hunters, making two extended hunts a year. Planting their crops in the spring, they would remain in their river villages long enough to give their corn crop one good hoeing before their first hunt. In the fall, they would harvest the crop before beginning their second hunt.

In addition to the Arikaras, the Caddoan linguistic family included several tribes of skilled agriculturalists, such as the Pawnees, Wichitas, and Caddos. Although by the 1700s the plains region was one of anthropologist Harold E. Driver's three principal agricultural areas in the United States, the East and the Southwest being the other two, little farming had existed in the Great Plains before the time of Columbus. Indeed, by the thirteenth century a series of droughts had driven most inhabitants out of this region. One of the first tribes to move back in after moisture conditions had improved was the Pawnees, a tribe that would be engaged in almost constant war with the Sioux by Red Cloud's day. The Pawnees had moved from eastern Texas into Nebraska about 1300 and, like the Arikaras, had developed buffalo hunting as a security net for their agricultural pursuits. Their early success in adapting to this once impossible environment, in fact, spurred other tribes to return to the Great Plains.

The coming of the Oglalas and Brulés to the Missouri country began a stormy relationship with the Arikaras which lasted for almost a generation. In their early contacts with these more sedentary people, the Sioux drove them upriver, employing the same aggressive tactics that made them successful against such tribes as the Omahas, Iowas, and Otoes and using the guns that had made the Crees, Assiniboins, and Chippewas successful against them. But by the late eighteenth century a series of developments eroded their initial advantages. For one thing, French guns and ammunition became scarce after France's defeat in the French and Indian War. The Sioux would not recover from this setback until English traders arrived to fill the vacuum. For another, the Arikaras began to flourish in their new homes farther up the Missouri River. In fact, by 1760 the population of the Arikara villages had risen to approximately twenty thousand, making them the most numerous of the Missouri River tribes and giving them a population about double that of the Sioux. Moreover, their agricultural safety net had strengthened their foothold on this stretch of the Missouri almost as much as their imposing earth walls and cedar log stockades had. Perhaps most important of all in helping the Arikaras resist the encroaching Sioux tide, however, was the introduction of another one of those important European imports, the horse.

Horses, the animals that would ultimately revolutionize the life of the Plains Indians, had been introduced in the Southwest by the early Spanish. But their widespread dissemination did not occur until after the Pueblo Revolt of 1680, when the Spanish were driven out of New Mexico for almost thirteen years. The victorious Pueblo Indians, being a sedentary agricultural people, did not see much value in these prized animals, but such nomadic neighbors as the Apaches and the Utes did. Those tribes began to acquire horses through "trades and raids," to use historian Alvin M. Josephy's expression. Eventually horses reached the vast buffalo plains to the north and east, where many tribes soon saw their importance for transportation and for the hunt or warfare.

Full integration of the horse into the life of the Plains Indians, however, did not occur instantly. It took about a generation before a transformation of this scope could happen; older Indians, for example, tended to resist the changes that this new mobility could provide. Nevertheless, use of the horse made its way up the broad expanses of the Great Plains, reaching the Red River by 1690. One of the first tribes in this area to acquire these animals was the Wichitas; by 1719 two Wichita villages in what is now Oklahoma possessed a herd of three hundred. The Pawnees were also among the earliest to obtain horses; by 1714, in fact, they were already regarded as excellent horsemen. They acquired their animals through trade with the Wichitas and in raids against those Apaches who roamed too close to their western borders. They also traded with a number of tribes that had been exiled to the Great Plains by the Sioux, such as the Omahas, Iowas, and Otoes.

The Kiowas, who in the late eighteenth century lived and hunted around the Black Hills, were probably the chief source of horses for the Arikaras. Indeed, until about 1790 the Kiowas made frequent visits to the Arikara villages in order to exchange their horses and Spanish goods for corn and other needed trade items. Because of the horses acquired through this trade, it soon became evident to the Oglalas and Brulés filtering into the Missouri country that the Arikaras were no longer a people with whom they could trifle. Mounted and armed with Spanish saber blades at the end of their sturdy buffalo lances, the reinvigorated Arikaras, numbering some four thousand warriors by 1760, could effectively rout the small bands of Sioux fighting on foot, regardless of whether the Sioux possessed European arms. Moreover, it became practically impossible for the Sioux to storm the formidable river fortresses built by the Arikaras; they often had to content themselves with a few horses and scalps and what corn they could steal from their enemy's cultivated patches. During these dreary years for the Sioux, as a matter of fact, many frustrated Lakotas came as suppliants, begging for corn, dried pumpkins, or tobacco. But they were never humble suppliants; the Arikaras knew that these same people could return later as enemies, which they often did during the long and stormy relationship between the two rivals.

What finally changed the balance of power between the Sioux and the Arikaras was the tragic arrival of that third European import, smallpox. Ethnologist John Ewers, who chronicled the

impact of this disease on the Blackfeet following the arrival
of white traders into their lands, has documented the misery
caused by this disease. In 1781, for example, smallpox killed more
than half the population of the Piegan Blackfeet tribe. A half-
century later, during the major smallpox epidemic of 1837, more
than two-thirds of the six thousand Blackfeet Indians died of
the dreaded disease. Smallpox was not the only infectious ill-
ness brought to the Blackfeet; scarlet fever also took its toll
in 1837, as did measles in 1864 and 1865. Because their villages
were more accessible to outsiders, the Arikaras were infected
by smallpox earlier than most; from 1772 to 1780 they suffered
from three devastating epidemics, which eliminated four-fifths
of their population and made them especially vulnerable to the
aggressiveness of the Sioux.

But the expansionist Lakota tribes were not immune to these
European diseases. According to Brulé winter counts, these
transplanted Plains Indians suffered from smallpox epidemics
in 1779–80, 1780–81, and 1801–1802. Because they lived in wandering bands, however, their losses were slight when compared
with those of the more stationary Arikaras, Hidatsas, and Mandans, who were often visited in their river homes by European
carriers of disease. During the nineteenth century, for example,
when great epidemics, such as the one in 1837, halved the population of the Plains tribes, the Lakotas, many of whom were
roaming in country far to the west of the Missouri, were suffering significantly fewer deaths. Indeed, because of their nomadic
life-style and their geographical dispersal, the Lakota or Teton
Sioux grew from approximately eighty-five hundred in 1805 to
somewhere in the range of twenty-five thousand by the 1850s.

Because of the disastrous impact of smallpox, the Arikaras retreated even further up the Missouri River, allowing the Oglalas
and the Brulés and their Yankton allies to settle along that stretch
of the Missouri below the Great Bend in present-day South
Dakota. In the meantime, the Saones, the five northern Lakota
tribes, were pushing toward the Missouri above the Arikaras.
Their migration to the west had been considerably slower than
that of the Oglalas and the Brulés. Living closer to the Crees and

Assiniboins was certainly one factor for this sluggish progress; from 1725 to 1750 they had been engaged in an almost constant struggle with those two rivals. By the 1770s, however, they were moving into the country adjacent to the Missouri, along with the Yanktonais, whose activities had paralleled theirs to a significant degree. The embattled Arikaras, as a consequence, now had hostile Sioux neighbors both to the north and to the south of them. But the upriver migration of the Arikaras continued, providing the Oglalas with a fairly safe site to cross the Missouri and head further west. In 1786 the Arikaras finally settled near the confluence of the Cheyenne and Missouri rivers, a better location but one that placed them directly in the path of the five approaching Saone tribes.

Although the westward migration of these northern Lakotas was delayed for ten years because of the Arikaras' new home, the Oglalas to the south were now moving across the Missouri with perfect impunity. From their foothold on the west bank, most of them traveled up the Bad River, a lonely watercourse whose source lay about 120 miles east of the Black Hills. The surrounding country was harsh even by Dakota standards. The river, which overflowed in the spring and dried up in the summer, had pools of brackish water, the existence of which probably accounted for its less than flattering name. The high, dry plains through which it flowed, while green in the early spring, were usually dry and brown by late May. As the year progressed, uncontrolled prairie fires would often sweep across the broad prairie landscape, blackening countless acres in the process. But there was abundant game along the river, a factor which might explain why the Oglalas followed this river rather than the White River south of them, which the Brulés used in their trek to the west.

The adventures of these pioneering Oglalas, whose numbers were small at first, soon had Sioux camps on the east side of the Missouri buzzing with excitement. Particular notice was taken of the successes enjoyed by these early bands; incidents of horse trading and horse stealing probably commanded most of the attention. Although the mobility these animals could provide was already appreciated, the fact that horses were now becoming available brought excitement to almost all Lakotas. No longer would they have to rely as much on women and children to act as porters or on dogs to pull travois overburdened with equipment for the next camp. Horses could haul longer poles to make for taller, more comfortable tipis. Moreover, horses would allow the westering Lakotas to travel more than five miles a day.

With horses becoming more available, the Oglalas were soon discovering new dimensions in this arid plains region that they had chosen for their next hunting ground. They eventually became aware of an extensive and remote region of clay buttes between them and their Brulé brethren to the south. Carved by erosion into exotic formations, this broken country would become known by its now famous name, the Badlands. Although the region was forbidding even for mounted travelers, horses made it easier for the Oglalas to explore it. These animals were also used for trips across the Missouri to acquire guns and other items of exchange at the coveted trade fairs, which were ultimately moved from the headwaters of the Minnesota River to the James River valley to be closer to most of the migrating Lakotas.

The history of this stage of the long Sioux trek west is even less documented than the earlier stages. While some information about Sioux movements east of the Missouri is provided by tribal tradition and a smattering of European written accounts, much of the information about movements west of the river is derived from the winter counts. Indeed, these counts probably comprise the most important source of information until white traders moving up the Missouri two decades later could provide additional knowledge. For example, American Horse's winter count, kept by an Oglala family, recorded the most significant event of these early trans-Missouri years, the discovery of the Black Hills by a party led by the Oglala leader Standing Bull in the winter of 1775–76. Even though Cloud Shield's winter count contends that the discovery was made the following year, the importance of both these pictographic records cannot be denied.

The Sioux attitude toward the new tribes encountered west of the Missouri provides an interesting insight into the strong likes and dislikes of these essentially warlike people. For example, when the Cheyennes, who had migrated across the Missouri even earlier than the Lakotas, attacked the Brulés in the early 1790s, the Oglalas joined their Sioux allies in capturing a Cheyenne village and killing many of its inhabitants. But they did not drive these temporary foes out of the region; in fact, for many years they were in league with the tall, stately Cheyennes, who increasingly shared a common interest with them. Yet in the case of most other rival tribes, the Lakotas showed no mercy; the Oglalas, for example, pushed the Kiowas out of the Black Hills, eventually forcing them southward to the plains country of Oklahoma. Sioux interaction with the Crows, whose hunting lands extended from the Black Hills northward, was about the same. Even though they spoke a Siouan language, the Crows, too, found themselves in mortal combat with the Lakota intruders, who eventually drove them out of their Powder River hunting lands and forced them to retreat even farther west.

The Sioux's relationship with the Arikaras, however, was often in a state of flux. Even though their recently established Missouri crossing was now comfortably south of Arikara country, the perennially restless Oglalas still had to cross the river twice a year to winter in Minnesota country. Consequently, it was good strategy for them to get along with the Arikaras, at least some of the time. Moreover, their continued appetite for the corn, pumpkins, and tobacco raised by the Arikaras only strengthened their motivation to avoid constant warfare with those still entrenched people.

But for the Saones, the northern Lakotas, the Arikaras posed a different problem. They were squarely in the path of the Saone migration across the Missouri. One result of this troubling standoff was an attack by the northern Lakotas in the summer of 1794 that drove one Arikara band up the Missouri to seek sanctuary with the Mandans and another down the river to join the Skidi Pawnees in Nebraska. But the plight of the once dominant Arikaras did not improve. The northern group had a falling out with the Mandans, who, in league with another agricultural people, the Hidatsas, forced the Arikaras southward, where, in 1799, they settled in three new villages above the mouth of the Grand River. With the Arikaras no longer blocking the Saones' passage to the west, the northernmost Lakotas were now free to join the Oglalas and the Brulés on the grasslands west of the Missouri. Their soon-to-be-busy Missouri crossing was at the mouth of the Cheyenne River, which was located about forty-five miles below the newest Arikara site. The river, which the Sioux called the Good River because it was one of the best routes to the west, would soon become another of those "old trails" that Red Cloud warmly recalled.

The number of Saones to reach the Oglalas and hunt with them in this new country became so large that by 1840 perhaps half of the Oglala Sioux had some Saone blood. Of the newcomers, the Miniconjous, who were the largest of the five northern tribes at that time, led the way, moving aggressively up the Cheyenne River. They were closely followed by the Sans Arc and Two Kettle Sioux. The Hunkpapas and Blackfeet Sioux, on the other hand, still engaged in a brisk trade with the Arikaras, lagged behind. In time, though, they, too, would make the crossing to become the northernmost representatives of this powerful Lakota alliance that would dominate the Northern Plains throughout much of the nineteenth century.

By 1795 the Sioux would finally encounter a group they could not dominate: European and American traders and explorers moving up the Missouri. French traders, arriving from Saint Louis on keelboats or pirogues in their ceaseless quest for furs, were the first to have personal dealings with the Lakotas. Although many of these Frenchmen preferred to trade with the more predictable Arikaras, contacts with the resolute Lakotas were unavoidable. In fact, the Lakota Sioux often harassed the French, making them pay tribute if they wanted to reach the Arikara villages upstream. Because of numerous problems with these more aggressive Indians, a number of French traders established fortified posts in the Missouri's Great Bend area for better protection.

Simultaneous with these French efforts to establish some reasonable basis for trade with the Sioux were the increasingly commonplace trips of these nomadic Lakota tribesmen from the Missouri River to the Black Hills and back. Because of this travel pattern, the Oglalas and the Brulés were just as apt to be encamped at the mouth of the Bad River as further to the west. Northern Lakotas, for their part, were often encountered by European traders near the mouth of the Cheyenne River. As for the Yanktons, they tended to gather below the Great Bend with a group of Lakotas who were later called Lower Brulés.

When Lewis and Clark arrived less than a decade later, many of these campsites had changed, revealing again the constant state of flux that characterized Sioux life. Although the Oglalas and Brulés still rendezvoused near the confluence of the Bad and Missouri rivers, almost all the Brulés, along with many Oglalas, were now living west of the Missouri on a more or less permanent basis, leaving the river's east bank for Yankton occupation. The Saone tribes, led by the Miniconjous, had pushed far up the Cheyenne River, the Arikaras no longer posing much of a threat to their Missouri crossing. But one thing had not changed during the past decade: the Sioux remained the unquestioned terrors of the river. Although the two resolute American captains, Meriwether Lewis and William Clark, refused to be cowed, they were among the first Americans to know that the Lakota Sioux should never be underestimated.

Lewis and Clark's initial encounter with the Sioux in 1804 gave the United States its first official glimpse of the Indian nation that would one day challenge its expansionist policies in this region. The first impression of these two men, however, gave little indication of the Sioux potential for making trouble. In fact, Lewis and Clark counted only 160 Oglala lodges during their visit that year, giving this most persistent of Lakota tribes only 360 members and allowing them to field only 120 warriors. Their unusual success in intimidating such formidable foes as the Crows and Kiowas may have been a result of their earlier acquisition of guns.

In 1825, American General Henry Atkinson, who was given

command of one of the early military expeditions up the
Missouri, reached a much more impressive tally; he counted
four times more Oglalas than Lewis and Clark had. His figure
is more in line with that of demographer Kingsley M. Bray,
whose 1994 study revealed that during the nineteenth century
the Oglalas grew more rapidly than any other Lakota tribe except the smaller Two Kettle. This dramatic population increase
probably was the result of the Oglalas' new mobility gained
through the introduction of the horse as well as to the influx of
other Lakotas into their ranks. Certainly the horse, along with
the gun, made the Oglalas not only more effective warriors but
also more efficient buffalo hunters. Because of this new mobility,
which all of the westering Lakotas eventually enjoyed, buffalo
meat became more abundant. Starvation, always a threat to a
subsistence culture, became less common. Moreover, the improved diet enjoyed by most nineteenth-century Lakotas was
matched by an easing of the tribal workload expected of the
women and children; horses could now haul the heavy loads of
equipment for the Sioux's nomadic life-style as well as provide
for a faster pursuit of their prey during the tribal buffalo hunts.

Life continued to improve significantly for the Lakota Sioux
throughout the first half of the nineteenth century. Because of
the horse, when bison herds became relatively scarce in one part
of their tribal range the hunters could move swiftly to another.
Unlike their allies, the Cheyennes, who may have been the major
source for horses acquired through trading rather than raiding,
the Sioux had probably never relied on cultivated fields as a security net as the Arikaras and Pawnees had done. Consequently,
the speed with which they could relocate was only impeded by
the physical limitations of the women and children in breaking
camp and moving elsewhere.

In a vast country such as the Great Plains, with its small
population and ordinarily abundant game, Lakota bands could
roam for miles in friendly country. Separating them from hostile
rivals, such as the Pawnees and the Crows, were zones of inde-
terminate size that historian Richard White has called neutral
grounds or war grounds. The boundaries of these zones, which

divided competing tribes from one another, were rarely firm, making the areas they encompassed dangerous ones where only well-equipped and well-prepared mounted war parties would dare stray. But because there was little pressure from hunters on the buffalo lands in these neutral zones, many animals from adjacent tribal hunting grounds would seek refuge in them, causing these areas to be temptingly rich in game.

Although the neutral grounds were never static, by the middle of the nineteenth century four of them directly affected the Lakota Sioux. One was the region between the forks of the Platte, often contested with the Pawnees, and another was the Medicine Bow–Laramie plains region, west of Fort Laramie. The third was the Republican River country along the Kansas-Nebraska border, and the fourth was the Yellowstone drainage for such rivers as the Powder and the Rosebud, which was initially Crow country but was transformed by the Sioux into a neutral zone during the 1840s and 1850s.

Because buffalo migrations were unpredictable, a serious reduction in the size of a herd in one tribe's territory could result in an invasion of one of these neutral grounds by that tribe. Whether the invasion was the start of some expansionist movement or simply a response to the loss of game, such an incursion was regarded with suspicion. When the use of the horse finally became widespread throughout the Great Plains, that animal became the solution in dealing with such problems; strong, fleet animals were soon regarded as indispensable for all war parties dispatched to deal with unwelcome intruders. Although horses were still relatively scarce when the Sioux started their slow crossing of the Missouri in the late eighteenth century, they eventually became commonplace; anthropologist Royal B. Hassrick, a scholar of Sioux culture, speculated that horses had already become crucial to the Lakota life-style by the turn of the century. Certainly by the 1820s, when Red Cloud was born, the mounted warriors of his tribe were already blazing those "old trails" so vivid in his memory and were becoming the dominant horsemen on the Northern Plains.

Long before they began to push aggressively into neutral

hunting grounds or into hunting grounds held by rival tribes, the Lakota Sioux had come to regard western South Dakota as their private preserve. They no longer wintered in Minnesota; indeed, their once important ties with eastern Sioux had been largely severed after the year 1785, when the Lakotas elected to stay year around on the less sheltered Dakota plains. During any time of the year, as a matter of fact, confident Lakota bands could be found hunting or camping somewhere on the great stretches of prairie between the Missouri and the Black Hills. In the northern part of this sprawling domain roamed the Saones, the northern Lakotas; the Miniconjous were in the vanguard of their slow but determined migration up the Cheyenne River. In the south hunted the adventuresome Brulés, traveling back and forth on the White River. In between these tribes, along the Bad River, wandered the restless Oglalas, who, during the years following 1805, had begun to winter at Bear Butte, a Cheyenne haunt located northeast of the Black Hills. Here they felt secure; they were near the Black Hills, which they called Paha Sapa, a place that had become increasingly important to them, and were surrounded by Sioux and Cheyenne tribesmen, whom they regarded as allies.

A new rhythm in Sioux life developed during these early Dakota years. The Oglalas, for example, would travel down the Bad River in the spring to its mouth on the Missouri, hunting buffalo and other game along the way. After reaching the Big Muddy, they would join either the Brulés to the south or the Saones to the north to harass white traders on their way upriver to the Arikara or Mandan villages. Sometimes they would even hold their sacred sun dance along the Missouri, even though the Black Hills was rapidly becoming the most popular place for this essential Sioux ritual. During the summer they would move far afield, attacking such traditional enemies as the Crows before returning to Bear Butte for their long winter encampment.

It was largely because of this free-wheeling life-style that the rapidly growing Lakota tribes and their Cheyenne allies would begin to extend their hunting grounds into the present-day states of North Dakota, Montana, Wyoming, and Nebraska. To the north, they would wage almost constant warfare against the hated Crows. They were not content to drive these rivals from their hunting grounds north and west of the Black Hills, thus turning Crow territory into a neutral ground, but they were determined to disrupt Crow life in any way possible; the trade the Crows had with the Mandan and Hidatsa villages at the mouth of the Knife River in North Dakota, for example, was almost completely stymied.

The Lakota Sioux also instituted frequent expeditions into Crow country to steal horses. Although the Crows, skilled mounted warriors themselves, would usually retaliate, sometimes their attempts at revenge would do them more harm than good. A Crow attack that wiped out a Cheyenne war party on the Tongue River in southern Montana sometime before 1820 provides a good example of how counterproductive such attacks could be. Angry relatives and friends of the vanquished Cheyenne band, after waiting the customary one winter before seeking help, went from one Lakota camp to another, where they passed around the war pipe and solicited aid. When they were ready, a large party of Lakota and Cheyenne warriors launched a surprise attack on a Crow village along the Tongue, resulting in the death of many Crow warriors and the capture of their women and children. It was through such aggressive actions as this that the Lakota Sioux ultimately transformed the Powder River country of eastern Wyoming and southeastern Montana from a neutral ground to a prized hunting ground for the Sioux and their allies.

The Kiowas were also plagued by the ever increasing presence of the Sioux. Even though they had been forced from the Black Hills, they still felt apprehensive about Lakota encroachments during the early years of the nineteenth century. Curiously, though, they did enjoy good relations with the Sioux's closest allies, the Cheyennes, many of whom camped regularly on the headwaters of the Cheyenne River in eastern Wyoming. In fact, the Kiowas and the Cheyennes often traded with each other at Horse Creek near the present Wyoming-Nebraska border. Along this tributary of the North Platte River the Kiowas and

Cheyennes peacefully encamped and exchanged horses, Spanish goods, and other trade items. In 1815, during one of their rendezvous, the Cheyennes brought a group of Lakotas with them, hoping to reconcile their Sioux allies with the Kiowas. But this particular trade fair had barely started when a bitter quarrel erupted between a Brulé and a Kiowa in which the Kiowa was killed with a war club. The result was a bloody fight in which the so-called guests drove the Kiowas west into the mountains near the head of the North Platte.

This event became quite significant because it represented the first important Sioux probe into the Platte River country, which by the 1830s would become a major hunting and trading area for the Oglalas and Brulés. It also led to the removal, at least in part, of one more detested rival. The highly resourceful Kiowa tribesmen, joined by friendly bands of Cheyennes and Arapahoes, migrated south to the Red River country, where they eventually combined with Comanches and Kiowa Apaches to form conglomerate groups of restless Indians who engaged in widespread trade up and down the Great Plains. While the Kiowas and their new allies would make temporary excursions into the Platte country, they were always wary of the Sioux, who by 1834 began to fill the void left by these departing tribes, making western Nebraska yet another extension of the exploding Sioux domain.

By Red Cloud's birth in the 1820s, Lakota dominance on the northern Great Plains was evident. These highly mobile buffalo hunters and warriors, through their greater aggressiveness and superior numbers, had become the scourge of much of the West. Armed as well as any of their neighbors, they were also superb horsemen who could still pioneer those "old trails" which Red Cloud boasted about to Cook in his poignant correspondence. The acquisition of the horse was especially important to them, for they had not been an agricultural people. This animal significantly increased their efficiency in hunting the huge buffalo herds that roamed the Great Plains, which may have numbered in excess of sixty million at that time. Because of their successes in controlling this great food commissary, the seven Lakota tribes reached a new level of power and prestige after they crossed the Missouri. Now better fed and healthier than their forbears, they could make convincing claims to a disproportionately large share of the buffalo-rich Northern Plains. Indeed, the triumphs that capped their epic migration west from Minnesota had placed them on the threshold of a golden age. But the ascendancy they derived from these glorious achievements would ultimately be threatened; by the 1860s they would be challenged by an equally expansionist people who coveted the same lands they did.

CHAPTER 2

The Making of a Warrior

RED Cloud was born in May 1821 on Blue Water Creek, a tributary of the North Platte River in western Nebraska. At the time of his birth, the banks of that creek were in a neutral hunting ground. Most Lakotas were still far to the north, roaming the plains of South Dakota. Pawnee hunting grounds were largely to the east; these soon-to-be bitter rivals of the Lakotas lived in earthen villages on the Platte and Loup rivers, where they not only cultivated patches of corn, squash, and beans, but from where they also made numerous hunting forays to the west. To the south and east roved a number of Plains tribes either in pursuit of buffalo or engaged in trade with other Indians.

Usually when a band of Plains Indians entered a neutral zone, such as the one surrounding the Blue Water, it came as a war party composed of wary fighting men. Yet Red Cloud's party obviously felt secure enough to bring women and children with them. The unusual confidence of this band could have been a result of the Sioux's awe-inspiring reputation as warriors; their rout of the Kiowas six years earlier at Horse Creek had undoubtedly discouraged other tribes from entering this region. But more than likely the Lakotas were aware that the Pawnees were still far to the east; traditionally the seminomadic Pawnees began their spring planting in early May.

Curiously, Red Cloud's claim to having been born in the spring of 1821 has been challenged by many historians. George E. Hyde, for example, has argued vigorously that Red Cloud was born somewhere between the Black Hills and the Missouri River, where almost all of the Lakotas lived and hunted at that time. His assumption is based on the belief that the southern

Lakotas, the Oglalas and Brulés, would not have strayed so far afield from their own hunting grounds unless they had embarked upon some important mission. Although there is logic to his supposition, it overlooks the extraordinary mobility and boldness of those two Lakota tribes. Their role in the great Sioux migration west from Minnesota had always found them in the vanguard. Moreover, they were rarely contained for long in any narrow perimeter.

Red Cloud also never wavered in his insistence that the Platte country was his place of birth. In 1870, when he made his first trip to Washington, he told officials of the Department of the Interior that he was born at the forks of the Platte, a remark that must have been made casually, in that the forks are approximately eighty miles east of Blue Water Creek. During Red Cloud's last Washington trip, however, he again cited Blue Water Creek as his birthplace, reminding members of the Senate Committee on Indian Affairs, whom he was taunting, that the site was only fifteen miles from where General William S. Harney humbled a band of Brulé Sioux in 1855 in the bitter Battle of Ash Hollow.

Hyde's differences with Red Cloud's testimony are based on two facts. First, Hyde believed that the Sioux chief deliberately misrepresented his birthplace in order to strengthen Sioux claims to the Platte country, even though such claims had been technically relinquished in the Treaty of Fort Laramie. And second, he was apparently unaware of the existence of Red Cloud's autobiography, an ignorance shared by many historians, anthropologists, and ethnologists until R. Eli Paul of the Nebraska State Historical Society authenticated that document in a 1994 article published in *Montana: The Magazine of Western History.*

The autobiography, uncommon because only Black Hawk and Geronimo of the major Indian chiefs left autobiographical accounts, was based on a series of interviews conducted with Red Cloud in 1893 by his old friend and Indian trader Sam Deon at the post office at Pine Ridge. The 135-page manuscript, organized in the "as-told-to" form characteristic of most Native American autobiographies, was eventually misconstrued as something else because it was written in the third instead of the first person. Deon, in translating Red Cloud's remarks, probably related the account in the third person when he told it to Charles Allen, the postmaster at Pine Ridge, who had hopes of writing a biography of Red Cloud.

Allen, anxious to publish his findings, sought the help of Addison E. Sheldon, superintendent of the State Historical Society in Lincoln, who also wanted to write a Red Cloud biography. Unfortunately, Sheldon virtually sat on this valuable manuscript for four decades; in fact, those who knew of its existence often referred to it as the Sheldon manuscript. They regarded it as an untrustworthy document based upon Red Cloud's reminiscences of his life before the great Sioux struggle with the U.S. government in the mid-1860s. One person who apparently never doubted the nature of the manuscript was Mari Sandoz, whose biography of Crazy Horse ranks high among her western writings. In 1932, as Sheldon's research assistant, she typed the long-ignored recollections of Red Cloud, feeling confident of their legitimacy. In a 1962 letter she referred to the product of her efforts as the "Red Cloud Autobiography."

With Sheldon apparently keeping the Red Cloud manuscript from Hyde, who lived in nearby Omaha, Hyde propounded a number of themes regarding the famous Sioux's origins. For example, he questioned 1821 as the year of Red Cloud's birth. He believed the Oglala chief was born on September 20, 1822, instead of in May of the previous year. His choice of this particular year has some prestigious support; the Lakota winter counts place Red Cloud's birth date sometime during the winter of 1822. The *Handbook of American Indians North of Mexico*, edited by F. W. Hodge, while conceding that Red Cloud was born on the forks of the Platte, has also concluded that 1822 was his birth year.

Hyde based his selection of September 20 as the birth date on the fact that a fiery red meteorite streaked across the sky, to the wonderment of many northern tribes, on the night of September 20. Indeed, this phenomenon gave Red Cloud his name, according to Hyde; after all, the ball of fire was red, and the

Sioux often used the words *sky* and *cloud* interchangeably. Thus, many Lakotas and Cheyennes, including Red Cloud's people, gave the name Red Cloud to infants born on that day.

Red Cloud in his autobiography, however, maintained that he did not receive his name until he joined his first war party at sixteen. Moreover, he unequivocally stated that Red Cloud was a family name; both his father and grandfather bore it. But there are other good arguments against Hyde's meteorite theory. For example, the Sioux, not having a gens or clan system, did not ordinarily name their children in such a ceremonious way. In fact, at that time individual Sioux usually earned their names by some trait or action that caught the fancy of the tribe. Names could also be applied later in life. Pine Ridge Indian agent Valentine T. McGillycuddy once argued that Red Cloud earned his name because at a single command he could get a large number of scarlet-blanketed warriors to cover "the hillsides like a red cloud." This explanation has been embraced by many Oglalas; even the famous Cheyenne half-blood George Bent accepted a version of this story, claiming that Red Cloud's band had been issued these red blankets by the U.S. government itself. The problem with this explanation is that if Red Cloud acquired his name at sixteen, he could hardly have been expected to command such a large entourage of followers at that time.

Red Cloud's birth west of the forks of the Platte provides an interesting example of how fluid Lakota society was in the early years of the nineteenth century. According to Red Cloud's nephew He Dog, the Sioux infant's father was Lone Man, the chief, or *itancan*, of a Brulé band that had merged with the Oglalas several years earlier, while his mother, Walks-As-She-Thinks, was probably a Saone, or northern Lakota. Of course the name Lone Man contradicts Red Cloud's insistence that his father's name was also Red Cloud. One possible cause for this disagreement is that Sioux men and women not only were named later in life on many occasions but also were sometimes given more than one name. According to Richard Williams, a Lakota descended from Red Cloud's band of Oglalas, there have been cases in which tribal members were given three or four

different names during a lifetime. Sioux activist Russell Means
was given four names, one for each stage of his life, ranging
from childhood to tribal elder.

Lone Man's band was called the Kuhee, which when translated means "standoffish"; perhaps that band's preference for
isolation explains why it was camping in neutral ground so far
from established Lakota territory when Red Cloud was born.
Old-Man-Afraid-of-His-Horses, who later became one of Red
Cloud's main rivals for control of the Oglalas, was born in this
same band of Brulés six years earlier.

While the Oglalas, Brulés, and other Lakota tribes were in-
termingling in this fashion, another threat of European origin
began to impinge upon the lives of the early Sioux. In 1817,
American companies, anxious for their share of the fur trade,
began to flood Lakota camps with liquor. Lone Man found
this potentially destructive trade item irresistible and, as an alcoholic, died of its effects in 1825, causing Red Cloud to be
a lifelong critic of white whiskey peddlers. Insisting that he
never touched strong drink, Red Cloud told at least one story in
his autobiography of how excessive liquor consumption caused
violence and death among his people.

After Lone Man's untimely death, Red Cloud and his siblings
were taken by their mother to live with her people. The leader of
Walks-As-She-Thinks's band was Old Smoke, a Saone who migrated from the north with his people to live among the Oglalas,
yet another example of Lakota fluidity. Red Cloud's mother presumably was a Saone herself because Old Smoke always called
her sister. According to some of the historical accounts, Walks-
As-She-Thinks died about the same time as her husband. Again,
Red Cloud's autobiography refutes that long-held conviction;
Red Cloud makes it clear that his mother was with him when he
went on his first war party at sixteen and when he was married
several years later.

Despite the tragedy that accompanied Red Cloud's early
years, most Lakota people during the 1820s were enjoying both
prosperous and fulfilling lives. Their adroitness in harvesting
the vast buffalo herds they encountered after crossing the Mis-

souri was probably the key to this better life. Buffalo meat was so abundant that the tribes often gorged themselves during certain times of the year. The mobility of fleet horses, of course, was one of the chief factors for this success.

Nevertheless, the growing use of the horse also had its disadvantages. Before the Missouri crossing, the Lakota tribes tended to stay together and cooperate for the common good, the northern Lakotas, or Saones, to the north and the Oglalas and Brulés to the south. But after the crossing, the better-mounted tribes began to disperse. The Miniconjou bands, for example, moved south, closer to the hunting grounds of the Oglalas and Brulés. Other bands of northern Lakotas, such as Old Smoke's, also drifted in that direction; his group would ultimately blend into Oglala life so completely that it would lose much of its original identity. Sometimes one Lakota tribe would share a hunting ground with another, but in most cases each tribe preferred to hunt in its own territory.

The structure of Lakota life at that time was a loose and tangled affair largely associating small bands—such as that in which Red Cloud was reared—which acted independently of one another. Yet, within each of these bands, there was an order, a system, that gave almost everyone a place in Lakota society. Each band, or *tiyospaye*, was ordinarily comprised of ten or more bilaterally extended families and was led by an *itancan*, a head chief whose overall responsibility was to provide for the basic needs of his people. Bolstering this man's authority was the war leader, the *blotahunka*, who protected the band from outside threats, and the enforcers, the *akicita*, who maintained order within the band's intricate social and political system, which ethnohistorian Catherine Price has so carefully described in her Oglala study. These leaders helped maintain the circle, or sacred hoop, which extended from the band's village circle to the circular-shaped entities that comprised the world around it, such as the sun and the moon and even the earthly rocks below. Thus, each circular-shaped Lakota lodge was a microcosm, centered in the universe, where Lakotas, as creatures of the earth, could commune with divine forces in circles surrounded by even larger circles. This sense of being a part of something greater also extended to less spiritual considerations. The seven Lakota tribes made genuine, but usually unsuccessful, efforts to have one great yearly encampment where all Lakotas could celebrate their sun dance and elect four respected leaders to represent their gathering for the coming year.

As the small band constituted the basis of Lakota life at that time, the family unit was also important. Indeed, one must talk of an extended family to properly characterize the social organization of the prairie Sioux. Lakota bands were organized around sibling cooperation and were directed by brothers and sisters who knew each other's needs and desires intimately. These leaders were often as concerned about their nephews and nieces as they were about their sons and daughters. By custom this solicitude was usually strongest on the distaff side. One of the most significant influences in Red Cloud's early life at Old Smoke's camp, for example, was his maternal uncle White Hawk, who would continually lecture the boy on the importance of controlling his unusually headstrong impulses.

Unlike Lone Man's case, many Lakota men lived with their wife's people after they got married; to this extent Lakota society was matrilineal. In most respects, however, the men got the lion's share of the respect and recognition. Younger warriors were often the driving force for these independent bands, although older men were listened to and revered for their wisdom and past experiences. A Lakota man in the prime of his life also enjoyed a great deal of freedom; he could compete for leadership, abide by the standards of tribal tradition, or, if disenchanted, leave and join another band. Indeed, the balance between the welfare of the individual and the welfare of the tribe or band in the 1820s was a healthy one.

When Walks-As-She-Thinks brought Red Cloud to Old Smoke's camp, the prospects for the future Sioux chief's life were not especially promising. His father had died of alcoholism, a death that probably brought disgrace to the entire family. Little Red Cloud, his brother Big Spider, and a sister (identified in Red Cloud's autobiography only as the future wife of Lit-

tle Bad Wolf) were now fatherless, a real liability in almost any
Sioux camp; their future would largely depend on how their
mother's people treated them. Fortunately, the Sioux tended to
lavish love and attention upon their children. But the competi-
tiveness of Lakota society could pose an impossible challenge to
any child who was meek or overly sensitive. Red Cloud, however, was anything but meek or sensitive. The tribal tradition
of training young Sioux to become self-sufficient warriors and
hunters found him to be an unusually apt pupil. Not only did
he have a fine mind, but his physical prowess was exceptional
as well. In fact, when he grew to manhood, his strength and
coordination became distinctive elements of his commanding
personality; his friend Captain Cook once likened him to a tiger
ready to pounce.

Red Cloud in his autobiography had little say about his early
life. Nevertheless, some reasonable assumptions can be made
about what it was like. If his experiences were typical of those
of most Sioux infants, for example, his first months were spent
in a cradle composed of a cushioned board with buckskin flaps
on either side. This familiar item of child care was often hung on
a tipi pole by a loop or was carried by his mother on her back
during one of those frequent trips made by Lone Man's nomadic band; according to Red Cloud, during his years with his
father's band and later with Old Smoke's band, he rarely stayed
in one place for more than two months except when the deep
snows and extreme cold of winter forced a longer encampment.

Because of the migratory nature of Red Cloud's life, the
young Lakota's growing-up years were spent traveling throughout much of the Northern Plains. As a consequence, he probably
became familiar with good portions of the country between the
Republican River in the south and the Yellowstone in the north.
According to historian Doane Robinson, he gained a full and
practical education based upon his experiences and the knowledge he acquired along the way. Like most young Lakotas of
both sexes, he became especially well versed in subjects such as
geography, topography, natural history, and biology. The intel-
lectually keen Red Cloud soon knew a great deal about many

of the landmarks in that expanding territory that most Plains tribes had to grudgingly regard as Lakota country. He could recognize the indigenous birds and animals that flourished on the prairie. He was able to tell which plants were good for food and which were good for medicine. He became, like so many of his young peers, a person perfectly at home in his environment.

But learning to be an intense and successful competitor was probably the most important aspect of this rough-hewn curriculum to which Red Cloud was exposed. Oglala boys, often as young as three or four, were encouraged to race against each other on ponies, sometimes clinging precariously to their animal's back but invariably learning to understand these valuable pets so well that they and their animals could become like one. A large percentage of their educational activities revolved around tests of strength and skill. When they were engaged in spinning tops, a popular game for Lakota boys, they were made to feel that keeping their tops going longer and having them fall closer to agreed-upon targets were of the utmost importance. When they were throwing javelins, distance and accuracy were insistently stressed. But the really crucial challenge faced by these young Lakotas was in the form of make-or-break endurance tests given when they were ready for manhood. They were sent on long, difficult trips to test their survival skills and gain that strong sense of purpose considered so essential in Lakota tradition.

Red Cloud emerged from this rigorous educational process as one of his band's most outstanding young graduates. Even though the system he went through was sometimes rough and brutal, the fatherless boy stood out as one of the keenest and sturdiest candidates for leadership in Old Smoke's band. In fact, he was so aggressive that his maternal uncle White Hawk was compelled to scold him from time to time. Fortunately for Red Cloud, this uncle, who enjoyed great status in the band, eventually handed his tribal rank over to Red Cloud, recognizing the great potential for leadership displayed by his willful nephew.

But the success of Red Cloud and his peers in this severe competition was never assured. A few of his young rivals even dropped out to become *winktes*, or male transvestites, fated to spend their manhood at the outer edges of the camp circle with those women and orphans who did not have anyone to champion their cause. Nevertheless, for the overwhelming majority of young Sioux males, the tribal educational system worked well, molding the well-trained and self-sufficient warriors that were essential for the survival of Lakota life.

When Red Cloud became a teenager, he faced a number of options opened to the young tribal members who aspired for leadership. He could gain the respect and admiration of his people by living up to the four virtues of his people: bravery, fortitude, generosity and wisdom. He could become a renowned warrior exhibiting one or more of these characteristics. He could be a successful buffalo hunter whom others would wish to follow. He could have stirring visions, as the spiritual Crazy Horse later did in his now legendary vision quests. Or he could belong to one of the important policing societies, such as the Badgers, the Kit Foxes, the Crow Owners, or the Brave Hearts, that existed among the loosely associated Lakota tribes; these prestigious groups supervised such essential communal activities for a Lakota band as moving the camp or organizing for a buffalo hunt.

Renown in one or more of these callings was always possible for a talented and determined person such as Red Cloud. But the prospects for success were usually better for a well-connected young man, perhaps a member or favorite son of one of the band's leading families. On this score Red Cloud was at a decided disadvantage; he was the son of a man who died of drunkenness, hardly an asset in a system of rivalry as intense as the Sioux's. Moreover, that Red Cloud's father was a Brulé probably prejudiced his aspirations. The family drawbacks for this exceptional young Lakota were such that Royal B. Hassrick has insisted that Red Cloud was deprived throughout his life of the kind of respect and recognition that he deserved.

Given the importance of family connections for the upward mobility of Sioux males, the role of warrior probably provided Red Cloud with his best chance for success. It was the tribal role least affected by external circumstances. In hand-to-hand combat with a Crow or Pawnee, family background obviously had little relevance; the outcome depended entirely on strength, courage, and daring, traits which Red Cloud had impressively shown during his difficult training as a warrior.

His first opportunity to demonstrate these traits occurred when he was only sixteen, during the late 1830s, when his people were camped on the North Platte above old Fort Laramie. A party of Sioux, which included his twenty-six-year-old cousin, had returned from a raid on the hated Pawnees. The war party's mission had been sadly marred by the death of the older cousin, who was also called Red Cloud. As was customary, a retaliatory party was organized to avenge the tragedy, and the teenager insisted on joining despite the protests of the women in his family.

When the aspiring youth failed to arrive in time to join the mission of vengeance, however, much sport was made of his failure. But before the war party could leave, shouts began to reverberate among the women in the village. "He is coming," they cried. "Who is coming?" some of them asked, reminding the village that this promising youngster had never been given a permanent name. "Red Cloud's son," one answered, using Lone Man's other name. "Red Cloud," shouted another. Fixedly the chorus of voices became general: "Red Cloud comes, Red Cloud comes!" The young Oglala soon burst upon the scene mounted on a fine spotted horse bearing the paint and feathers reserved for a warrior's mount. He even brought along a handsome bay as his extra steed. The incident was the beginning of Red Cloud's long career as a great warrior; in fact, he took his first scalp during this expedition.

Red Cloud was highly elated by his first exposure to real combat. Because his party had returned with fifty horses, including a horse taken by Red Cloud himself, and four scalps, they were given an exuberant welcome. The returning heroes were invited to one lodge after another to relate their experiences, answering the endless questions showered on them by their excited hosts, who fed and lauded them for days. Yet Red Cloud was also aware of the negative side of combat. The families of the two warriors who did not survive the Pawnee raid were the source of mournful cries, their lonely lodges being darkened by the smoke from extinguished fires.

Red Cloud went on to exhibit even more impressive deeds of valor during the coming months. In the month of March, following his first taste of conflict, his band attacked a party of Crows somewhere between the Laramie and North Platte rivers. Fourteen trapped Crow warriors, fatigued from their attempted flight and weak from exposure, drew their blankets over their heads and dropped into the snow, ready to accept their fate. Red Cloud, who was one of the first upon the scene, struck three of these prostrate Crows with his bow, not killing any of them but exposing himself to possible retaliation, because it was considered braver to strike a living enemy than to kill one.

These three coups, probably earned in 1838, were among the first of some eighty attributed to him, an astonishing record if true. A coup was an act of bravery, such as touching or killing an enemy in combat, stealing his horse, or performing some other deed generally recognized as being courageous. Consequently, if Red Cloud accumulated anything near eighty coups, he would have to be regarded as the greatest nineteenth-century Lakota warrior before the legendary Crazy Horse achieved that reputation. Even the formidable Sitting Bull claimed only forty-five coups, which he proudly celebrated by drawing pictographs of each one. Whether Red Cloud was indeed responsible for eighty coups, he did admit once, while being questioned by a tactless white teacher from the East regarding how many whites he had killed during his long career, to being involved in eighty battles.

Red Cloud continued to show exceptional valor after he reached his early twenties. There was, however, one new twist in his budding career. He was beginning to show an unusual resourcefulness to match his boldness. On one horse stealing expedition against the Crows, for example, he showed an impatience for caution and a contempt for danger. On this occasion he was in a war party headed by two prominent Lakota chiefs, Old-Man-Afraid-of-His-Horses and Brave Bear. The warriors were headed toward the Yellowstone River near the mouth of

Rosebud Creek, where they expected to find a large Crow camp
with a fine herd of horses. The party moved slowly through a
series of protected valleys and steep gorges, hoping to avoid
detection. Red Cloud soon became edgy about their glacial
progress. Yearning for action, he chose a young Miniconjou
who enjoyed his confidence and pushed ahead of the group to
a grassy plateau where a herd of fifty Crow horses was located.
These prized animals, grazing peacefully below them, were
guarded by one unsuspecting Crow Indian. The sentry proved
no match for Red Cloud, who charged him on horseback,
stabbing and scalping him with terrifying speed.

When the rest of the Sioux party caught up with Red Cloud
and his companion, both men expected to be whipped or "sol-
diered" for their unauthorized conduct. But Old-Man-Afraid
and Brave Bear thought otherwise; the two daring young warriors had captured a sizeable herd without warning the main
Crow camp, which was successfully attacked the following day.
The results of this Lakota mission were exhilarating; some three
hundred Crow horses were brought back. As for Red Cloud,
he not only had another coup to his credit, but, along with his
comrade, he could account for fifty of the horses taken.

But the resolute young Oglala warrior was not invincible.
During the early 1840s, when Red Cloud was barely twenty, an
event occurred which almost ended his life. He was placed in
charge of his own war party, probably for the first time, his mission being another foray into Pawnee country to steal horses.
Fighting Pawnees had become increasingly popular among his
people since they had made the Platte country their new hunting ground in the mid-1830s. During this campaign Red Cloud
made a confident attack on a Pawnee village along the Middle
Loup River in present-day Nebraska. But he and his men had
badly miscalculated the strength of their adversaries and were
convincingly repulsed.

In the midst of this bloody struggle, Red Cloud became separated from the rest of his party and incurred an almost fatal
arrow wound below his rib cage. His loyal comrades, however,
were able to rescue their new leader by dragging him from the

field on a blanket tied to one of the party's sturdier horses. After reaching a place of safety, one of the older warriors abruptly removed the arrow, causing Red Cloud to hemorrhage badly. The young Sioux's wound, nevertheless, was gently bathed and a travois was prepared for his eventual escape; fortunately, the Pawnees did not pursue the Sioux with their usual relentlessness. By the following morning, Red Cloud, who was finally able to take some nourishment, was ready for his party's long fifteen-day trip back to the main camp. Even so, for two months after his return he hovered between life and death. But his sturdy constitution and steely will ultimately made the difference; he was able to recover slowly, although his near-fatal wound would bother him for the rest of his life.

Sometime after this nearly disastrous incident, Red Cloud assumed another important responsibility of Sioux manhood: he got married. He chose for his mate a strong and loyal woman named Pretty Owl, who remained with him into old age; indeed, she was the only wife Red Cloud ever acknowledged. This commitment to one woman was rather unusual for a Sioux leader of Red Cloud's stature; many of his peers had more than one mate. The wife of Red Cloud's good friend Captain Cook, who probably knew the Oglala chief and his family as well as her husband did, concluded from an interview with one of Red Cloud's daughters that Red Cloud had at least one other wife; in fact, Mrs. Cook eventually reached the conclusion that Red Cloud had six wives, the last of whom he married when he was only twenty-four.

But Red Cloud's insistence that he was monogamous is quite convincing. His strong belief in that principle was an outgrowth of a tragic event that he inadvertently caused. According to his own testimony, Red Cloud, who was willing to give as many as twelve horses to Pretty Owl's father to win her hand, had intended to take as a second wife Pine Leaf, a young woman who loved him very much. He wanted the proper amount of time to elapse before he proposed to her, however, so he never told her of his intention. Brokenhearted, on the night of Red Cloud's wedding the young Sioux maiden hanged herself in despair on the branch of a tall tree overlooking a lodge especially prepared for the newlyweds by members of the tribe. Red Cloud, severely distraught over this unnecessary death, vowed never to take another wife.

Testimony regarding the number of Red Cloud's siblings and offspring is as contradictory as the testimony regarding the number of his wives. Given the importance of sibling cooperation in the governance of many nineteenth-century Lakota bands, young Red Cloud, who claimed to have had only one brother and one sister, probably regarded some of his cousins (the offspring of solicitous aunts and uncles) with the same warmth and devotion as if they were brothers or sisters. Consequently, the report that Red Cloud lost a brother named Yellow Lodge in the brawl that resulted in Chief Bull Bear's death in 1842 may have referred to an especially close cousin, not a brother.

As for Red Cloud's children, he claims that by the 1850s he had three: two daughters born in 1850 and 1854 and a son, Jack, born in 1852. The fact that he mentions only Jack by name says a great deal about the significance of boys in a warrior society such as the Sioux's. Indeed, for many years Red Cloud worked diligently to have Jack be his successor as chief of the Oglalas. Until recent years the consensus was that Red Cloud ultimately had five children; the only disagreement among tribal scholars, according to historian James C. Olson, was whether he had one son and four daughters or two sons and three daughters. Pretty Owl told the wife of Pine Ridge agent John R. Brennan in 1904 that she and Red Cloud had one son and five daughters. A probate document from the South Dakota State Historical Society verified that number, listing as Red Cloud's heirs Jack and five sisters named War Bonnet, Leading Woman, Plenty Horses, Charges at Him, and Tells Him.

But Red Cloud's emphasis in his autobiography was not on the details of his personal life but on his exploits in warfare, a rather typical approach for a Native American autobiography from that period. And by the 1850s, when Red Cloud had his first three children, he already had achieved the exalted status of a *blotahunka*, or war leader. In fact, the system he developed for the Oglalas, in which war parties of only eight to twelve men were dispatched to engage the enemy, had become widely accepted. If he wanted to lead one of these parties, moreover, few would dare challenge his authority.

Once, in 1849, a jealous warrior named Black Eagle plotted to sabotage a Red Cloud–led raid on the Shoshones, or Snakes, as they were often called. But the charismatic Red Cloud promptly won over a majority of his warriors, surrounding Black Eagle and his fellow conspirators and forcing them to return to the main camp in disgrace. There were very few cases when Red Cloud's authority was questioned. Indeed, by the late 1850s his reputation had extended throughout much of the sprawling Lakota world. In 1857 a band of remote Brulés on the upper Missouri gave refuge to Red Cloud after a disastrous campaign against the Arikaras, feeling honored to have the renowned warrior as their guest.

By his own admission, not all of Red Cloud's war exploits were successful. Just before the winter of 1856, for example, Red Cloud, who was thirty-five years old at the time, was encamped on one of the branches of the distant Little Missouri River. As the weather got colder in this more northern region, his Oglala band became impatient for one more tilt with the Crows or Shoshones before the advent of snow. Red Cloud, leading one of his last war parties of the year against enemy bands, unknowingly camped near a Crow party, which was simultaneously heading toward Red Cloud's camp. The Crows discovered this fact first and stealthily seized all the Lakotas' horses, which had been carefully picketed near the edge of a wood. When the surprised Lakotas discovered this catastrophe, they were compelled to make the humiliating trip home on foot. Fortunately, another small band led by Young-Man-Afraid-of-His-Horses returned home at the same time from a successful raid against the Shoshones which netted them almost a hundred horses and a number of buffalo robes.

There were also negative aspects to Red Cloud's exploits; these were embodied in charges of cruelty leveled against him, usually by white antagonists. One episode of his alleged vengefulness occurred during the summer of 1857, when his band, while still in the north country, moved toward the upper Missouri, where game was more plentiful. Encamped at a new site far from their traditional hunting grounds, these adventuresome Oglalas decided to break the monotony by making war against some of the tribes in the area. They sent small parties to the west to conduct raids against the Shoshones or Crows. Another party, a large one of twenty-four led by Red Cloud, headed east to attack some old enemies from the past, the Arikaras, or Rees, as Red Cloud usually called them. When they finally reached the Missouri River, however, they found a village of Gros Ventres instead of a village of Rees. Although outnumbered, Red Cloud and his warriors attacked the unsuspecting Gros Ventres three times but were repulsed with surprising vigor on each occasion; the raid was considered a success, though, because they were able to seize one hundred horses.

One member of Red Cloud's party was killed and three were wounded, and although Lakotas, like most Plains Indians, were extremely sensitive to losses of this kind, thirteen of Red Cloud's men decided to go on with their leader while the rest of the party returned to camp with the stolen horses. On the following day, Red Cloud's smaller party discovered downriver a large Arikara village where a herd of horses, gathered at the side of the mud-daubed huts that comprised the Ree settlement, made an inviting target. But their surprise attack on these Arikaras was destined to fail; the Gros Ventres had already warned the Rees that there were Sioux in the area. As a consequence, the charge was broken up, the Sioux party losing about a third of its members; and Red Cloud escaped with his life by desperately paddling down the Missouri in a stolen Ree canoe for four days before reaching a friendly Brulé village.

During the following summer, in 1858, when Red Cloud and his Oglala band decided to move toward the Black Hills, they encountered a large band of what they thought were Cheyennes or Arapahoes some twenty-five miles east of Slim Buttes, one of the familiar landmarks in that part of the Northern Plains. The Oglalas, already irritated by their frustrations of the past two years, decided that if the strangers, stretched out in a long mounted procession, were Cheyennes, they would let them pass in peace, but if they were Arapahoes, distant relatives of the treacherous Gros Ventres who had warned the Arikaras of the recent Sioux attack, they would make war. To determine the identity of this winding caravan of travois, comprised of about fifty families, Red Cloud and a dozen of his warriors rode to the top of a nearby hill and asked in sign language who they were. When the spokesman for the nervous band admitted that they were Arapahoes on a trip to visit their relatives, the Gros Ventres, they unwittingly sealed their own doom; the vengeful Lakotas promptly attacked the peaceful party, deliberately killing all but the women and children.

Incidents of this kind are the cause for much of the criticism directed against Red Cloud, particularly by white critics, who have found him to be an unnecessarily heartless warrior. For example, Dr. James R. Walker, a physician at Pine Ridge and a student of Sioux culture in his own right, told Judge Eli S. Ricker, who conducted eighty-nine interviews of both Indians and whites at Pine Ridge from 1906 to 1907, that Red Cloud's cruelty was so blatant that through the years it had cost him the respect of many Lakotas. Mari Sandoz probably did the most damage to his reputation, however. Reacting negatively to the allegedly self-serving nature of Red Cloud's autobiography, Sandoz, in her book on Crazy Horse, tended to match every sterling quality possessed by Crazy Horse with a negative one possessed by Red Cloud. Nevertheless, to excel in a warrior culture, such as that which characterized Plains tribes of the nineteenth century, required a certain degree of ferocity; indeed, this trait was often essential for survival.

Whether Red Cloud showed less pity than other warriors is probably a matter of perception. But his outstanding success as a competitor in warfare is indisputable. American Horse, one of Red Cloud's contemporaries and a formidable warrior himself, once boasted proudly that Red Cloud killed four Pawnee warriors singlehandedly in one battle. On another occasion, he stampeded fifty Crow horses by killing the boy responsible for herding them and then killing the leader of the Crow party who pursued him. Yet, although warfare was often brutal among Plains tribes, Red Cloud's conduct could at times be especially ruthless. His attack on a Ute enemy about to drown in a stream because his horse was badly wounded is most illustrative. No doubt eager for another coup, Red Cloud charged into the water, grabbed the struggling Ute by the hair, and brought him to shore, where he promptly scalped him. Such brash and frightening conduct prompted even Captain Cook to admit that Red Cloud was truly a "terror" in combat.

Nevertheless, Red Cloud did change from a terrifying young warrior to a strong and prudent leader. Much of his life's remarkable evolution was dictated by the aging process. By the late 1850s, when Red Cloud was in his mid-thirties, he was beginning to pass his prime in the physical sense of that term. By the 1860s the process had reached a point in the forty-year-old warrior's life at which he was ready to let younger warriors, such as Crazy Horse, do the most dangerous fighting and take the most serious risks. In short, he was preparing for a new role in his life: that of an active political leader in peacetime and major strategist in wartime.

The question of when Red Cloud achieved significant leadership among the Lakota people is shrouded by the same controversy that has marked so many aspects of his personal life. In 1893, when Red Cloud gave the interviews that resulted in his unpublished autobiography, he insisted that he was made an Oglala chief in 1855. In fact, he described in great detail the elaborate pipe-dance ceremony by which he and his family were inducted into their new social category as tribal leaders; his description even specified the kinds of personal possessions he was expected to give to qualify for the honor. But his testimony was given after his people were defeated and their adversaries in the U.S. government had redefined the role of chief, giving it more power and prestige than it had ever had under the Sioux. Curiously, Red Cloud, in his account, failed to designate whether in that ceremony he had been made a shirtwearer or some other kind of Lakota leader.

George E. Hyde and Mari Sandoz in their Sioux studies have

both insisted that Red Cloud's rise to power occurred during the 1860s rather than the 1850s. Hyde has alleged that Red Cloud achieved the status of a shirtwearer by 1865, while Sandoz has insisted that he was passed over as a shirtwearer that year. The title of shirtwearer (so called because any man chosen for that position was entitled to wear a distinctive, often colorful, shirt) was an important one, for there were rarely more than four shirtwearers chosen from each Lakota tribe.

Regardless of whether Red Cloud was a shirtwearer or some other kind of Sioux tribal head, he was, by the 1860s, ready to assume a commanding position of leadership among his people. He had already accumulated enough brave deeds to be recognized as one of the greatest of the Sioux warriors. Among Oglalas he was an exceptionally able *blotahunka*, or war leader. His physical appearance seemed to dramatize as well as fulfill that reputation. One young army wife described him as being about six feet tall and looking very impressive. Although he does not appear to be conspicuous in size or height in the group photos taken later by whites, there was evidently something imposing about him. Perhaps it was his demeanor; although confident in manner, he was often a quiet person, responding to others only when addressed. When he rose to speak, however, almost everyone felt his charisma. His keen intelligence also marked him as an exceptional person. Certainly if any Lakota warrior could have perceived the ultimate threat posed by the increasing influx of whites into Sioux country by the 1840s and 1850s, it would have been Red Cloud. In fact, his interaction with traders, soldiers, and immigrants during those years probably prepared him for the greatest challenge of his life: leadership against an enemy more formidable than any the Sioux had ever faced before.

CHAPTER 3

The Coming of the Whites

IN 1834, when Red Cloud was only thirteen, he and his people moved south into the Platte River country. At that time the forks of the Platte constituted one of those neutral hunting grounds that rival Plains tribes often contested but rarely controlled. But things were bound to change, for the power of those Lakota bands to the north was even greater in 1834 than it was in 1821 when Walks-As-She-Thinks gave birth to Red Cloud. Moreover, Sioux successes in raiding and hunting in this neutral zone had made other Plains tribes increasingly wary of it. Even so, although game was plentiful, the potentially rich area was still a kind of no-man's land largely restricted to small and occasional war parties.

The Lakota tribes that lived and hunted along the northern fringes of this stretch of the Central Plains were, of course, aware of the lack of pressure put on the buffalo population in that region compared to the persistent pressure put on their own herds. By the mid-1830s the Oglalas and Brulés were more than ready to move into the game-rich Platte country and transform it from a neutral hunting ground into a Lakota one. Chroniclers of early Sioux history have argued for years that white trappers and traders were the ones who lured the Lakotas into the once disputed locale, but historian Richard White has argued that it was the other way around: profit-wise traders had followed the wandering Lakota bands into this new buffalo country to trade with them. According to White's version, frontier entrepreneurs such as William Sublette of the Rocky Mountain Fur Company were the first to realize that the choice hunting grounds of the Oglalas and Brulés were now closer to the Platte than to the

Missouri; in essence, these traders were just taking advantage of the trade opportunities with those Lakotas gravitating toward the unspoiled hunting lands along the Platte and North Platte rivers.

Regardless of who initiated this crucial migration to the Platte country, the Lakotas who settled near the forks of the Platte would again come in contact with the aggressive white newcomers they had first encountered along the Missouri thirty years before. Although this could be a cause for conflict, relations between the whites and the Lakotas were fairly benign at first; the trappers and traders offered the Sioux goods that made their lives significantly more comfortable. But a few years later, when the Platte Valley became a corridor to the Pacific Coast for an endless number of California- or Oregon-bound emigrants, this new relationship became more complicated.

Red Cloud's skills as a warrior grew significantly during his early years in the rich grasslands of the Platte Valley. Although he devoted most of his energies to hunting buffalo and raiding the camps of rival tribes, his contacts with white traders were nonetheless unavoidable. The major responsibility of dealing with the new competitors, however, fell to the chiefs and older men of the tribe. One Lakota chief particularly anxious to act as the spokesman for his people was Bull Bear. This willful person, who was also a respected holy man, had been the most powerful of the Oglala *itancans* for almost a decade. Indeed, for the past several years he had shown an unfaltering determination to make himself the final arbiter in almost all tribal matters. Because Bull Bear and his band held sway over Old Smoke's people during the 1830s, his often arbitrary conduct affected Red Cloud's life just as it did the lives of other young Oglalas.

Probably the first important historical reference to Bull Bear was made in 1825 when Red Cloud was only a child. In that year the Oglalas made their first treaty with the U.S. government; they negotiated a friendly pact with Brigadier General Henry Atkinson, who had led an impressive military expedition up the Missouri River. This event, made more memorable because the Sioux saw their first steamship, which provided part of the transportation for Atkinson's ambitious expedition, involved Saones, or northern Lakotas, as well as Oglalas. The records for this early treaty session listed the four bands that comprised the Oglalas at that time. The two most important were the True Oglalas, whose members probably constituted the head band, and the Koyas, who were later called the Kiyuksas. Bull Bear, who was designated as head warrior of the Koyas, undoubtedly became the most notable of those Oglalas listed in the treaty; his people, who probably lived near the headwaters of the Des Moines River before they crossed the Missouri, would become the most important of the four bands, largely because of Bull Bear's forceful personality.

Bull Bear's meteoric rise to leadership had a major influence on all the Oglala bands as well as the white traders moving westward to exchange furs for European goods popular with the Sioux since the early Minnesota years. But throughout the years of his ascendancy the great chief proved no diplomat. Described by his critics as being a blustering tyrant, he intimidated his followers by bellowing at them and taking the knife to anyone who would question his authority. He was even accused of ignoring the established Sioux custom of paying for a wife; indeed, he would allegedly take any young maiden who caught his fancy, leaving the parents without their customary recompense.

Beyond this highly negative picture is the same confusion and contradiction that seems to dog so many Lakota leaders, Red Cloud being no exception. Accounts from white sources cannot even agree on Bull Bear's physical appearance. American artist Alfred Jacob Miller's painting of the chief provides just one example. He presents Bull Bear as a handsome, heroic-looking chief with a long Roman nose and flowing black hair. Yet the German traveler Wislizenus, after a chance meeting with Bull Bear in 1839, described the Oglala leader as a "squat, thick figure." But there was a strong consensus on one thing: Bull Bear was trusted by the white traders, who attributed much of the stability among the Oglalas to his leadership.

Bull Bear's life span overlapped a period of more frequent contacts with whites moving into the area. From the Lewis and

Clark expedition in 1804 to the treaty sessions with General Atkinson in 1825 interaction increased. But the real upsurge in contacts with the newcomers occurred when the American Fur Company got involved in some serious trade arrangements with the Lakotas. Using an old Oglala trading site on the Missouri at the mouth of the Bad River, this company established a trade monopoly that lasted for almost a decade. Its approach was in sharp contrast to that used by its chief competitor, the Rocky Mountain Company, which sent brigades of fur trappers into the high country to gather beaver pelts. When the American Fur Company became aware of the success of its aggressive rival, however, it too began to send employees into the field. The result was a brisk trade war that marked the final years of the fur business, which began to decline in the late 1830s when silk hats replaced beaver ones.

In 1834, William Sublette and Robert Campbell, two men anxious to do business with the Rocky Mountain Company, entered the scene. Their plan was to bring supplies by way of the Santa Fe Trail to the fur company's trappers in the high country, the Platte River route being temporarily blocked by hostile Arikaras. Encountering frustrating delays along the way, the two decided that Sublette should push ahead in time for the company's annual rendezvous in the Rocky Mountains. Sublette's hasty mission ended in disappointment, however, as the Rocky Mountain Company purchased the supplies it needed before he arrived. Campbell, in the meantime, reached the mouth of the Laramie Fork of the North Platte and, while waiting for Sublette's return, built a little stockade, calling it Fort William to honor his partner.

Disappointed by his and Sublette's failure to do business with the Rocky Mountain Company, Campbell decided to entice the Oglalas southward to trade at their new post. His decision was not a difficult one, given the fact that many southern Lakotas were already moving toward the Platte as part of their desire to hunt for more bountiful game. But it did alarm Lucien Fontenelle of the American Fur Company, who wrote his firm an urgent letter warning of this new competition.

Despite the anxiety generated by Campbell's aspirations, subsequent events would significantly alter his plans and vitally affect the destinies of the Oglala people. Shortly after Fort William was constructed, two traders, C. E. Galpin and John Sabille, traveled to the plains east of the Black Hills to parley with Bull Bear's band at Bear Butte. Bull Bear was urged to move his people into the Platte country, where buffalo herds were still abundant and where the Oglalas could bring their trade goods to the new fort. As a consequence, Bull Bear led approximately a thousand Oglalas (about a hundred lodges) southward in 1834, to be followed by another thousand of his tribal brethren in the spring of 1835. Old Smoke's people, including Red Cloud, were a part of this important migration; indeed, by the mid-1830s the followers of both Old Smoke and Bull Bear were known as the Bear people, an impressive testimony to the remarkable power already achieved by Bull Bear.

Although the future for this new fort seemed bright, Campbell and Sublette had a change of heart and abandoned their ambitious plans, turning Fort William over to the Rocky Mountain Company. That company, not finding the new venture profitable, sold it to its perennial rival the American Fur Company, which renovated the post and renamed it Fort John. As a result, the newly arrived Oglalas, who for the past decade traded almost exclusively with American Fur Company, found themselves once again engaged in commerce with their familiar trading partners. From such modest beginnings the famous Fort Laramie emerged; in 1849, Fort John was converted into a military post to provide protection for the constant stream of emigrants heading west.

Red Cloud was only a teenager during his first years in the Platte country, but with the passage of time he, along with other Bear people, became enamored with the rolling hills and nutritious grasslands of this new home. They also appreciated their access to the enormous herds of buffalo; the shaggy beasts were especially plentiful to the south, where the Republican and Smoky Hill rivers drained much of the Central Plains. Access to Fort Laramie was certainly another attraction; the post soon assumed great importance to the transplanted Sioux. Red Cloud's understanding of white people, whether traders, soldiers, or emigrants, probably developed at the same time that Fort Laramie was becoming a center of the Oglala world.

Because the bands of both Old Smoke and Bull Bear were often camped near the fort, Red Cloud undoubtedly spent some important time at Fort Laramie, even after it became a military post. There he gained keen insights into the character of the light-skinned newcomers, who would one day become the chief adversaries of his people. In many respects, Red Cloud and the other Bear people gained a twofold advantage from this interaction. They could acquire the superior trade goods at the fort and yet still lead the restless life of a Plains band, being able to come and go as they pleased.

During these years the members of Red Cloud's band acquired the less-than-flattering name of Bad Faces. Lieutenant Caspar Collins, a soldier who knew the Sioux quite well, claimed that Red Cloud and his people got the name because they quarreled so often with the other Lakota bands. Yet Red Cloud, in an interview given to Judge Ricker many years later, categorically denied that negative connotation. He insisted that his people were called Bad Faces because, with their heads hanging low in a dejected fashion, their faces often looked downcast or bad. He Dog, himself a Bad Face, provided another version more consistent with the traditional Sioux approach in coining names. He claimed that Old Smoke's son had a jealous wife, who continually berated him for his unfaithfulness. Her favorite characterization of her mate was that he had a bad face, which reflected his bad faith. She repeated this epithet with such frequency that their heated encounters became known to everyone living in the camp. In fact, the henpecked Young Smoke eventually acquired the nickname Iteshicha, or Bad Face; soon the entire band was saddled with the name.

Even though the lives of Red Cloud and his comrades were still centered around hunting, coup taking, and horse stealing, they could no longer ignore the intrusion of traders and trappers into their world. These people were becoming more evident with each passing day. But by the 1840s, even some white traders felt overwhelmed by the thousands of Oregon-bound emigrants who constituted the next wave of frontier migration. While almost all of the emigrants were just passing through, their presence was a harbinger of things to come. Moreover, Sioux interaction with the newcomers was not nearly as harmonious and beneficial as it had been with the traders and trappers.

The fur trade, of course, was not a new form of commerce for the Lakota tribes; they had been dealing with white traders off and on for more than a century. The relationship had not been a bad one, either. Employees of the American Fur Company, along with those trappers and traders who acted as independents, had goods to trade that the southern Lakotas really wanted. Their textiles, household goods, guns, and liquor were willingly exchanged for the fur pelts and buffalo robes the Lakotas could offer.

The traders also understood the psychology of the Plains Indians. They knew enough to make their transactions appear like an exchange of gifts. They understood that their Indian trading partners would never comprehend the free-market forces that ordinarily determined the prices they set. They were careful to avoid any kind of price variation that would unduly anger their Indian counterparts. More important, they knew the importance of always appearing to be a "friend" no matter how tough the bargaining got. Many of these men married into Sioux tribes; most Lakota women were honored to marry a man who possessed as many goods as the traders did. Thus, during Red Cloud's time a number of these enterprising traders—men such as Sam Deon, Nicholas Janis, and John Richard and the controversial son who bore his name—became vital links between the whites and the Sioux.

When the fur business began to decline in the late 1830s, trade relations with the tribes of the West became more fragile. This deterioration was, for the most part, a reflection of the dwindling supply of beaver. But even the buffalo, which still numbered in the millions, were beginning to show signs of decline. In short, the reckless and wide-open aspect of the early fur trade was coming to an end. Yet the industry did not retrench or attempt to harmonize with the law of supply and demand; instead, new companies replaced those that had already failed. Also, a large segment of the fur business tended to splinter into smaller, more competitive units. More ominous, perhaps, liquor became an increasingly important factor in the Indian trade.

Liquor had always been a trade item that the Sioux found hard to resist. Many tribal leaders, such as Red Cloud, who had lost a father to alcoholism, had seen the damage that whiskey could do, but they did not know how to stop it; indeed, the farflung tribes of both the Great Plains and Mountain West had little or no cultural experience with the consumption of alcohol. As a consequence, violent, drunken brawls often broke out among members of the tribe, sometimes leading to injury and death and sometimes dividing friends and families. On the upper Mississippi in 1822, for example, a number of Oglala tribesmen were killed in bloody, liquor-caused riots.

Beginning about 1840, traders, a number of whom were waging a trade war against the American Fur Company, began to discount the price of liquor in order to gain advantage over the fur giant. One of them was John Richard, who eventually managed to get close to Red Cloud and significantly influence him. Richard, who worked for Pratte, Cabanne & Company, one of the American Fur Company's most determined rivals, launched an effort to smuggle whiskey from some of the Mexican communities south of the Arkansas River. Using these supplies of whiskey, Richard's firm, which built a post near Fort Laramie (then called Fort John), began to entice customers away from the American Fur Company, using liquor as the bait.

The older company, in retaliation, lobbied to get one of its employees appointed as Indian agent in order to stop the practice, hypocritically increasing its own supply of liquor to reverse its losses and putting laudanum in the whiskey to calm rather than stimulate the unfortunate victims of John Barleycorn. These measures, however, did not slow the enterprising Richard; he embarked on a trading mission to the Black Hills, where he left a trail of dead Lakotas wherever his liquor was traded.

The disruption from the liquor trade eventually caused a serious cleavage among the Oglalas. During the six years that followed their migration into the Platte country, they began to divide themselves into two camps: those who followed Bull Bear and those who followed Old Smoke. Although there were other bands, these two were the most important. Unfortunately, a great deal of animosity had resulted from this division, much of it a result of Bull Bear's arbitrary use of power. Because many white traders were grooming the plump and good-natured Old Smoke as a rival to the arrogant Bull Bear, the suspicious Koya leader was becoming even more testy. The introduction of whiskey into tribal affairs only aggravated an already bad situation. Fortunately, separate hunting grounds kept the two antagonistic groups apart much of the time. Bull Bear's people tended to hunt on the Laramie Plains at the head of the North Platte, while Old Smoke's band hunted near the forks of the Platte, where they were often joined by Brulé bands down from the north.

But this geographical division could not indefinitely stem the growing feelings of animosity. Bull Bear, who could no longer contain his frustration over the new rapport Old Smoke was enjoying with some traders, caused one particularly disruptive incident. He boldly marched into Old Smoke's camp, stopping in front of his rival's lodge and daring him to come out and fight. When Old Smoke refused, the enraged Bull Bear grabbed the chief's favorite horse, which was tethered in front of Old Smoke's lodge, and killed it. Although Old Smoke was deeply offended, he was afraid to respond. The incident, however, would not be forgotten; many members of Old Smoke's shocked camp, including the belligerent Red Cloud, vowed to get even.

The ultimate vengeance against the arrogant Koya chief occurred in November 1841. According to historian Francis Parkman and the ubiquitous frontiersman Rufus B. Sage, Bull Bear and his followers rode into Old Smoke's encampment on the Chugwater, a branch of the Laramie River, for an allegedly peaceful visit. Old Smoke's people apparently began to ply their unpopular guests with liquor from Fort John, which predictably resulted in a noisy quarrel. When Bull Bear tried to break up the drunken brawl that resulted, he was killed, along with seven other warriors.

Red Cloud's version differs from that account in several ways. He blamed Bull Bear for starting the fight, insisting that the headstrong chief and his followers came to Old Smoke's camp with malice in mind. They were angry because of a controversial kidnapping: a young man from Old Smoke's camp had seized a young Koya woman with matrimony in mind. This act was a perfectly acceptable one if those involved were friendly, but it could constitute a dangerous insult to the bride's family if they were not.

Because the young woman was related to Bull Bear, who strongly disliked the would-be groom, the Koya chief decided to end the affair once and for all. His people, in order to help their leader succeed in his mission, invited a Bad Face warrior named Trunk to their camp. Trunk, who was one of Red Cloud's uncles, was considered a particularly savage fighter, and their purpose was to get him drunk so that he would not be at Old Smoke's camp when they attacked. But Trunk, who apparently had more tolerance for alcohol than most Sioux, returned to camp in time to confront Bull Bear's party. In fact, when Bull Bear's men killed the father of the aspiring groom, it was an angry Trunk who taunted Old Smoke's young warriors to retaliate. "Are you going to lay there and be killed?" he screamed. "Where are all the young men? Where is Red Cloud? Red Cloud, are you going to disgrace your father's name?"

Spurred by the older warrior's taunts, the young Bad Faces opened fire on their largely intoxicated kinfolk. One shot struck Bull Bear in the leg, bringing him to the ground in a sitting position. Red Cloud, never one to give quarter in battle, rushed to the fallen chief and shot him in the head, saying, "You are the cause of this."

Red Cloud's version of the incident was obviously a self-serving one. Although he may have been swept up by the emotion of the moment, he had plenty of reasons to hate Bull Bear. In addition to insulting Old Smoke, the imperious Bull Bear had killed Red Cloud's favorite uncle, White Hawk, in another drunken brawl. Another motive for Red Cloud was the prolonged history of bitterness between the two Oglala factions. Even so, it is difficult to give much credence to the speculation of longtime Sioux observer Dr. William F. Gerton that Red Cloud plotted to kill Bull Bear so that he could assume Bull Bear's position of leadership. Red Cloud was only twenty years old and had not been chosen as a shirtwearer or as any other kind of tribal leader at the time.

Regardless of Red Cloud's motives, the incident did elevate him among Old Smoke's followers. Shortly after Bull Bear's death, he was given leadership in the raid on the Pawnees that almost cost him his life. Although his own band was not especially popular among the Oglalas, Red Cloud's role in this controversial affair gave him a visibility few warriors his age could ever expect. His subsequent exploits as a warrior only enhanced that envied reputation.

Although Red Cloud may have benefited from Bull Bear's death, the old chief's demise was truly devastating to many Oglalas. Whether or not Old Smoke had realistic aspirations for leadership, he could not replace Bull Bear, who was one of the few Sioux leaders who could compel obedience among the independent-minded members of the tribe. In fact, the bitterness between the two Oglala bands continued well into the reservation period.

Both feuding groups even moved to different hunting grounds as far apart as possible. Ultimately Bull Bear's Koyas, along with a Brulé band headed by Red Water, an old chief who had helped Bull Bear gain control of all the Oglalas, seceded from the rest of the tribe. The vacuum they created constituted fully half of the Oglala population. Although these disenchanted Oglalas continued to wander throughout the far-reaching domain appropriated by the aggressive Lakotas, they finally gravitated toward the buffalo-rich lands between the

Platte and Smoky Hill rivers, where they began to hunt with
the Southern Cheyennes. The remaining members of the Oglala
tribe—those who had followed Old Smoke—also continued
their restless ways, ultimately ending up in the Powder River
country, where they hunted with bands of Northern Cheyennes
and those of another Lakota tribe, the Miniconjous.

Red Water's son told Francis Parkman five years after Bull
Bear's death that the Oglalas had not recovered from that event;
they were like children who did not know their own minds.
Many of them were wandering about without direction or purpose. Bull Bear's people seemed to suffer the most in this regard.
Although the slain chief's son was recognized as their leader for
a time, he never became the kind of strong and dominant chief
they required. One sign of this disillusionment occurred when
Bull Bear's Koyas changed their name, a decision that was allegedly made at a council meeting to elect Bull Bear's successor.
During those important proceedings, an older man picked up a
small garter snake wriggling nearby, put it in his mouth, and bit
it in two, saying, "This shall be our name—Ki-ya-hsa." Although
the new name literally meant "bitten in two," it was later translated into "cut-off." Thus, Bull Bear's crestfallen people acquired
a new identity; they became known as Cut-Offs or Kiyuksas.

This bitter schism, which divided the Oglala bands so profoundly, could not have occurred at a more unfortunate time.
In 1841, the year of Bull Bear's death, the first sizeable wagon
train made its way westward on the newly developed Oregon
Trail; the emigrant party divided at the Bear River, with one-
half going to Oregon and the other half, the Bartleson-Bidwell
group, going to California. During the remainder of the decade
the number of emigrants heading west would increase significantly. Most of them were heading for Oregon, but Brigham
Young's large wagon train passed through the Platte Valley in
the summer of 1848, marking the start of the great Mormon
migration to Utah. In 1849 the California-bound gold seekers
also came in impressive numbers; in fact, during that year approximately fifty thousand emigrants crossed the hunting lands
of the southern Lakotas.

The problems caused for the Sioux by these travelers were enormous. That these wagon trains had an adverse effect on the herds of buffalo that stood in their path seems obvious. Even the white traders did not like to see this many new people; although the hordes of emigrants were just passing through, many traders felt they would ultimately ruin the country and destroy their livelihood. The once comfortable relations enjoyed by the Lakotas with most white traders and trappers also started to deteriorate. An increasing number of Sioux attacks on the Shoshones and Crows, for example, involved trappers; many of those men, who were experienced frontiersmen, had remained with those two tribes when the fur business played out in the early 1840s and regarded attacks on the Shoshones and Crows as attacks on them.

Actually the influx of westward-bound emigrants was an addition to already disturbing trends that had begun years before. Indeed, the destruction of buffalo herds was not a new problem. In 1832, George Catlin saw a herd of fifteen hundred buffalo slaughtered by Indians near Fort Pierre on the Missouri because one trader wanted to send a boatload of salted tongues to the Saint Louis market. John C. Frémont estimated that in the decade before 1843, ninety thousand buffalo were brought to market annually by the fur companies. But many Indians were also responsible for this reckless slaughter. Motivated by the enticing prices that traders were willing to pay, they, too, took their toll of these animals, which had been like a great commissary for most of them. Nevertheless, it was the emigrants who incurred the greatest wrath, even though they had only disturbed that segment of the Oregon Trail extending from the Grand Islands in the east to the forks of the Platte in the west. Although the herds that roamed this one-hundred-mile stretch had significantly declined, the tribes of the region could still profitably hunt in the grounds north of the Platte, which the Sioux called Buffalo North, or in the grounds south of it, which they called Buffalo South.

Asiatic cholera was another grievance that the Plains Indians had against the emigrants. Not the first European disease to plague American Indians, smallpox having been a scourge for years, this new disease, with its severe cramps and usually fatal dehydration, was brought westward on the Oregon Trail in 1849 after having been carried up the Missouri River by steamship. The Sioux winter counts of that year record the disastrous effects of this disease. In many camps the population was absolutely devastated; an army officer, Captain H. Stansbury, observed a Sioux camp at Ash Hollow where there were five lodges filled with dead Lakotas. The effects of cholera lasted for over a year, and serious epidemics of smallpox and measles followed. The spread of these diseases only aggravated relations between emigrants and Indians; in fact, during those dreary months many sick and frightened Indians lined the Oregon Trail to beg for food and medicine.

Red Cloud's Bad Faces did what people have done for centuries in the face of a life-threatening pestilence: they fled. Seeking the White River country north of the Oregon Trail, close to where the Pine Ridge Reservation is now, they put as much distance between them and the spreading sickness as they could. While living in that more isolated area, Red Cloud devised a remedy to counteract the fatal effects of cholera. His concoction was composed of boiled cedar leaves, the residue of which was to be drunk or used for bathing. This apparently successful decoction has been cited as proof that, like Sitting Bull, Red Cloud was a medicine man. There is very little basis for such a contention, however; although he may have given relief to some sufferers, this medicine-making phase of his long career was a passing one.

Even before the cholera epidemic, the influx of emigrants was creating problems that could no longer be ignored. In 1845, the ubiquitous Frémont heard the Sioux claim that these intrusive emigrants had already driven most of the buffalo from the North Platte area, compelling them to hunt in the Laramie Mountains. Emigrants, for their part, insisted that in the summer of the same year, threats and attacks were made against them by the Lakotas. Indeed, many hungry Sioux found it impossible to desist from begging and stealing from the wagon trains, which continued to cross their lands in increasing numbers. Even though few fatalities had resulted from these incidents, they were occurring too often in the mid-1840s as far as the U.S. government was concerned.

To deal with these problems, the government sent Colonel Stephen Watts Kearny into the Platte country in 1845. Kearny rode into Fort Laramie four years before it became a military post with five companies of well-equipped and smartly mounted dragoons. The no-nonsense colonel, with his penchant for strict discipline, put on an impressive parade geared to command the respect of those bands that had gathered to parley. His approach with these suspicious Indians was a carrot-and-stick one. Kearny told them that the Great White Father loved his Indian children. He urged them to reject the whiskey being plied by unscrupulous white traders. But his most compelling message was a warning that the Oregon Trail was to remain open and its travelers were not to be molested. Kearny concluded the parley by giving the Plains tribesmen some eagerly received presents, such as blankets, knives, and beads. He left the meeting feeling it had been an unqualified success.

Although Red Cloud claimed that he and other members of Old Smoke's band were present at the gathering, Bull Bear's alienated followers were apparently hunting on the Laramie Plains. Because approximately one thousand Sioux were present, Kearny may not have noticed Red Cloud, even though this "magnificent specimen of physical manhood," to again quote Captain James Cook, was in his prime as a warrior. But with older men such as the Brulé chief Bull Tail doing most of the talking, there was probably little reason for Red Cloud to attract any special attention.

Red Cloud's impressions of this show of military power would have been interesting because of his early interaction with whites. It also would have differed from Crazy Horse's and Sitting Bull's views in many significant ways. Although Crazy Horse was an Oglala, he was from a band whose contacts with whites were not as frequent as those of the Bad Faces. He was sometimes seen along the Oregon Trail with other Lakota warriors; indeed, he was so light-skinned that Crazy Horse, originally called Curly, was often mistaken for a white man. There were, in fact, many who believed that he had been taken captive by the Sioux as a boy. As for Sitting Bull, far to the north with his Hunkpapas, he was even more remote from whites than Crazy Horse and probably less familiar with them.

But Red Cloud had been living near whites off and on since Bull Bear led his migration into the Platte country in 1834. Although Old Smoke's band often hunted downriver from Fort Laramie or on the High Plains west of it, they routinely camped on the lush river bottoms near the fort. This closeness gave Red Cloud many opportunities to know and understand the often perplexing, strangely clad, and different-looking white people. Old Smoke was even more familiar with the members of this new culture. Long after most Oglalas had left Fort Laramie, Old Smoke remained in the vicinity of the post, almost becoming a fixture. When he died in 1864, a scaffold was erected for him on high ground outside the fort.

The conference with Kearny did little to stem the mounting tensions. Soon prominent people were warning of the disaster that would ensue unless some decisive action were taken. Among these gloomy prophets was the famous mountain man Thomas Fitzpatrick, who had been appointed Indian agent for the tribes on the upper Platte in 1845. Two years after he took office, Fitzpatrick urged federal authorities to locate a military post "at or in the vicinity of Laramie," where most of the "formidable tribes" were gathered and where, because of the decrease in buffalo herds, the danger to travelers was greatest. In 1849 the government responded by purchasing Fort Laramie from the American Fur Company and transforming it into a military post. This step, however, failed to convince Washington that travel in the Platte Valley was now safe.

A peace conference with the Plains tribes was another solution aggressively advanced at this time. One of the major advocates of this approach was Thomas H. Harvey, superintendent of Indian affairs in Saint Louis. As early as 1847, Harvey warned about the dangers of intertribal warfare and the decline in buffalo herds which aggravated that problem. Sioux winter counts had clearly shown that intertribal warfare commanded more attention among the Lakotas than their growing confrontations with whites. It was not only the kind of warfare which harmonized with the ritualistic life of a Sioux warrior, but it also was considered essential for horse stealing, which fueled the economy of most Plains tribes. But the increasing scarcity of the buffalo was making intertribal warfare intense at the same time more emigrants were crossing Indian lands on their way to the West Coast. The buffalo's diminution as a commodity was, indeed, becoming an ominous fact; by the 1850s many Lakotas were managing their herds like semidomesticated animals, driving them into areas where only the Sioux could hunt and starting fires in the grasslands of their Pawnee rivals in order to drive their herds into Sioux country.

Harvey's ideas for peace were implemented by his successor, Colonel David D. Mitchell, whose lobbying convinced Congress finally to appropriate money for a peace conference in February 1851. With this vital funding secured, the federal government's Indian Office sent messengers throughout the Great Plains to bring northern tribes to a conference somewhere in the Platte Valley. This effort, noble as it was, was not an easy one. Crows, Shoshones, and Pawnees were afraid to travel anywhere in Sioux country; indeed, the Pawnees absolutely refused to participate. The deaths from the cholera epidemic of 1849, which caused such devastation along the Oregon Trail, were still fresh in the minds of many tribal members. In fact, not even the presents promised to prospective delegates could completely overcome this widespread reluctance. Continued persistence on the part of the government, however, eventually bore fruit; a large peace gathering finally assembled in September 1851 at Horse Creek, a tributary of the North Platte, several miles down from Fort Laramie.

Eight suspicious tribes, including the Crows, Shoshones, Cheyennes, and Arapahoes, along with several of the river tribes and most of the Brulé Sioux, attended the Horse Creek conference. As all the bands of the Oglala tribe came, it may be presumed that Red Cloud was there. But the major voice for the Sioux at Horse Creek was the Brulé leader Conquering Bear (or The Bear), whom Mitchell had chosen to represent all the Lakotas at the conference. This chief, who was employed by the American Fur Company in 1841, had been close to white traders and trappers for many years. In some respects his position was not unlike that of Bull Bear. Traders had complete confidence that he could maintain good trade relations with them. Even though he was a Brulé and this meeting was held in Oglala territory, Conquering Bear's signature on the treaty was considered one of the government's biggest accomplishments. As for the Oglalas, none of them even "touched the pen."

The government's basic motive for the Horse Creek council was to get the tribes to live and hunt in certain assigned areas, in return for which they would receive one hundred thousand dollars in annuities each year for fifty years. But to qualify for these payments, the tribesmen had to lessen the dangers to travelers on the Oregon Trail by promising not to make war against each other. Of course, compelling the tribes to live at peace was a highly unrealistic goal at that time, and a number of them were decidedly unhappy about such a commitment. Avoiding war with the Crows, for example, was unthinkable as far as most Lakotas were concerned; when the Hunkpapas heard about this stipulation in the treaty, they steadfastly refused to abide by it. Even more distressing to the Sioux was the fact that the Crows had been assigned the Powder River country, a region that Red Cloud and other followers of Old Smoke would soon occupy as their new hunting ground.

In the end, the intertribal peace that the U.S. government had hoped to achieve failed to live up to its expectations. When the feasting and socializing of the eighteen-day conference ended, most tribal members went back to raiding, fighting, and competing for the dwindling buffalo herds. But, happily, open warfare between the Indians and the U.S. government did not erupt until several years later.

In August 1854, three years after Horse Creek, the disruptive Grattan affair occurred. It involved a weary cow that had strayed away from its Mormon owner on the Oregon Trail and wandered into a Brulé camp. There it was killed and eaten by a visiting Miniconjou. The culprit, a head warrior for the Miniconjous named High Forehead, was the grandfather of Clarence Three Stars, an important source for information about the Sioux around the turn of the century. The incident, which should have been a minor one, was twisted out of proportion by a brash young lieutenant named John L. Grattan; this officer, who was fresh from West Point and anxious to achieve distinction, took a detachment of twenty-nine men from nearby Fort Laramie to arrest the offending Miniconjou.

When Grattan's men reached the Brulé camp, Conquering Bear, along with the Oglala leader Old-Man-Afraid-of-His-Horses, tried to intervene on High Forehead's behalf. It was at this point that Grattan made his most foolish decision. He ordered his troops to fire their two howitzers into the tense Indian camp, fatally wounding Conquering Bear. In the melee that followed, Grattan and several of his men were immediately killed, and the efforts of the rest of his party to escape ended in disaster; all but one of Grattan's soldiers were slain as they retreated back to Fort Laramie. Red Cloud, according to his own testimony, was camped near the fort at the time of the incident but probably refrained from getting involved, as the attack was against a Brulé, not an Oglala, encampment.

Notwithstanding the provocative nature of Grattan's mission and the death of Conquering Bear, who had won the confidence of most traders, the attitude of federal authorities toward the Sioux hardened; they were determined to retaliate for the death of Grattan and his men. Moreover, the true story of what happened never reached Washington; a number of white traders, fearful that Conquering Bear's death marked a sinister turn in Lakota-white relations, twisted the events of the Grattan affair to make the Sioux appear to be the real aggressors; an attack on a mail wagon the following November by two of the Brulés' future leaders, Spotted Tail and Red Leaf, only added credence to the charge of Sioux aggressiveness.

In retaliation, the U.S. Army launched a surprise attack on a

Brulé encampment on the Blue Water near Ash Hollow, not far from Red Cloud's birthplace. The twelve-hundred-man force was commanded by Brigadier General William S. Harney, a seasoned officer whose fury in battle won him the Sioux nickname Mad Bear. Harney struck the unsuspecting Lakotas, who were under the leadership of Conquering Bear's successor, Little Thunder, on September 3, 1855. The results of his attack were disastrous: eighty-six members of the tribe were killed, and seventy women and children were captured. The victorious Harney then marched north and in the spring of 1856 forced a number of northern Lakotas at Fort Pierre to promise not to interfere with emigrant traffic through the Platte Valley.

Harney's brutal, give-no-quarter campaign had far-reaching consequences. The two main bands of the feuding Oglalas, who had dominated much of the area in the Platte Valley for two decades, continued to draw away from each other. As a consequence, the well-traveled Oregon Trail, or the Emigrant Road, as it was often called, was free from much of the interference attributed to the divided Oglalas. The Brulés, who suffered the most from Harney's campaign, also moved expeditiously from the path of the Oregon Trail.

The Kiyuksas, Bull Bear's people, moved from the Laramie Plains, where they had probably wintered before Ash Hollow, to the Republican River country in the south. There they joined the Brulés under the leadership of Little Thunder and Spotted Tail in Buffalo South. Bands of Southern Cheyenne were also there to share that hunter's paradise. These tribes also engaged in hunting excursions as far south as the Arkansas River, making it increasingly difficult for them to return to Fort Laramie for the annuities they were promised at the Horse Creek conference in 1851.

The migrations of Old Smoke's people were also far-reaching, although they tended to occur north of the Platte Valley. After Ash Hollow, they were often found camping along the South Fork of the Cheyenne River, southwest of the Black Hills, or spending the fall on the Clear Fork of the Powder River further north. In his autobiography, Red Cloud, who claimed that his Bad Faces camped on the Clear Fork in late 1855, carefully traced their extensive wanderings during the late 1850s, which took them as far east as the Missouri River and as far north as the country between the Little Missouri and Heart Creek. They ultimately ended up in the Powder River country east of the Bighorns, an area that had been assigned to the Crows in the 1851 treaty. There they, along with the Miniconjous and North-ern Cheyennes, enthusiastically renewed their warfare with the hated Crows.

The Bad Faces, including Red Cloud, were probably among the last to break their once close association with the traders and soldiers at Fort Laramie. In fact, L. B. Dougherty, one of the fort's traders, placed Red Cloud there in 1856, probably a mistaken date, as Red Cloud claimed to be many miles north of the fort that year. Nevertheless, Dougherty, who described Red Cloud as being almost a fixture at the fort, related an in-cident that showed how comfortable Red Cloud had become with whites by that time.

The proud Lakota warrior, then in his mid-thirties, wanted to feast some prominent chiefs who were visiting the fort. Al-though generally against alcohol, Red Cloud was anxious to please his guests with strong drink. He, therefore, asked the post surgeon for a bottle of whiskey, which he was willing to exchange for two beautifully ornamented buffalo robes. When the much anticipated feast began, Red Cloud ceremoniously handed the new bottle to the most prominent of his visitors. The man took a drink, looking at Red Cloud in a puzzled way, and handed the bottle to the next guest, who reacted similarly. When the bottle finally reached Red Cloud, he discovered, to his dismay, that he was serving nothing but water, the cork hav-ing been soaked in whiskey to trick him. In anger, he left the party and headed for the surgeon's office, but the wary officer had already made himself scarce. The dispute was settled several days later when the surgeon made amends by presenting Red Cloud with gifts impressive enough to restore his pride. Nev-ertheless, as long as Red Cloud remained at the post, he was known as Two Robes for the pair of lavish gifts he had given for just a bottle of water.

This episode not only shows that Red Cloud maintained close contacts at the fort after most Oglalas had deliberately put ample distance between them and their increasingly aggressive white adversaries, but it also reveals a surprising intimacy between Red Cloud and many officers at the post; the post surgeon must have felt quite secure to pull such a trick on a warrior with a reputation as intimidating as Red Cloud's. Despite such cases of familiarity, however, Red Cloud's Bad Faces should not be confused with those Lakota outcasts known as Loafers (or Waglukhe, to use the Sioux name), a makeshift band of Indians who for many years hunted near the Oregon Trail, often begging from emigrants, or encamped close to Fort Laramie, often begging from soldiers. That group usually included the families of daughters who had married white traders or who had established intimate relations with army officers. Although at one time the Loafers comprised a rather large and important band, as Red Cloud's visits to the fort became less frequent only a few Bad Faces, such as Big Mouth and Blue Horse, remained with these increasingly isolated Indians; in fact, their numbers dwindled to fewer than fifty lodges by the time of the Civil War.

The actual departure of most of the Bad Faces from their campsites around Fort Laramie, however, was part of a gradual process. This increasingly dominant Oglala band would continue to wander throughout the far-flung Lakota hunting ground to the north as it had apparently done during much of the late 1850s. But after 1856, the Bad Faces did not return to camp in the immediate environs of the fort. Often they were not far from it—their winter camp in 1861–62 was only sixty miles from Fort Laramie—but they no longer centered their lives around this post, which had been their winter home for more than two decades.

The get-tough policy of the U.S. government following the Grattan affair was probably one reason why Fort Laramie no longer appeared a safe and comfortable place for these northern

Oglalas. But the Mormon War of 1857–58 was certainly another reason for this change of heart. When President James Buchanan sent federal troops to Utah to deal with the allegedly rebellious Mormons there, a number of officers at the fort with whom Red Cloud was on friendly terms were reassigned to become participants in the Utah Expedition. No doubt the post lost much of its warmth because of this personnel change.

An even more important reason for Red Cloud's ultimate disenchantment with Fort Laramie was Indian Agent Thomas Twiss's decision in 1857 to move the Oglala agency from Fort Laramie to a new post on Deer Creek, some one hundred miles to the west. Twiss, a fascinating figure who decided to live permanently with the northern Oglalas after Lincoln removed him as agent in 1861, seemed as much motivated by commercial considerations as sentimental ones when he selected an old Mormon way-station on the Overland Trail for the new site of his Indian agency. Located close enough to the Powder River to supply the Sioux with arms and ammunition for another war with the Crows, the Deer Creek post soon became a bustling place.

While Red Cloud may have known some army officers at Fort Laramie fairly well, his closest friends among the whites were almost always sympathetic traders such as Twiss. Indeed, with Twiss's departure from Fort Laramie, those Bad Faces who remained at the post may have felt vulnerable, given the indifferent attitude of the military garrison there. At Deer Creek, however, things were different. Twiss, an honor student at West Point who became a longtime employee of the American Fur Company, had been close to the followers of Old Smoke. Even closer was the older John Richard, who, ironically enough, was the trader who pioneered the destructive liquor trade among the Sioux in 1840. Richard, who became a particularly close confidant of Red Cloud, also established a post on Deer Creek, making handsome profits supplying goods to such Lakota tribes as the Oglalas, Miniconjous, and Sans Arcs, along with their allies the Northern Cheyennes, for a new conflict with the Crows.

Despite their long and sometimes profitable association with whites at Fort Laramie, Red Cloud's Bad Faces, who had raised him from a four-year-old child to a renowned warrior, had not degenerated into Loafers. In truth, by the early 1860s, when most members of the Loafer band would have been terrified to join the "wild camps" of those Lakotas in the north, all but a small number of Bad Faces were eager to drive the Crows out of the Powder River country. Using the supplies they traded for at the posts along Deer Creek, they joined their fiercest warrior, Red Cloud, who in 1861–62 led a large war party that, according to Cloud Shield's oft-cited winter counts, resulted in an impressive Crow defeat and the death of an important Crow chief named Little Rabbit.

Notwithstanding Red Cloud's newly refurbished reputation as a war leader during the early 1860s, his credentials as a chief were still shrouded in controversy. His alleged installation as a chief in 1855 certainly had failed to persuade the astute soldier Lieutenant Henry E. Maynadier of his importance. Maynadier, who later became the commandant at Fort Laramie, insisted that when he saw Red Cloud at Deer Creek trading with John Richard in the winter of 1959–60, Red Cloud was not a chief. In fact, the recognized leader, or *itancan*, of the Bad Faces was not Red Cloud but one of Old Smoke's sons. Yet in reality, whenever the Oglalas were seriously threatened, Red Cloud would become the de facto chief of the Bad Faces. The big question on the eve of the Civil War was whether Red Cloud would be as effective in fighting the whites, with whom he had a long history of friendship, as he was in fighting his Indian rivals.

CHAPTER 4

Red Cloud's War

THE early years following Red Cloud's departure from Fort Laramie were relatively peaceful ones for both the Sioux and their new white rivals. Most of the Oglala bands were now many miles away from the stream of emigrant traffic on the Oregon Trail, a situation which allowed these Sioux time to resume their more traditional way of life. They could now hunt and camp in peace with only the presence of largely cowed rival tribes to constitute a threat. For the Sioux the only drawback to this happy arrangement was the decline in their trade with white entrepreneurs; the exchange of goods at Deer Creek and the visits of white traders to the Lakota camps could not fill the void created when Fort Laramie ceased to be their main trade outlet.

These were satisfying years for Red Cloud. His prestige as a warrior was now firmly established; the decisive leadership he showed in the Crow wars of 1861–62 only enhanced this reputation. But by the end of the Civil War he knew he would have to make a new adjustment in his life; he was in his mid-forties, and his style of fighting would have to change. No longer could he be expected to head risky war parties or lead the decoy forces necessary to lure the enemy into an ambush; these dangerous activities were more appropriate for younger men eager for the coups and special distinctions that Red Cloud had already achieved. In short, Red Cloud, still a powerful man moving grudgingly into his middle years, would now have to be more of a strategist than a tactician in warfare. Still, he was a man whose judgment was highly respected, given his formidable war record.

During the years before the Civil War, those Oglalas now living in the Powder River country had organized into three

principal bands. Probably the most important was the Hunkpatila band, whose leader, Old-Man-Afraid-of-His-Horses, was
designated by Conquering Bear as his successor after Conquering Bear had been fatally wounded in the Grattan affair. Man-
Afraid's leadership, which lasted for more than a decade, was
reassuring to most whites, given the Sioux chief's strong commitment to peace. One of Man-Afraid's Hunkpatilas, however,
perceived the growing strength of the whites quite differently.
Crazy Horse, who was only twenty years old in 1862, was already a bitter and confirmed enemy of these new adversaries.
The young warrior had been with the Brulé band that carried off
the dying Conquering Bear in 1854 and had barely missed being at camp when "Mad Bear" Harney had launched his attack
on Little Thunder's Brulés near Ash Hollow in 1855. Another
formidable Lakota leader was Red Dog, head of the Oglala band
called the Oyukhpe; he was an able warrior whom the whites
would one day find most intractable. As for the third band, the
Iteshicha or Bad Faces, their war leader, Red Cloud, was still an
unknown quantity as far as his attitude toward the whites was
concerned.

The motivations of these three bands in choosing the Powder
River country for their new home has been the subject of some
debate. One account claims that the decision was a product of a
grand council convened for all seven of the Lakota tribes at Bear
Butte during the summer of 1857. The gathering was called to
deal with the now widely recognized threat of a white invasion.
Because it was impossible for that many tribes to congregate together for long—the damage done by the huge herds of horses
alone was just one of the negative factors—it was decided at Bear
Butte that each tribe should choose its own hunting ground to
develop and protect. Thus, those Oglalas who had followed Old
Smoke chose the Powder River.

This story given as the reason for picking the Powder River
as a new home is highly suspect. Lakota tribes tended to make
unilateral decisions when it came to major geographical moves.
Also, it was difficult to bind all seven tribes to any commitment
of this magnitude; Lakota tribes had customarily operated on

their own or sometimes in tandem with one or two close allies.

The Powder River, particularly the region around the head-waters of that coveted watercourse, was the most natural place for the Oglalas to choose as a new home. It was fairly close to the North Platte River, for one thing. It was also easy for white traders to move from Fort Laramie to the meandering banks of the Powder. But, most important, the Powder River country was one of the last of the unspoiled hunting regions left to the Lakotas. Large buffalo herds still roamed the area from the Black Hills to the eastern slope of the Bighorns; the steep thickets and woodlands of the latter range virtually teemed with small game. The entire area, which was shared in the north by such Lakota tribes as the intransigent Hunkpa-pas, extended throughout much of the present-day states of Wyoming and Montana and encompassed such game-rich val-leys as those of the Yellowstone, Tongue, and Little Missouri rivers and Rosebud Creek.

These early years in the Powder River country were good ones for Red Cloud; the white threat was temporarily stymied by the nation's growing sectional conflict and the outbreak of the Civil War. Red Cloud's obvious assets seemed to be receiving more recognition. Although Old-Man-Afraid-of-His-Horses was still the leader of the Powder River Oglalas, Red Cloud, who was only five years his junior, had achieved a special niche in tribal affairs by virtue of his war exploits. It could be said that Man-Afraid, the principal *itancan* of the northern Oglalas, was the peace chief, while Red Cloud, whose status at that time probably did not exceed that of a shirtwearer, was the leading *blotahunka*, or war chief.

Red Cloud faced some serious obstacles in his quest for lead-ership, however. His key role in the demise of Bull Bear had left its mark; although the old chief's controversial death had occurred twenty years earlier, many Oglalas had not forgotten it. Red Cloud's extraordinarily willful personality only added to this long-standing liability; throughout much of his career he was a man who was often more feared and respected than liked. His own band, the Bad Faces, were also immersed in controversy. His people had gained a reputation among many

Lakotas as being the least cooperative of the northern Oglala bands. Their tardy departure from Fort Laramie, where for two decades they had been enchanted by the white man's hardware and whiskey, was also used against them. Had Red Cloud and his Bad Face comrades not been so successful in the rekindled Crow wars that preceded the Civil War, their negative image would have been even greater.

This unfavorable reputation was strong among many of Man-Afraid's Hunkpatilas. One incident in particular aggravated relations between them and Red Cloud's Bad Faces. It involved Red Cloud and Crazy Horse, who was then a rising young Hunkpatila warrior. Crazy Horse had fallen in love with Red Cloud's niece, Black Buffalo Woman. Their courtship was apparently a happy and passionate one until Crazy Horse became the victim of a cruel ruse involving Red Cloud and several Bad Face warriors. Crazy Horse, who may have been only eighteen at the time, was on a raiding party, sometime about the year 1860, when a Bad Face warrior named No Water left the group on the pretext that he had a toothache. He promptly returned to camp and, taking advantage of Crazy Horse's absence, managed to convince Black Buffalo Woman to marry him. When Crazy Horse discovered that he had been duped, he could hardly contain his bitterness; this event no doubt caused long-lasting ill feelings between him and Red Cloud, who he felt had been involved in the deception.

Although the Oglalas both to the north and south of the Platte Valley were leading more isolated and traditional lives during the late 1850s and early 1860s than had been the case for years, emigrant traffic was continuing to flourish, notwithstanding the interruption of the Civil War in the westering process. The number of people using the Holy Road, as the Sioux sometimes called the Oregon Trail after the U.S. government sanctimoniously decreed that no one could interfere with the travel of its users, could now proceed with greater safety than ever before. The normally peaceful Pawnees to the east and the Cheyennes and Arapahoes to the west were the only Indians who could possibly interfere with the migrants' progress. Thus, emigrants continued to come by the thousands, some

going to Oregon and Utah but most going to California. In
1858 gold was discovered in Colorado and a new group of gold
seekers, the Fifty-Niners, started to move along the busy banks
of the Platte; they were scurrying down the river's south fork to
Cherry Creek, in what later became Denver, before scrambling
into the gold-rich Rockies to the west.

With the bustling Platte Road free from Sioux obstruction,
entrepreneurs began to build way-stations along the river for
the famous Pony Express, which began to carry its mail westward at record speed in April of 1860. A few months later
the U.S. Congress passed the Pacific Telegraph Act to encour-
age private enterprise to string telegraph wires for even faster
communication with settlements on the coast;the now famous
Western Union Telegraph Company contracted for the project
that same year, completing it in October of the following year
with very little interference. When the Civil War erupted in
1861, the Overland Mail Company, which had been deprived
of its southern mail route through Texas, relocated to a route
through the central plains; it too began to use the increasingly
busy Platte corridor for its mail deliveries and passenger service.
By the early 1860s the United States was already making plans
to build its first transcontinental railroad line; the initial tracks
for this new enterprise would be laid through the once pristine
Platte country.

The Sioux were also being outflanked in other directions during this deceptively calm interlude in their history. To the east,
white settlement was creeping toward their hunting grounds
from such sparsely populated border states as Minnesota and
Iowa. Whites in the newly created Dakota Territory were largely
confined to the Yankton area in the territory's extreme southeast corner, but the westward direction of their migration did
not augur well for the Lakotas. Although most white settlers in
Nebraska, which was given territorial status in 1854, still resided
along the Missouri River, some of them had started such settlements along the Platte River as Columbus, Grand Island, and
Kearny City. These ambitious communities were established to
supply goods and services to westward-bound emigrants. Aid-

ing them in this endeavor were newly developed ranch spreads to provide livestock for the travelers, freighting stations to supply their material needs, and army posts to protect them. Starting in 1859, other facilities of this kind were established along the South Platte to accommodate the Fifty-Niners.

An even more immediate threat to Red Cloud's surprisingly serene Sioux was the trail, developed by John M. Bozeman in 1863, that extended from Julesburg on the South Platte through the Lakota hunting grounds in the Powder River country to Montana's newly discovered gold fields. Although the Oglalas eventually reacted violently to this shortcut to Montana— Bozeman lost his life in 1867 on the trail that bears his name—the fact that they allowed the whites to develop it at all is an indication of their indifference toward what was going on outside their hunting grounds.

The tranquil mood of these indifferent Lakotas shifted only slowly. Perhaps they were too distant from the Platte forts to assess the disturbing changes in personnel caused by the outbreak of the Civil War. Nevertheless, the replacement of army regulars with less efficient volunteers could not indefinitely escape their notice. But it was probably Little Crow's War in 1862 that brought the first real inkling of the grave dangers that faced them. After the failure of the Santee or Dakota Sioux to drive the largely German-speaking settlers out of the Minnesota River valley, a number of refugees from this exceptionally bloody war reached the country across the Missouri to tell their old allies about the duplicity and insatiable appetite for land of the aggressive newcomers. Although many of the demoralized Santees sought refuge in Canada, a number of them chose to live among the northern Lakotas, where they became a constant reminder of the seriousness of the situation.

During the summer of 1863, hostile bands of Cheyennes and Arapahoes, who had remained in the Platte and South Platte valleys, launched a series of sporadic attacks against such symbols of white intrusion as wagon trains, telegraph offices, stage stations, and ranch houses. It was first believed that these raids were the work of irresponsible warriors and that tribal leaders would eventually control them. But in light of the earlier disaster in Minnesota, there was little patience among western settlers for restraint; many began to agitate vigorously for better protection. Government officials responded as promptly as Civil War conditions would permit. Military escorts were furnished for travelers west of Fort Kearny. Fort McPherson was built that fall on the South Platte, eight miles above the forks of the Platte. The Eleventh Ohio Cavalry was dispatched to strengthen the undermanned garrison at Fort Laramie. Many of the troops sent, however, were both unseasoned and poorly disciplined; a number of them were "galvanized Yanks," former Confederate soldiers who wore the blue uniform of the frontier trooper for mercenary reasons. But there was a handful of good officers, of whom Colonel William O. Collins, commander of the Eleventh Ohio, was probably the best.

The small, unauthorized attacks of 1863 grew into a general Indian war in 1864. At first the bloodshed did not involve Red Cloud's Sioux in any direct way; most of the Indian raids were conducted in the fledgling Territory of Colorado. There, gold seekers headed for Denver were scrambling through some of the finest hunting lands still left to the Cheyenne and Arapaho tribes; the result was a series of violent confrontations involving soldiers and Indians. In April the oxen of the freighting firm Irwin and Jackson were allegedly driven off by Cheyennes. This incident was followed soon after by an encounter at Fremont's Orchard on the South Platte between a Cheyenne party and the Colorado Volunteer Cavalry. In response to these frightening episodes, Major General Samuel R. Curtis, commander of the troops along the Platte and Arkansas rivers, ordered Colonel John M. Chivington of the Colorado Volunteers to pursue those Indians, a major mistake given the fact that Chivington, a zealous former Methodist preacher, was an unregenerate Indian hater. The result of his unyielding attitude was a series of bloody Cheyenne and Arapaho attacks that lasted throughout the summer. But he really destroyed any hope for an early peace by his surprise dawn attack in November on a Cheyenne encampment on Sand Creek in southeastern Colorado which resulted in the brutal deaths of two hundred people, mostly women and children.

Chivington's attack on that bloody morning brought national repercussions. There was outrage in the East, resulting in an investigation by a congressional committee headed by Republican Senator James R. Doolittle of Massachusetts in March 1865. The work of the committee led to Chivington's condemnation and an attempted court-martial, which was only thwarted by the fanatical colonel's resignation. The Indian response, however, was much more serious. The survivors at Sand Creek, under the leadership of Black Kettle, who was, ironically enough, a peace chief, fled to another Cheyenne camp on the Smoky Hill River. There, a large war council was held. One result was the prompt dispatch of a war pipe, the sure symbol of direct action or revenge, to the other Indian encampments of the area, including a large Sioux camp on the Solomon Fork and a Northern Arapaho one on the Republican River. The outcome of all this frenzied activity was the gathering in late December of some eight hundred lodges, more than half of which belonged to Brulé, or southern Oglala Sioux.

These new allies launched a series of devastating attacks on settlements, ranches, and stage stations along the South Platte, culminating in an attack, involving as many as a thousand warriors, on Julesburg in northeastern Colorado on January 7, 1865. Throughout the remainder of the month, while Red Cloud and his warriors still were rather passive, raids were made with such ferocity that a disapproving Black Kettle left with his band of Cheyennes for the Arkansas. In February the avenging warriors moved their offensive to the North Platte Valley, attacking Julesburg again during their bold wintry march. The makeshift army later fought a sharp encounter with the members of the Eleventh Ohio Cavalry at Mud Springs before crossing the icy North Platte in western Nebraska, with their women and children and stolen livestock, and heading for the Black Hills. Once they reached their destination, the rest of the Cheyennes and Spotted Tail's Brulés went their way, while the southern Oglalas traveled westward to join Red Cloud and his Oglalas in the

Powder River country. This epic march, which covered about
four hundred miles, probably resulted in the deaths of more
whites than the number of Cheyennes killed at Sand Creek.

The Oglalas hunting along the Powder River were already
alarmed by the bitter fighting in Colorado. Crazy Horse and
a group of warriors, in fact, went south to participate in the
second attack on Julesburg. But the peace faction led by Old-
Man-Afraid-of-His-Horses counseled against any rash action. It
was becoming increasingly difficult to assume a neutral position,
however. On April 30, 1864, about the time the Cheyenne-
Arapaho war started, northern Lakotas under the leadership of
Sitting Bull, Four Horns, and Black Moon warned the whites
that they would no longer be allowed in Lakota country. In
July, on the Upper Knife River, the Battle of Killdeer Mountain
was fought with the army under Brigadier General Alfred Sully;
substantial losses were inflicted against the Sioux in this engagement. During that same summer, the Hunkpapas attacked an
armed wagon train of Montana gold seekers east of the Little
Missouri River.

This growing warfare both to the north and south of Red
Cloud's Oglalas could not be ignored indefinitely, especially in
light of the Sand Creek Massacre. Younger warriors such as
Crazy Horse were ready to fight, and many of the tribe's fire-
eaters were already turning to Red Cloud for more aggressive
leadership than Man-Afraid was willing to offer. The arrival in
March 1865 of the victorious Lakotas who had participated in the
great Indian campaign of the previous winter only strengthened
the war faction among the restless Powder River Oglalas. The
tales of deceit and callousness on the part of the white soldiers
brought by these new heroes triggered the expected emotions of
rage and anger. But the booty those Sioux had gathered, which
included large herds of prized horses, provided an even more
persuasive lure.

In May, Red Cloud and Young-Man-Afraid-of-His-Horses,
who was much more militant than his father, met with other
Lakota and Cheyenne war leaders on the Tongue River to plan
a joint strategy. There it was decided to send a large expedi-

tion against some strategic military fortification along the North Platte, using the same kind of highly formal organization employed during the second Julesburg attack. In short, they would organize as one large, well-disciplined war party similar to the type they would send into Crow or Pawnee country if they were involved in a major war with either of those tribes. Once the purpose was accomplished, they would return without further plans for warfare until the next summer.

In July 1865 the much anticipated expedition was ready; the small army garrison at Upper Platte Bridge, the present site of Casper, Wyoming, was the target. The enthusiasm was especially great because during the previous month Crazy Horse and a party of Oglalas had arranged for the escape of a terrified band of Loafers who were being marched from Fort Laramie against their will through dangerous Pawnee country to get them out of an area the military regarded as too sensitive. Further stoking the expedition's exuberance was the triumphant return of those Sioux and Cheyenne war parties sent by Red Cloud and other war leaders in May to harass the new enemy throughout much of the Platte Valley.

The members of this huge expedition were as well trained in the ceremonial aspects of warfare as they were in the tactics and strategy of combat. Older men demonstrated for younger warriors the proper care of weapons and the proper application of war paint to their sturdy mounts. Equally ceremonial was the organizational plan for the expedition's approximately one thousand newly constructed lodges, which were to be occupied by such Lakota tribes as the Oglalas, Miniconjous, Sans Arcs, and Brulés and by Cheyenne warriors of both the northern and southern tribes. The lodges for each tribe were arranged in a large circle, where formal parades were organized before the entire body gathered in columns for the trip south. When this large, ornamental war force began its march, war chiefs were in the lead, carrying war pipes and setting the expedition's pace. Surrounding the columns on all sides were tough Cheyenne Dog Soldiers chosen to keep order among all members of the party.

To sanction this elaborate expedition, religious ceremonies, including the sun dance, were held before the group's grand departure. The leadership of this almost unwieldy war party, which proved one of the last of its kind, was impressive. According to George Bent, the astute mixed-blood Cheyenne who was also a participant, Red Cloud and Young-Man-Afraid were chosen to lead the Powder River Oglalas. Other leaders included High-Back-Bone (sometimes known as Hump), who represented the Miniconjous; Pawnee Killer, who represented the southern Oglalas; and the Northern Cheyenne leader Roman Nose, whose previous exploits had already given him an almost legendary status.

On July 25, 1865, this formidable expedition reached the hills above the Upper Platte Bridge. A decoy party of twenty, including Crazy Horse, was dispatched to lure the troopers, who manned the garrison on the south bank, across the bridge and into the hills, where most of the Indians waited in ambush. The effort failed; although some of the infantrymen took the bait, the garrison's cavalrymen refused to follow. A second decoy party was more successful, enticing a column commanded by Lieutenant Caspar Collins to cross the bridge. But instead of chasing the decoys into the hills, Collins's men galloped upriver to rescue a wagon train that had just come under attack. The Cheyennes, who had more experience fighting white soldiers, were able to cut them off; indeed, Roman Nose and his warriors had already killed most members of the luckless wagon train. The Lakotas, eager for action, left their positions of concealment in the hills about that time to swing behind the cavalry force and close the trap. The desperate cavalrymen, however, did manage to charge through the Sioux ranks and recross the bridge with only the loss of Lieutenant Collins and four of his troopers.

At that point the Sioux-Cheyenne force decided to declare victory, making no further attempt to cross the bridge and destroy the garrison. Although the members of the expedition were short of guns, this decision had more to do with their style of fighting. They elected to spend the night exchanging war stories and holding victory dances before a vast majority of them returned home to resume a normal life. It was, after all, almost time for the fall buffalo hunt.

This encounter was probably Red Cloud's first major experience fighting whites. Little did he and his comrades realize how inconsequential in the grand scheme of their turbulent future this victory would be. Much more ominous to the welfare of the Lakotas were the troops under General Patrick E. Connor which had been committed as early as April to invade the Powder River country and put an end to a perceived Sioux threat. By the late summer of 1865, General Connor, who was the new commander of the Platte, had three armies wandering through those vast Sioux lands, which sprawled from the headwaters of the Powder River to the Yellowstone in Montana. The main frustration of Connor's armies, ironically enough, was that they could not find a large Lakota force to attack. About the best that General Connor's Pawnee guides could do was to locate the campsites of those Sioux returning from the Upper Platte Bridge campaign.

Although there was some enthusiasm among Connor's men, Connor having chalked up a good record fighting Indians in the Far West, the morale of the columns under Connor's associates, Colonel Nelson Cole and Colonel Samuel Walker, was very low; in fact, Walker's men, exhausted by their long Civil War service, had revolted earlier against being sent on this expedition. To compound their frustrations, the demoralized forces of these two commanders were attacked after they had rendezvoused near the mouth of Powder River. Sitting Bull and his Hunkpapas, who had unsuccessfully tried to lure soldiers from Fort Rice on the Missouri in much the same way that Red Cloud and his people had tried with the garrison at the Upper Platte Bridge, turned on the discouraged Cole-Walker force with a vengeance. In the end, this hopeful but costly Powder River Expedition, whose major activities occurred during the month of September, ended with a whimper; the harassed men under Cole and Walker's leadership, in their vain effort to find Connor's army, finally reached a makeshift fort constructed in mid-August by General Connor's bewildered force. But not even this fortification, which bore Connor's name, would give him or the members of his expedition any enduring fame; the post was renamed Fort Reno on November 11 of that year.

About the same time that Connor's three columns were wandering through the Powder River country in search of the Sioux, Red Cloud became embroiled in another incident involving white intruders. A large wagon train bound for the gold fields of Montana was intercepted by an Indian party in the broken countryside around Pumpkin Buttes in northeastern Wyoming. The wagon train was carrying a road building party headed by James A. Sawyer, a former army officer from Sioux City, Iowa, who had acquired an army escort and a governmental subsidy on the basis that he would construct a road through Sioux country. The party had followed the Niobrara River past its source before it was spotted, east of the Powder River, by scouts who reported the wagon train's whereabouts to Red Cloud and Northern Cheyenne chief Dull Knife. When these two arrived at the head of a large war party, Red Cloud told Sawyer that his road builders could not travel through the Powder River country because they would disturb the buffalo. Yet the canny Red Cloud, who probably knew the white man better than did almost any other Lakota leader, allowed Sawyer's party to continue their trip provided they skirted the better hunting lands. But there was a price: the Sawyer party would have to give Red Cloud and Dull Knife one wagon full of provisions. Sawyer, over the strenuous objections of the army officer in charge of his military escort, met Red Cloud's demand, but his appeasement led only to more humiliation. A few days later his wagon train was attacked by other Indians because he refused to give them their share of provisions.

Perhaps the most surprising thing about this incident was that when it occurred, sometime in late August, the Lakota Sioux, including Red Cloud, were evidently not aware that the U.S. government was planning to build a road to Montana through the Powder River country. Their lack of preparedness in this regard was baffling, given the importance of their beloved hunting grounds. Just as shocking was the fact that Red Cloud was probably not even aware of Connor's recently initiated Powder River campaign.

Fortunately for the Powder River Oglalas, the great western campaign launched against the Plains tribes in 1865 was going badly throughout much of the Great Plains. Directed by a mediocre Civil War officer, Brigadier General John Pope, the campaign had largely discredited the concept that a military solution was the best one for the Indian problem. Although six thousand soldiers organized in regiments and brigades were involved, and thousands of others assumed back-up positions (guarding forts, settlements, and travel routes), the basic effect of the Pope campaign was to discourage an already war-weary nation. Nevertheless, important lessons were being learned. The army discovered, for example, that large columns of blue-coated soldiers operating in the wilderness needed much better logistical support than they usually received. In the case of Connor's units in the Powder River campaign, the loss of starving horses and mules because of miserable weather conditions almost resulted in the death of many of the commander's soldiers. Moreover, the long supply trains often needed for a Pope offensive sometimes caused such delays that the element of surprise was lost.

Other forces unleashed in Washington made the costly Indian campaign of 1865 even more unacceptable. Because of the staggering costs of the Civil War and the limited funds available, appropriations for the army seemed better directed toward the reconstruction program in the South, which by 1867 would become a military one. Moreover, humanitarian considerations had joined cost-cutting ones in the Indian policy being developed in Washington at that time. Senator Doolittle of Massachusetts, chairman of the Senate Committee on Indian Affairs, was one of the key personalities in this shift; in 1865 he authored a measure to send three congressional groups to the West to investigate the conditions of the western tribes. One important result of this effort was the cancellation of a major offense that Pope had planned against certain tribes south of the Arkansas River.

Doolittle's approach provided the motivation for other peace efforts in the Great Plains country. The governor of Dakota Territory, Newton Edmunds, was deeply concerned that an impending Sioux war would discourage further settlement of his territory. In October 1865, Edmunds, in charge of an ambitious commission that bore his name, traveled up the Missouri River to negotiate peace treaties with the more friendly of the Sioux; not one chief who put his mark on an Edmunds treaty, however, had resisted the three-year effort by such generals as Henry H. Sibley and Alfred Sully to militarily subdue these northern Lakotas. Edmunds's new peace initiative, moreover, did not represent any important change in the attitude of white settlers, who remained the most hostile of the anti-Indian groups in the country.

A conviction was evolving in Washington during these post-war years that peace with the Indians could be achieved without resorting to violence. The army's role would still be important, of course, but it would be far less proactive. On August 23, 1865, General Pope, sensing the new mood, wrote Major Frank Wheaton, the new commander of the District of Nebraska, that the frontier army should "return to a purely defensive arrangement for the security of the overland routes." This renewed commitment to defend the Platte Road also included a commitment to defend the new transcontinental railroad being built west from Omaha. Although this new dedication to peace was embraced by such leaders as Senator Doolittle and a majority of President Andrew Johnson's cabinet, it did not preclude the development of travel routes outside the Platte Valley (especially if gold were involved). The improvement of the Bozeman Trail, the two-year-old road to the Montana gold fields, thus became a legitimate goal even for those with the purest of intentions.

But cooperation with the Sioux was essential if any road were to be built through the Powder River country. Connor's Powder River expedition, of course, had already complicated things almost beyond repair. Nevertheless, to win Indian concessions through peaceful rather than warlike methods required new negotiations with the Lakotas and their allies. With this objective in mind, General Pope informed Secretary of the Interior James Harlan that he had ordered a council to convene in the spring of 1866 at which the Powder River tribes could conclude a peace treaty with special commissioners appointed by the president.

The prospects for Pope's lofty plan, however, were not very promising. In fact, a proposal to send a mission into the Powder River country to persuade the Sioux to participate was considered so dangerous that no white man would undertake it. Finally, Colonel Maynadier, then commandant at Fort Laramie, convinced Big Ribs, a member of the fort's Loafer band, and four other friendly Lakotas, including the influential Big Mouth, to take on the difficult assignment. Three months elapsed before any news about this mission reached the fort. But when it finally came in March, the government was elated. Not only would Red Cloud participate with some 250 lodges under his leadership, but he had also requested that the Northern Cheyennes and Arapahoes be allowed to join him in the peace negotiations. Also scheduled to arrive about the same time were two prominent Brulé leaders, Spotted Tail and Swift Bear.

When Spotted Tail reached Fort Laramie, Maynadier (promoted from lieutenant to colonel since his encounter with Red Cloud six years earlier) was particularly pleased. This powerful Brulé chief, once friendly to whites but now alienated because of mistreatment, wanted to bring the body of his favorite daughter to the fort for burial; she had tragically died from some disease. The diplomatic Maynadier, sensing a real opportunity to win Spotted Tail's support, arranged a touching sunset funeral for her at Fort Laramie. In the process, he convinced the grateful Spotted Tail of his genuine commitment to peace and of his belief in the fair treatment of all Lakotas.

Colonel Maynadier had some interesting impressions of both Red Cloud and Spotted Tail at that time. He believed Red Cloud had more status and power before the outbreak of hostilities in the Powder River country than has generally been recognized.

Indeed the part played by this rising Oglala war leader, or *blotahunka*, during the mid-1860s has been subject to the same controversy that has surrounded much of his early life. For example, his role in the Tongue River meeting, which launched those fateful attacks against whites in the Platte Valley, and his role in the Battle of the Upper Platte Bridge, which involved the leaders of the most intransigent of the Plains Indians, can be validated only by the Southern Cheyenne mixed-blood George Bent. Yet George Bird Grinnell, who relied heavily on Bent in his history of the Cheyennes, failed to mention Red Cloud's name in connection with either of these important events; only Red Cloud's role in extorting provisions from the Sawyer party is acknowledged by both Bent and Grinnell. Nevertheless, in March 1866, Maynadier regarded Red Cloud and Spotted Tail as the two most important Sioux leaders; these "two rule the nation," he asserted in a letter to Commissioner of Indian Affairs D. N. Cooley.

Because of Red Cloud's status at that time, Colonel Maynadier and Vital Jarrot, the Indian agent on the Upper Platte, were anxious to please him. In fact, when Red Cloud arrived at Fort Laramie for peace talks, he was taken to the telegraph office to hear a peace message from E. B. Taylor, head of the new presidential commission appointed to negotiate with the Lakotas. Taylor promised Red Cloud, via the singing wire, a trainload of presents by June 1 if he and his people would meet with the commissioners that day.

Red Cloud's willingness to negotiate over the objections of young warriors such as Crazy Horse was largely a result of the plight of the Sioux at that time. The winter of 1865–66 had been a difficult one for the Lakotas in the Powder River country; many of them were almost destitute. Wild game, which had been declining for years because of the reduction of hunting lands, was especially scarce. Conditions were so bad, as a matter of fact, that many Sioux stayed around the fort for three months to be fed until Taylor and his peace commissioners arrived. Maynadier and Jarrot, for their part, provisioned these hungry Indians as best they could. Red Cloud was even encouraged to return to his village and bring back more Indians for the council; his absence was regarded as a measure to meet the food crisis. Even small amounts of powder and lead were given so that the Indians could hunt during their long wait at the fort. The government's awareness of this sad state in Sioux life probably encouraged it to be less than candid about its intention to improve the road through the Powder River country; it did not clearly communicate, for example, that Indian cooperation, in allowing the road to be maintained by the government, was an absolute condition for the presents they were promised by Taylor.

On May 30, 1866, Taylor and his peace commissioners reached the fort, allowing the conference to begin five days later its efforts to achieve "a lasting peace." Taylor was delighted. Not only was Red Cloud there, but Old-Man-Afraid-of-His-Horses and Red Leaf were also present. The now conciliatory Spotted Tail was one of the Brulé spokesmen, while the Cheyennes and Arapahoes had their own small but forceful delegations. Taylor enthusiastically opened the council by assuring the Indians that his government had no intention of purchasing their lands; it simply wanted to "establish peaceful relations" and "make and use through their country such roads as may be deemed necessary for public service and for the emigrants to mining districts of the West." Clearly this reference to the Bozeman Trail, or the Powder River Road, as it was also called, was rather vague. In fact, it appears that Red Cloud and other Indian leaders at the conference were never briefed about any plan to improve or fortify the Bozeman Trail.

Because of the federal government's confidence in the new peace policy, it honestly believed that a simple reorganization of its western forces would constitute a sufficient step to open up the Powder River country for the irrepressible Montana gold seekers. With this objective in mind, a new Department of the Platte had been organized two months earlier, and Colonel Henry B. Carrington, a cautious garrison officer with no experience in Indian warfare, had been almost simultaneously put in charge of a newly established "Mountain District." Feeling optimistic, the government ordered Carrington to take the Second Battalion of the 18th Infantry from Fort Kearny on the Platte to

the Powder River country. There he was to develop the Boze-
man Trail into an important thoroughfare linking the Oregon
Trail with the new Montana gold fields. No problems with the
Sioux were anticipated.

But on June 13 the peace council at Fort Laramie came in for a
surprise. Red Cloud, who had just returned from the headwaters
of the White River, where he had gathered more Sioux participants for the conference, encountered Colonel Carrington, who
for the past several weeks had been marching his troops up the
Platte and North Platte for patrol duty along the Bozeman Trail.
Carrington's awkward timing could not have been less fortu-
nate; when Red Cloud learned of Carrington's mission, he was
outraged.

Red Cloud's fury virtually broke up the conference. According to one version, when he heard about Carrington's orders
he leaped off the platform on which he was standing, picked
up his rifle, and angrily pointed to it, saying, "In this and the
Great Spirit I trust for the right." A wife of one of Carrington's
lieutenants described Red Cloud's outburst in equally colorful
terms. The enraged Lakota wrapped his blanket around him, she
testified, and refused to be introduced to Carrington, angrily
berating the bewildered officer with these words: "The Great
Father sends us presents and wants us to sell him the road, but
White Chief goes with soldiers to steal the road before the Indians say Yes or No." George Hyde, on the other hand, insists that
Red Cloud's surprise could not have been that great. According to his version, Carrington had earlier informed a friendly
Brulé chief about the nature of his mission while he and his men
were encamped a few miles below Fort Laramie. The chief com-
municated this message to the other Sioux camps adjacent to
the fort, where Red Cloud presumably heard it before he met
Carrington.

But the account that best fits Red Cloud's style and personality was provided by William Murphy, one of the enlistees in the
18th Infantry. Red Cloud, according to Murphy, gave an absolutely impassioned speech before he bolted the conference with
Old-Man-Afraid and those other Indians who felt as he did. He

accused the peace commissioners of treating all the chiefs at the conference like children, "pretending to negotiate for a country which they had already taken by conquest." He denounced the callous treatment of his people: they had been progressively crowded northward into an ever smaller area until now their women and children were faced with starvation. He urged his conference allies to fight rather than starve, feeling confident that they could ultimately prevail. Probably the most important thing about this powerful performance, however, was his insistence on presenting all points in support of his position before issuing dire warnings against any intrusion into Sioux territory and stalking out of the conference. For those who would hear him speak and debate in the future, this kind of forceful presentation was almost vintage Red Cloud.

When Red Cloud and his irate followers headed north into the Powder River country, they included the most important participants of the now failed conference. Their emotions were almost as high as those of Cheyenne and Arapaho warriors eighteen months earlier when they had first heard about Sand Creek. Although the still-respected Old-Man-Afraid-of-His-Horses was with him, Red Cloud was now the unquestioned leader for most Oglalas; even the younger, more militant warriors looked to him for direction.

During the next six months, the Powder River Lakotas under Red Cloud's leadership engaged in guerrilla warfare; more formalized attacks, such as the much heralded one at the Upper Platte Bridge, were not attempted. Most Sioux, in fact, aside from their occasional forays against foolish intruders, were leading fairly traditional lives. The sun dance was held a few weeks after the collapse of the Fort Laramie conference. The annual fall buffalo hunt began later that autumn. During the waning months of 1866, Red Cloud and Man-Afraid spent much of their time encamped along the Tongue River; there were five hundred lodges under their control. Another camp of "hostiles," as the military now called them, was on the Powder River north of Clear Creek. Joining them were a number of disgruntled Northern Cheyennes and Northern Arapahoes; the Arapahoes, under the leadership of the once peaceful Medicine Man, had been reluctantly drawn into this essentially Lakota quarrel because of an unwarranted attack by Connor's soldiers the previous year.

But it was becoming increasingly obvious that Red Cloud meant business. He and Man-Afraid had even gone so far as to visit the Crows in order to gain their support against the army; they had promised to return Crow hunting lands as a reward for Crow cooperation. According to Jim Bridger and Bill Williams, two legendary mountain men now serving as army scouts, Crow chiefs had told them that some young Crow warriors were actually considering the Sioux offer. Indeed, during one of Man-Afraid's visits to a Crow camp, he urged these would-be allies to wait before taking any action; because he had received some prized tobacco from Fort Laramie, often a gesture made in behalf of peace, he wanted to go to the fort first to investigate the possibilities for some kind of accommodation.

In the meantime, peace commissioner E. B. Taylor attempted to put the best face on his collapsed peace talks. He tried to blame Red Cloud for his failure at Fort Laramie and tried to isolate the Oglala war chief and his band from the other Lakotas in his reports to superiors. Red Cloud was characterized as the head of about 250 "desperate characters of various tribes of Sioux" known as Bad Faces, who comprised only one-eighth of the total number of Oglalas and Brulés involved in this controversy. Refusing to recognize the authority of most other Powder River bands, they were responsible for most of the depredations that had occurred since the failure of the Fort Laramie conference. Seeking to impress federal authorities in Washington, Taylor convinced as many friendly Indians as he could to sign the treaty drawn up at Fort Laramie. Such "friendlies" as Big Mouth and Blue Horse of the Laramie Loafers, along with Swift Bear, the Brulé leader of the peaceful Corn Band, were persuaded to put their marks on the treaty. But Spotted Tail was considered his most important prize, even though this Brulé chief was already committed to peace and was far more interested in the hunting lands south of the Platte than those adjacent to the Powder River. What limited success Taylor did enjoy was

primarily because of the federal government's financial inducements: the Sioux were offered annuities amounting to seventy
thousand dollars a year for twenty years, while the Cheyennes
were offered fifteen thousand dollars a year for the same period.

In the meantime, Colonel Carrington remained almost oblivious to the impending danger caused by the breakup of the Fort
Laramie conference. With only seven hundred infantrymen, including the members of his battalion band, and with a quiet
confidence he resolutely marched toward Fort Reno following
his unpleasant meeting with Red Cloud. He had apparently
given little thought to the fact that Fort Reno was built by a
man, General Connor, who could not subdue the Sioux with a
force three times larger than Carrington's. After arriving at the
post, the colonel calmly promulgated regulations for the wagon
trains waiting there for a military escort to the Montana gold
fields. He urged all gold seekers to stay close together and avoid
antagonizing the Indians. Although the businesslike colonel,
displaying one of those flourishing beards much in vogue at
that time, had left the impression that he could handle all emer-
gencies, two days after his arrival seven Lakota warriors boldly
ran off a large herd of horses kept by the post sutler.

Carrington left Fort Reno on July 10 and marched about forty
miles north to a high plateau between the forks of Piney Creek,
a meandering stream fed by tributaries that plunged down from
the steep Bighorns. There he decided to construct a post where
he could protect those travelers taking the Bozeman Trail. His
confidence during the uneventful three-day trip to this location
was boosted by the fact that he did not see one Indian along the
way. Soon after his arrival, however, a messenger representing
some friendly Cheyennes came into camp to inquire about his
intentions. Carrington invited this Cheyenne and the rest of his
party to come and confer on the site of Fort Phil Kearny, the
name he proposed for his new fort to honor a Union general
killed during the Civil War. Two days later, when the obviously
peaceful Cheyennes arrived, headed by Black Horse and Dull
Knife, they gave Carrington and his men plenty of reasons to
worry. The Indians painted a bleak picture of the prospects for

peace. The Sioux had already visited them with dire warnings about how treacherous the whites could be. The Sioux had also applied tremendous pressure to get the Cheyennes to join Red Cloud's campaign to close the Bozeman Trail. Although Carrington was sympathetic toward the plight of the Cheyenne warriors, who were clearly not belligerent themselves, he did not feel threatened enough to take exceptional steps. Nevertheless, he gave the party food, tobacco, and a promise of assistance if they were attacked for not supporting the Sioux cause.

These friendly Cheyennes paid an awful price for this visit. On the day after their meeting with Carrington, they encountered some of Red Cloud's warriors at the nearby trading post of Pete Gasteau (better known as "French Pete"). A nervous Black Horse admitted to the Lakotas that his party had gone to Colonel Carrington's camp to talk peace. He probably did not admit, however, that he and Dull Knife and the other warriors had even offered Carrington the services of a hundred of their young warriors. No doubt hoping to pacify the Sioux party, Black Horse also told the suspicious warriors that there were presents at Fort Laramie for those Lakotas willing to sign the new peace treaty. But the Sioux were outraged at what they saw as a betrayal; they contemptuously whipped the humiliated Cheyennes on their backs and faces with unslung bows. Probably among the fiercest Indians on the Great Plains, the Cheyennes in this party were outnumbered and had to bear this insult in silence. Before departing from Gasteau's camp, however, they warned the veteran trader that he, too, was in danger. But French Pete, who was married to a Sioux woman, was too secure and comfortable to move fast enough; as a consequence, he and all of his men were killed the following day.

Being warned by the same Cheyennes that Red Cloud had already sent warriors south to cut off travel on the Bozeman Trail, Carrington began to consolidate his tenuous position at Fort Phil Kearny. He moved as quickly as possible to complete his stockade; a formidable installation, it would eventually comprise seventeen acres. The prudent officer, who thrived on garrison duty, also worked to strengthen his position all along the Bozeman Trail. With this objective in mind, he sent two of his infantry companies on a dangerous ninety-two-mile trek northward along the Bighorn Mountains to establish another fortification. Successfully avoiding Red Cloud's wary scouting parties, the soldiers promptly began construction on a new post in southern Montana, Fort C. F. Smith, on August 12; there were now three posts to guard the Bozeman Trail: Fort Reno, Fort Phil Kearny, and Fort C. F. Smith.

But Carrington's mobility in the Powder River country grew less and less as the summer wore on. The Sioux had instituted the practice of attacking travelers on the Bozeman Trail on a daily basis. They even had the audacity to lay siege from time to time to both Forts Phil Kearny and C. F. Smith; wagon trains and troop columns were harassed and wood supply trains were jeopardized within sight of the two posts. Yet Carrington remained surprisingly serene; his reports to superiors did not reveal any great alarm. Although he did ask for reinforcements, he honestly believed he could accomplish his mission with only one additional battalion.

Although Carrington was complacent, the popular Civil War general William Tecumseh Sherman, now commander of the Military Division of the Mississippi, was not; he ordered a full regiment from Saint Louis to strengthen Carrington's precarious position in eastern Wyoming. With the amazing Red Cloud apparently organizing the Lakotas and their allies for full-scale warfare, Carrington's vulnerability was causing growing concern in the army.

Carrington's new garrison at the edge of the Bighorn Mountains was hardly prepared for an offensive war. Most of the soldiers at Fort Phil Kearny, in fact, were raw recruits. Only two hundred of the colonel's infantrymen could ride horses, a weakness the officer readily admitted; as Carrington put it, "infantry make poor riders." The garrison's lack of mobility was especially important because of the immense area of land under its jurisdiction. Also, Carrington's troops were armed primarily with aged, muzzle-loading Springfields, which were impractical for mounted warfare and inferior to the few arms the Sioux possessed. There were only twelve officers under his command, two of whom were detached for recruiting duty. Fortunately for the safety of his under-armed and highly inexperienced troops, Carrington was more than content to maintain a defensive posture. He actually preferred garrison duty to battle duty. His love for the details of military life were well known; one of his main concerns during the height of the crisis was to keep his men from walking on the newly planted grass at Fort Phil Kearny. In many ways, the colonel's temperament harmonized well with Washington's new peace orientation toward the Indians.

But Red Cloud was cautious, too. Despite the burning desire of many of his warriors to attack the army directly, Red Cloud tended to restrain those younger, more impetuous souls. He also wanted to maintain the Lakotas' traditional way of life as much as possible, even in the face of an impending war. Thus, the revered sun dance was to precede any major fighting. The fall buffalo hunt was to be completed before launching a really big attack. Indeed, Sioux strategy before the wintry weeks of December was basically to make the Bozeman Trail as unsafe as possible. Nevertheless, as early as the summer of 1866, intelligence from Crow and friendly Cheyenne sources reported that the Lakotas and their allies were planning major assaults against Forts Kearny and Smith.

Throughout the summer and fall months of 1866, Red Cloud was involved in most major activities to disrupt the government's plan to guarantee a safe federal road through the Powder River country. In July he led a war party in the vicinity of Fort Reno against those gold seekers who had the temerity to use the Bozeman Trail in spite of the Sioux threat. On December 6, the veteran warrior was involved in a major effort to entrap Carrington's soldiers almost within the shadows of Fort Kearny; indeed, Red Cloud was seen on a hill directing this battle with various hand signals. Even though his ambush failed, it did reveal certain vulnerabilities among the troops at Fort Kearny, namely, a careless eagerness on the part of many soldiers to pursue the enemy even into well-protected Indian strongholds.

On December 21, Red Cloud's warriors were given another

chance to strike a blow before the coming of more severe weather. This opportunity involved the last wood-gathering party of the season; more than eighty men, including a group of woodcutters and the soldiers that comprised their military escort, were dispatched by Colonel Carrington for that purpose. The Lakotas and their allies were banking on the fact that the garrison at Fort Kearny was anxious to pursue any Indian party that would jeopardize the safety of this wood supply train; in an ambush attempted two days earlier, a military escort was almost lured across a high ridge known as Lodge Trail Ridge, behind which a large war party waited in anticipation. The Sioux were thus determined to make this attack work; it had become their top priority.

The assault would be a more formal affair such as the one employed at the Battle of the Upper Platte Bridge. Like that campaign, it would be led by older chiefs. Its participants would be carefully supervised by police societies so that the ambush would not misfire because of some premature action. The crucial decoy force would be its centerpiece; to ensure a representative involvement, this party was comprised of six Lakotas, two Cheyennes, and two Arapahoes. Crazy Horse was given the honor of leading this body, the main bait for the trap that had been carefully set. His choice was a natural one, given the fact that his respected mentor, the Miniconjou leader High-Back-Bone, was responsible for the overall strategy. Another important participant was the Northern Cheyenne leader Two Moons, who would become the basis for much of the testimony about Crazy Horse's vital role in this attack forty-six years later.

Red Cloud's role in what whites would later call the Fetterman Massacre has always been shrouded in controversy. The chief would insist until his dying day that he was directly involved in the struggle. Moreover, a number of Oglala combatants, while admitting that High-Back-Bone was the chief military strategist, would later endorse Red Cloud's claim that he was a participant. Most Miniconjous, however, have categorically denied that he was present. As for historians, a number of them would place him somewhere on the Tongue River that day, directing the overall campaign against the army.

When the large wood-gathering party was attacked on that cold December day, the predicted restlessness inside the fort erupted. Carrington, remaining true to form, ordered Captain James W. Powell to relieve the besieged wood train but insisted that Powell not pursue the attackers over Lodge Trail Ridge; this customarily cautious officer had followed such orders two days earlier in response to another attack. But before Captain Powell could begin his rescue, a brash young captain, William Judd Fetterman, who had arrived at the fort on November 3 with a company of cavalry, stepped forward, insisting that, because he had been brevetted a lieutenant colonel during the Civil War and thereby outranked Captain Powell, he should be given the command instead. But Carrington was apprehensive about Fetterman's qualifications. This thirty-one-year-old officer with muttonchop whiskers distinctive even for the Gilded Age had allegedly boasted that he could conquer the entire Sioux nation with eighty men. Moreover, he had been consistently critical of Carrington's prudent course. Unfortunately, Carrington, who was a stickler for military protocol, felt he had no other alternative but to accede to Fetterman's insistent demands. Even so, he warned Fetterman, as passionately as he had warned Powell, not to cross Lodge Trail Ridge in pursuit of the attackers.

When Fetterman left the fort he had about eighty men under his command. Supremely self-confident and openly disdainful of Indian warriors, Fetterman was the perfect candidate for an ambush. He was constitutionally unable to resist the taunts and obscene gestures of Crazy Horse's noisy decoy force, which successfully distracted him as he was on his way to relieve the embattled wood party. Fetterman pursued Crazy Horse with an almost foolhardy determination, crossing the forbidden Lodge Trail Ridge in reckless haste. His confident romp ended along a high spur of land behind Lodge Trail Ridge, where he and his men found themselves strung for almost a mile along the top of a steep ridge, his faster cavalry substantially ahead of his infantry. On both sides of this treeless ridge, excited Indians hid in the grass or behind the rocks that dotted the slopes. When the de-

coy party reached the end of the ridge, now called Fetterman or
Massacre Ridge, the Lakotas, Cheyennes, and Arapahoes waiting in ambush charged up the steep slopes and showered their
surprised victims with great numbers of deadly arrows.

In less than half an hour, every member of Fetterman's command was killed. Fetterman, who had desperately retreated with
a group of mounted troops to a pile of rocks on the ridge, was
found dead near Captain Frederick H. Brown, another reckless
fire-eater. Many historians have concluded that Fetterman and
Brown shot each other in the head to avoid an agonizing death
at the hands of the Indians. The post surgeon, who reported a
bullet hole in Brown's left temple, however, never mentioned
seeing such a wound on Fetterman's head. American Horse, a
close comrade of Red Cloud and married to one of his daughters, insisted that he had killed the overconfident Fetterman,
smashing him to the ground with a club and then cutting his
throat with a knife; in fact, the post surgeon discovered a cut
in Fetterman's throat and neck so deep that it reached his cer-
vical spine. Curiously, Red Cloud, in an interview given forty
years later, could not remember that his friend American Horse
was there, bringing into question the extent of their mutual
involvement.

When the violent struggle was over, the celebrating victors,
who were zealously taking scalps and mutilating bodies, looked
up toward a high ridge where Captain Tenedor Ten Eyck and
a seventy-six-man rescue force watched in horror. The warriors
angrily challenged the soldiers to come down and fight. But
Ten Eyck wisely declined to accommodate them; his men estimated that there might be as many as two thousand triumphant
warriors ready to back up this challenge. Curiously the victorious Lakotas and their allies seemed perfectly satisfied with what
they had done that day; there was something in their nature that
did not require an attack on Ten Eyck's hesitant column or the
storming of Carrington's frightened stockade three miles away.

This major Indian battle, which the Sioux sometimes called
the Fight of One Hundred, because they believed that there
were twenty soldiers under Fetterman's command who were

not counted, could have had more serious consequences. But by the end of this feverish day, the shortest of the year, most of the jubilant warriors were ready to return home and stock up for the long winter season. As American Horse put it in an interview given many years later: "After the battle [all] the Indians scattered . . . [with] various tribes going in different directions to secure game for food." In fact, all the tribes implicated in the Fetterman affair spent that very cold winter of 1867 scattered throughout the Powder River country, living off the buffalo caught during the previous fall hunt. There was, however, one new element for that year's winter encampment: the victorious Lakotas, Cheyennes, and Arapahoes could extol their great feats around a campfire made warmer by memories of their great military success.

Throughout the rest of the country, however, there was outrage over the so-called Fetterman Massacre. The army, of course, viewed this tragic development in more personal terms than did other governmental institutions involved in implementing Indian policy. General Sherman called for a vigorous winter campaign against the Sioux and their allies. These Indians "should be punished with vindictive earnestness, until at least ten Indians are killed for each white life lost." A frenzied effort on the part of some senior officers to shift the blame for the army's failure to successfully prosecute Red Cloud's War, as many were beginning to call this bloody impasse, resulted in Carrington's replacement as commander of the Mountain District. Colonel Henry W. Wessells, who was already on his way to Fort Phil Kearny with reinforcements, was the man put in charge.

Officials in the Department of the Interior were also embarrassed by this tragic event. Commissioner Taylor's confident assurances that most tribes supported the Fort Laramie Treaty had proven utterly baseless. But there were civilians in government who insisted that the military's negative attitude toward the Indians was one of the chief causes for the violence. Commissioner of Indian Affairs Lewis V. Bogy even blamed the army for the December 6 fight near Fort Kearny, which Red Cloud personally directed. According to Bogy's dubious version, Red Cloud's party, hungry from lack of food and needing guns and ammunition for the hunt, was just making a friendly visit to the fort when hostilities erupted.

Settlers on the Northern Plains, however, showed little patience for this futile finger pointing; they wanted immediate action. In April 1867, Acting Governor Thomas F. Meagher of Montana Territory, disappointed that the army did not launch the kind of major winter offensive that Sherman had called for, urged civilian volunteers to make their own war against Red Cloud. Two months later a mass meeting of Colorado citizens subscribed five thousand dollars for the purpose of buying Indian scalps, a surprisingly intemperate action even for fanatical Indian-haters but one which won the support of Colorado's territorial governor.

Faced with deep divisions throughout the country, Congress, in February 1867, appointed a commission to investigate the causes that led to Fetterman's tragic demise. This body, sometimes called the Sanborn-Sully commission because of the prominent participation by Generals J. B. Sanborn and Alfred Sully, was balanced by a civilian viewpoint because it was under the direction of the Department of the Interior. Its members were also anxious to achieve some accommodation with Red Cloud; when two of them visited Fort Laramie in April, they tried to lure Red Cloud to the fort for peace talks.

Although a meaningful dialogue with Red Cloud was never achieved during the early months of 1867, there is evidence that this new power among the Lakota peoples did visit Fort Laramie in June. In fact, on the twelfth of that month a conference was held at the fort between the new peace commissioners and several chiefs, such as Old-Man-Afraid-of-His-Horses and Iron Shell. According to Indian agent M. T. Patrick, Red Cloud, who preferred to stay in the background, was also there. Big Mouth, one of the better-known Laramie Loafers, was another who testified concerning Red Cloud's presence. Historians have speculated that this meeting may have meant that Man-Afraid and other chiefs, perhaps even Red Cloud himself, were softening their opposition to the use of the Bozeman Trail. There is, however, virtually no basis for such a claim; indeed Man-Afraid left an impression at the fort that he was there to get badly needed ammunition to hunt rather than to make peace.

Red Cloud's alleged presence at this conference prompted even greater controversy. His actions during the months that followed this June meeting are a sure indication that he was not ready for any accommodation with whites. As for his comparative silence at the fort, it was probably self-imposed; by June of 1867 he had long since eclipsed Man-Afraid as the spokesman for his people. In fact, his name had become so synonymous with Indian resistance in the Powder River country that many Lakotas and their allies were jealous of him. The Miniconjou opinion that this new Lakota savior was not present at the Fetterman Fight may simply have been a product of envy.

Red Cloud's exact role in the struggle over the Powder River may never be known, but almost all the testimony places him in the area around Fort Kearny during those weeks that preceded Fetterman's convincing demise. More important, he was the unquestioned leader of those who planned the overall strategy against the army during the fall of 1866; whether he did it from a campsite on the Tongue or at the site of Fetterman Ridge itself does not seem that critical for his reputation as a warrior-statesman. He was undeniably the major personality in whom Lakotas, Cheyennes, and Arapahoes could comfortably lodge their confidence. He was also the man who could most effectively speak for this Indian alliance until some satisfactory settlement of their bitter dispute with the U.S. government could be arranged.

CHAPTER 5

A Treaty at Last

THE efforts of the Sanborn-Sully commission to restore peace to the Powder River country achieved few satisfactory results. Although the panel attempted to negotiate with a number of Indian chiefs, it failed to get its most important adversary, Red Cloud, to the peace table. This disappointment was a major setback, because persuading the Lakota leader to agree to the treaty he had contemptuously rejected at Fort Laramie the year before was an essential first step. As a consequence, the commission, which was also called the Fort Phil Kearny commission, could boast of few successes.

It did, however, have many opportunities for travel. After its organizational meeting in March 1867, the commission traveled to Fort McPherson, near the forks of the Platte, to interview the now controversial Colonel Carrington. Fort Laramie was its next destination, but that was a disappointing journey because none of the leaders involved in shutting down the Bozeman Trail, including Red Cloud, were there. Members of the commission even dispersed to locations in the upper Great Plains to achieve some kind of accommodation with the Sioux. General Sully, for example, accompanied by fellow commissioner Colonel E. S. Parker, journeyed north to parley with northern Lakotas gathered at Forts Rice and Berthold on the Upper Missouri. They encountered the same problem that their parent body did during its futile negotiations in the Platte Valley; only friendly, relatively unimportant Indians would talk to them. Even more galling to the ubiquitous commission members was the fact that many of the tribesmen who had signed the Fort Laramie Treaty in the summer of 1866 now wanted to sign it again for the annuities and presents still being offered to Red Cloud and his followers.

Symbolic of the commission's frustrations was its failure to submit a formal report. Rather, by consensus, its members agreed that Sanborn and N. B. Buford should travel to Washington as individuals and report the committee's finding. Of these two commissioners, Sanborn was probably the most blunt. He made it clear, for example, that a state of war still existed between the more intransigent Sioux and the U.S. government—a sad result, in his opinion, of the army's failure to supply Colonel Carrington with enough men and supplies during the autumn months of 1866. Yet Sanborn and his colleagues refused to censure any of the officers involved in Fetterman's fatal ambush; fault finding of this kind would be left to the president and the secretary of the interior.

Sanborn and the other commissioners, however, were most concerned about the overall Indian dilemma, and their recommendations on that score played right into the hands of the more militant peace advocates. For example, the commission called for a special federal tribunal to deal with wrongs inflicted against the Indians. It also recommended that a special tract of land be set aside for the Sioux. Its most immediate demand, however, was to put an end to "aggressive war" against the Indians, an objective that could be best attained by the dispatch of a new commission to the West.

The upshot of these important recommendations was the creation of the Indian Peace Commission, one of the landmark developments in federal Indian policy during the nineteenth century. This new body, created by Congress on July 20, 1867, was the product of an ambitious effort to balance the opinions of those who wanted to make peace with the Indians against those who were willing to risk war. Although the new commission was a direct consequence of Red Cloud's obdurate refusal to sign the Fort Laramie treaty, its mission went far beyond achieving peace with the Lakotas and their allies; the Indian Peace Commission was authorized to deal with tribes throughout the entire Great Plains region. One of its objectives was to remove all causes for hostility that would endanger the frontier settlements or imperil the much publicized transcontinental railroad being built to the Pacific.

The long-range goal for this new commission, however, was to civilize the Indians so that they could be assimilated instead of destroyed through war. The Indian Peace Commission was determined to initiate a system of small reservations for this purpose. Through the use of land set aside by these reservations, Plains Indians could learn to be farmers instead of restless hunters. Yet the commissioners must have anticipated that forcing the Sioux to become farmers was contrary to everything Red Cloud and his people believed; consequently, this new legislation authorized the president of the United States to call for four regiments of mounted troops to deal with any opposition encountered by the Indian Peace Commission.

The head of the new Peace Commission was Senator John B. Henderson of Missouri. Selecting him as chairman of the Senate Indian Affairs Committee made good sense; indeed, he had sponsored the legislation which created the new body. The other three civilian members appointed by Congress were Sanborn, whose work on the Sanborn-Sully or Fort Phil Kearny commission was appropriately recognized by his designation; the commissioner of Indian affairs, Nathaniel G. Taylor, an ample, bewigged man who would be accused more than once of pampering the Indians; and Samuel F. Tappan of Colorado, a staunch supporter of most of Taylor's pro-Indian views, who had headed the commission that had investigated the Sand Creek Massacre several years earlier.

The other three members of the Peace Commission were military men appointed by the president. This strong-willed trio, quite naturally, tended toward a military solution to the Indian problem. Of the three, Lieutenant General William Tecumseh Sherman was the most prominent, if not the least inclined to temporize. He also knew that his views would be supported by Brigadier General Alfred H. Terry, commander of the Department of Dakota, and retired General Harney, whose reputation as an Indian fighter before the Civil War could hardly have been reassuring to the Sioux and their allies. When Sherman was recalled to Washington after the Peace Commission's disappointing failure to gather the northern tribes for a meeting at Fort Laramie in 1867, Colonel Christopher C. Augur, who had been appointed commander of the Department of the Platte shortly after the Fetterman disaster, was added to the commission.

Conditions were not conducive for the success of the Indian Peace Commission at that time. Red Cloud had already refused to meet the old Sanborn-Sully commission, and there was little evidence of enthusiasm on his part for the new commission. Moreover, the resistance he had inspired in the Powder River country was manifesting itself in many ways. Colonel Augur admitted to Sherman on May 21 that there would be no more travel on the Bozeman Trail that year except by "our own trains." The army, in fact, was having trouble contracting freighters who would supply the embattled forts along the Bighorn range, a development that was causing freight rates to soar. But trouble was not confined to the Powder River country. In the Platte Valley to the south, Indian depredations were becoming so commonplace that authorities were accused of losing interest in solving the problem. Most alarming to the federal government, however, was an ominous January 26, 1867, letter sent to General Grant by Thomas C. Durant, the man in charge of the Union Pacific's rail construction westward. Durant solemnly warned that, unless some immediate governmental "relief can be afforded," the laying of railroad tracks along the Platte River would be suspended.

The apparent Indian threat to the Union Pacific would have a real impact on government policy toward Red Cloud. Earlier, Grant had emphasized to Sherman the importance of protecting the nation's first transcontinental railroad. He had also warned that any delay in construction would give the builders of the Union Pacific another pretext to ask for more governmental assistance. Although Sherman admitted that the transcontinental railroad had become the nation's top priority in the West, he denied that any military expedition against the tribes in the Powder River country would unduly stretch army supply lines, making the Union Pacific more vulnerable to an attack. Indeed, in May 1867 the still lionized Civil War hero ordered Colonel Augur to go on the offensive, even though his frustrated subordinate had already complained that his forces were barely able to maintain an acceptable defensive posture.

But Sherman and Augur must have realized that there was little sentiment in the East for a major Indian war. National attention in 1867 was largely directed toward the reconstruction of the South through military means, a controversial program launched by Congress in March of that year; this legislation, which carved the South into five military districts, put yet another strain on the nation's resources, which had already been overburdened by five years of Civil War. To the Radical Republicans in Congress, particularly, troops could be much more effectively employed in the South than in the West. Also, there was the increasingly bitter feud between President Andrew Johnson and Congress that marked this stormy Reconstruction Era, a struggle that resulted a year later in the failure of the Senate by one vote to remove the scrappy Johnson from office.

The nation's distraction over the southern question, however, was only one obstacle to General Sherman's determination to end the Sioux threat. A strong element of the population in the East was sharply critical of the way the federal government was handling Indian affairs. These people, who had been outraged by the treatment of Plains tribes since the bloody Sand Creek incident, were keenly at odds with the anti-Indian views prevalent on the frontier. More relevant, they had significant influence among both the Radicals and their opponents in Congress; the creation of the Indian Peace Commission was convincing testimony as to their growing strength.

With pacifistic views gaining more acceptance in Washington, rumors for peace were eagerly devoured by the American public. The *New York Times* reported as late as July 28 that Spotted Tail had persuaded Red Cloud to listen to the federal government's latest peace overtures, a breakthrough that was responsible for the quiet mood that now prevailed over Sioux country. Such optimism, however, was absolutely without foundation; in fact, with the weather improving, Red Cloud and his allies were planning to renew warfare sometime during the summer of 1867.

The only obstacle to a major attack in the Powder River country was the indecision among Sioux and Cheyenne leaders about which post on the Bozeman Trail should be the target. Red Cloud insisted that Fort Phil Kearny was the logical choice; he undoubtedly recognized the symbolic importance of gaining another victory at the same place where Fetterman was ambushed. During the Lakotas' great sun dance, sometime in June or July, an apparently heated debate occurred among the two tribes over this question. Such Cheyenne chiefs as Two Moons and Dull Knife argued that Fort C. F. Smith to the north was much more vulnerable to a successful assault. In the end, the Lakotas and the Cheyennes decided to carry the war to both outposts; the Sioux would attack Fort Kearny, and the Cheyennes, Fort Smith.

As a result of this fateful decision, a band of five hundred Cheyennes and Arapahoes, along with a few Lakotas, attacked a haying party three miles northeast of Fort Smith on August 1. The party, which was working in a meadow of tall grass along the Bighorn River, was made up of six hay cutters and nineteen soldiers, who were there to provide a military escort. The jittery hay makers, who had already been harassed by smaller war parties, were shocked at the size of this new Indian group. They desperately lashed their teams into a nearby corral built to keep the horses and mules inside at night. The corral provided excellent defense against the mounted warriors, who continually circled the makeshift fortification, clinging precariously to their fleet ponies and firing continually at the embattled defenders. Fortunately for the besieged group, the lowest logs of the wooden corral rested on the ground, making them excellent gun rests for anyone firing in a prone position. Moreover, the thick logs acted as an effective barrier against both bullets and arrows. After a fire set to the grass around the corral failed to break this stubborn resistance, a reckless attack on foot was made through the smoky haze. When this assault also foundered, the noisy war party reluctantly withdrew, ending several hours of intense fighting.

The Hayfield Fight, as terrifying as it was to the nervous guardians of the Bozeman Trail, did not prove particularly decisive. Casualties were comparatively light; the besieged party suffered only three deaths and three injuries. Although the haying party's successful resistance was later trumpeted as a glorious victory, the response of Fort Smith's commander was much more indicative of the conflict's true nature. Lieutenant Colonel L. P. Bradley, the man in charge of the isolated outpost, absolutely refused to go to the aid of the endangered party. He even closed the gates of the fort and categorically denied permission to one officer who wanted to lead a relief column to rescue the imperiled corral. It was only after the frustrated war party had withdrawn that the shaken Bradley finally sent any help.

One advantage that the army had on this occasion, which it lacked at Fetterman Ridge, was possession of the Model 1866 Springfield-Allen breechloader. This modified Springfield rifle, which reached the fort about a week before the attack, was much faster than the old muzzle-loader; its use in the Hayfield Fight undoubtedly came as an unpleasant shock to the attackers.

At the same time that this predominantly Cheyenne band was preparing to attack Fort Smith, a much larger force of warriors from Sioux camps along the Tongue River and Rosebud Creek was making a confident trek toward Fort Phil Kearny. Red Cloud rode at the head of the long column, according to some accounts of this affair, although High-Back-Bone and Crazy Horse were also among the leaders. The force, which numbered between eight hundred and a thousand, was basically an Oglala one, despite the prominent presence of the always tenacious Miniconjous and Sans Arcs.

Their ultimate target was a woodcutting party from Fort Kearny, which they assaulted in a surprise attack about five miles north of the fort on August 2, the day after the Hayfield Fight. The large Sioux party struck at seven in the morning, burning the woodcutters' camp and forcing the survivors to take refuge in a makeshift corral. Like the one near Fort Smith, this corral was built to protect livestock. It was made of fourteen wagon boxes stripped of their canvas covers and removed from their chassis to form a protective enclosure. Inside the oval-shaped perimeter these boxes formed, twenty-six enlisted men, two officers, and a handful of civilians held out under one of the few prudent officers involved in the Fetterman affair, Captain James Powell. As was the case with the Hayfield Fight, the first attack was a mounted one; Powell estimated that the large Lakota party, stirring up clouds of dust, may have numbered as many as five hundred.

With the odds decisively on Red Cloud's side, it would seem that success was assured. But again, the breech-loading Springfields made a difference. The attacking warriors, circling the wagon-box corral in a seemingly endless procession, waited anxiously for that pause when Powell's men would have to reload; at that time they could burst into the circle and overwhelm the courageous defenders. But the pause never came; indeed, the discharge of the new rifles continued almost unabated. With their modified Springfields the soldiers quickly ejected their empty cartridges and slapped new ones into the breech; they hardly needed to take their eyes off the target. The result was a withering volley of gunfire, causing an unacceptable loss of life for a people who would not tolerate high casualties.

Some accounts of the Wagon Box Fight have been highly critical of Red Cloud and the other Sioux leaders. These men allegedly witnessed this bloody setback from a gentle rise near the battle site, doing nothing to intervene or stop it. Finally, somewhere on that confused battleground, a desperate council of war was held to devise a more successful strategy. The result was a new attack, this one on foot. It was launched by scores of screaming Lakota warriors, who moved up a ravine just north of the corral. Some were firing guns, many no doubt gathered after the Fetterman battle; others were shooting flaming arrows to ignite the bales of hay stored in the encircled wagon boxes. Attacking in a compact wedge, the warriors got within five feet of their goal before they broke and retreated in the face of unforgiving gunfire.

The Sioux had to withdraw before achieving anything decisive, just as the Cheyennes had to do the day before. When the welcomed relief column finally arrived from Fort Kearny, the small knot of defenders, still secure behind their wagon boxes, had taken few losses; only three were killed and two were wounded. Lakota casualties, on the other hand, although difficult to ascertain because of the Indian practice of carrying off the dead and wounded, were considerable. Estimates range from as few as five killed to as many of sixty; figures for the wounded also start at 5, but some estimates exceed 120.

The army, eager to improve its tarnished image, proclaimed the Wagon Box Fight a victory, exaggerating assessments of Lakota casualties. One account placed Sioux losses higher than a thousand. These estimates were matched by equally bloated ones regarding the size of the Sioux force; Captain Powell, for example, judged Red Cloud's attacking force to be about three thousand. Red Cloud's recollections, recorded many years later, did not clarify the situation. Although in one report he declared his force to number three thousand, of which he lost half, in another he scaled down his losses to six hundred. All these estimates were unduly high and ran counter to the Indians' philosophy of warfare. White Bull, one of the Lakotas at the fight, insisted that his people rarely tolerated losses greater than 1 or 2 percent. George Sword, known as Hunts the Enemy at the time of the battle, flatly stated much later that no more than three hundred Lakotas fought on that fateful August day and only two were killed. Also, the Sioux, having captured a large number of mules and horses, just as the Cheyennes did at the Hayfield Fight, could never regard the Wagon Box Fight as a defeat. Nor would they agree that the prompt dispersal of their warriors after the battle was the result of a disastrous setback. Victorious Lakotas also scattered their camps throughout the Powder River country after destroying Fetterman's ill-fated column in December. There was the fall buffalo hunt to prepare for after the Wagon Box Fight, just as there was a winter encampment to prepare for after the Fetterman Fight.

The warlike activities of the Sioux during the following months provide even more evidence that they had not been routed. Lakota war parties continued to attack unescorted settlers on the Bozeman Trail. Concerned army leaders established Fort Fetterman some eighty miles northwest of Fort Laramie in order to better protect traffic on the precarious trail. Even more ominous was an attack on a Union Pacific freight train approximately forty miles east of Fort McPherson, in west central Nebraska, an assault which prompted further threats by Union Pacific officials to suspend building operations until better security could be provided.

Although Red Cloud never fought the army again after the Wagon Box Fight, his reasons probably had more to do with the benefits he perceived in using the diplomatic approach than anything else. He had already been approached by federal agents anxious to make peace and please him in the process. Whether or not he was advised by friendly white traders on the importance of an early peace, he had to be aware of the unusual attention being paid to him. Indeed, he was now the focus of almost all news coverage regarding the struggle that most people were calling Red Cloud's War. This inordinate attention and these nervous peace overtures undoubtedly persuaded him to try a new tack in his dealings with the federal government.

Fortunately for Red Cloud, the diplomatic approach was still favored by many of his white adversaries. Only elements of the army and the perennially hostile western settlers still wanted to conduct a holy war against the Sioux and their allies, who were perceived as vulnerable after the Wagon Box and Hayfield fights. Most influential whites, however, still embraced the view that peace was the best way to achieve an accommodation with the Plains tribes. This lingering attitude, which stemmed back to the Sand Creek Massacre, had remained especially strong among more pious and educated groups of the East.

But the conscience of a Christian nation was probably not as strong a motivation as the political and economic ones embraced by people along the eastern seaboard. Politically, the need to reconstruct the South had become the government's top priority. Economically, the need to complete the first transcontinental railroad had become paramount to most of the country's business interests. In fact, building the Union Pacific was much more important than maintaining a road through the Powder River country, which might ultimately require thousands of troops. Hence, the government decided to continue its patient negotiations, offering generous presents and annuities to induce the Indians to make peace. This policy, largely self-serving, harmonized well with the prevailing government belief that it was cheaper to feed Indians than to fight them.

The Indian Peace Commission reflected this more pacifistic mood when it gathered on August 7 at Saint Louis for its organizational meeting. Members at this session not only expressed their commitment to peace but also their desire to negotiate two sets of treaties instead of one. The first would be with the Powder River Sioux and their allies, who had created the crisis, and the second would be with the restless tribes in the lower Great Plains. Their strategy was to meet with the northern tribes at Fort Laramie on September 13. The commissioners, of course, were anxious that Red Cloud be there; in truth, the general public now regarded the Sioux leader as the indispensable factor in achieving peace on the Northern Plains. October 13 was the date set for meeting the southern tribes; Fort Larned in Kansas was to be the location. Although anxious to succeed, the commissioners had scant reason for optimism. Colonel Augur told his fellow commissioners in a later meeting at Omaha that he expected a general war to result from Red Cloud's latest campaign on the Powder River. He also added, ominously, that he would need twenty thousand men to fight that war.

But most members of the Peace Commission were undaunted by these gloomy prognostications. Employing the savvy of G. P. Beauvois, an experienced Sioux trader, they traveled up the Missouri for friendly talks with upriver tribes. The commission's tardy return to Omaha on September 11 made it late for the planned meeting with Powder River tribes at Fort

Laramie. General Sherman telegraphed Fort Laramie to see if the commissioners should rush to the fort in order not to lose momentum in their efforts to win over the warring Lakotas. The response he received was discouraging; runners from the back country reported that Red Cloud's people were not planning to be there.

The commissioners were desperate to achieve more substantial results. They took the Union Pacific to North Platte on September 14 for a meeting with those Lakotas and Cheyennes considered more peaceful. Spotted Tail, who had already signed the 1866 Fort Laramie treaty, was the principal spokesman for these tribesmen. Although his main concern was to get guns and ammunition so his people could hunt buffalo along the Republican River, he did demand that the Bozeman Trail be closed. At the North Platte council, which almost turned chaotic because the Indians got hold of a barrel of whiskey, General Sherman was often grim and intimidating. But N. G. Taylor, the commission's civilian president, was sympathetic to the point of providing guns and powder so that Spotted Tail's people could hunt until the Fort Laramie conference convened.

From North Platte the commissioners traveled to Medicine Lodge Creek, seventy miles south of Fort Larned, to parley with the southern tribes. There, in mid-October, the commission members, accompanied by a large corps of eastern newspapermen, negotiated with colorfully garbed representatives of the Cheyenne, Arapaho, Comanche, Kiowa, and Kiowa-Apache tribes who roamed the Southern Plains. Presents were generously distributed and agreements were reached with tribal leaders in which the distasteful concept of living on reservations was reluctantly accepted.

Although many of these treaties were rejected shortly thereafter, the Indian Peace Commission, flushed with success, started for Fort Laramie to negotiate similar agreements with northern tribes such as the Crows and Arapahoes as well as the Lakotas and Cheyennes. When they arrived on November 9, 1867, they were promptly jolted back to reality: only a few friendly Crows were on hand to greet them. The disappointed commissioners, nevertheless, went through the motions of a formal council meeting. But Red Cloud remained uppermost in their minds. He had evidently sent word that, because the Powder River country was the last good hunting ground left to his people, he would not make peace until the military garrisons at Forts Kearny and C. F. Smith were closed. The Peace Commission, as a consequence, departed for Washington, leaving two special agents from the Indian Bureau, A. J. Chamblin and H. M. Mathews, to communicate to the Sioux the commission's desire to meet with Red Cloud the next summer.

Reports from the hostile Lakota country north of the fort were of a mixed nature. Some were reassuring, most were not. For example, one of the more ominous ones claimed that selfish white traders had promised Red Cloud all the powder and lead he would need to resist all intruders. But there were optimistic reports, too. Special agent Mathews, for one, boasted of a meeting with a group of Bad Faces, which included a man who claimed to be Red Cloud's brother. This party insisted that Red Cloud would make peace if the government would abandon the Bozeman Trail and evacuate the offensive forts that guarded it.

Mathews rushed to Washington convinced he had made a great breakthrough. Ironically, Mathews's revelations were nothing new; Red Cloud had opposed the opening of the Bozeman Trail since the first Fort Laramie conference in 1866 and had opposed the forts along the trail from the day they were built. What made Mathews's Washington mission important was that the federal government was now willing to settle on Red Cloud's terms after months of stalemate.

Indeed, Red Cloud was about to become the first Indian leader to force the federal government to back down in a truly major controversy. It was not a sign of weakness on the part of the government, for the army was stronger than ever; it was merely a matter of priorities. The federal government could not occupy the South and protect the Union Pacific at the same time it was defending the Powder River Road, in the opinion of an economy-minded Congress. Besides, there were new options for Washington. With Union Pacific tracks now being laid farther to the west, there were opportunities to establish routes to the Montana gold field west of the Powder River country. Moreover, the Northern Pacific Railroad, which had been chartered four years earlier, would soon provide an eastern access to Montana. Peace with Red Cloud was being increasingly regarded as an opportunity rather than a liability.

The new resolve to end Red Cloud's War was quickly implemented. General Grant wrote Sherman on March 2, 1868, telling him to close Forts Kearny, Reno, and Fetterman. Grant added Fort C. F. Smith to his list the following day. Colonel Augur, acting on Sherman's instructions, implemented Grant's orders, except for the inclusion of Fort Fetterman, which Sherman knew Grant had never intended. Taylor, the head of the Indian Peace Commission, enthusiastically telegraphed Augur to inform him that the commission would return to Fort Laramie on April 7. Runners were again dispatched northward to bring Red Cloud to this new treaty council.

The peace message to Red Cloud this time was most compelling. All of his major demands had been met. In fact, the new treaty to be signed at Fort Laramie specifically called for the closure of the Bozeman Trail and the forts built to protect it. Moreover, an immense tract of land would be set aside for the Sioux; it would extend from the Bighorns eastward to the Missouri River and from the forty-sixth parallel southward to the Dakota-Nebraska boundary. The eastern portion of it would be reservation land and the western portion unceded Indian territory. The Lakotas were also granted hunting rights along the Republican River and on the lands above the North Platte "so long as the buffalo may range thereon in such numbers as to justify the chase." As a further enticement, the treaty promised Red Cloud and his people rations and annuities for thirty years.

When the commissioners arrived at Fort Laramie on April 10, however, none of the Lakota leaders, including Red Cloud, were there. Once again the frustrated commissioners held a formal conference, and once again the tractable Spotted Tail was part of the negotiations. Again, the prominence of the peace commissioners was in sharp contrast with that of the tribal representatives. There was the illustrious Sherman, the most conspicuous of the hard-liners, and there was the pro-Indian Taylor, whose size and persuasiveness had already marked him as a prominent spokesman in earlier conferences. Opposite this high-powered delegation was a group of Indians considered to be friendly, such as Spotted Tail and most of his Brulés, who were ready to agree again to the terms discussed seven months earlier at that North Platte meeting.

Most of the peace commissioners were humiliated by what they regarded as another snub by Red Cloud and his followers. Their feelings were only partially eased when Mathews arrived on May 1 with news that Red Cloud and Man-Afraid would arrive in ten days to confer with the commissioners. But even this promise proved groundless; Red Cloud declared later that he would not meet with the commission until those reviled Powder River forts were evacuated. "When we see the soldiers moving away and the forts abandoned," he reportedly said, "then I will come in and talk."

Furious with Red Cloud, a majority of the commission's members left Fort Laramie, leaving only Sanborn and Harney there in case a set of more favorable circumstances developed. Those two, in reward for their perseverance, reached agreements with the Northern Cheyennes, the Arapahoes, and the always more accommodating Crows. On May 25 and 26 they even got some ordinarily hostile Oglalas, Miniconjous, and Yanktonais to put their marks on the treaty. The two finally returned to the East, leaving the treaty with Fort Laramie's commandant, Lieutenant Colonel A. J. Slemmer, with instructions that he get Red Cloud's agreement whenever possible. Yet the government now seemed reconciled to the fact that Red Cloud would not come to the fort until all the posts along the Bozeman Trail were surrendered.

Closing the forts did not prove an easy job. The army's effort to sell post supplies to the Bureau of Indian Affairs failed, forcing a public sale, which also failed; prospective buyers, nervous about Red Cloud's intentions, were afraid to go to Fort C. F. Smith, where the sale was to be held. In the end, what was not abandoned was sold to the freighting firm of McKenzie and Story or given to the Crows, who had been cooperative throughout the entire crisis. Finally, on July 29, Fort C. F. Smith was evacuated, and at dawn on the following day Red Cloud and his warriors, who had been in the mountains watching the troops as they filed out, swept down on the deserted fort and torched it. Forts Reno and Kearny were abandoned a few days later, and the latter post, an even more detested symbol of the invasion of Sioux lands, was also set afire.

Federal officials were now much more confident about peace, and preparations for the much-delayed conference with Red Cloud proceeded with special energy during the month of August. Two respected clerics, Father Pierre Jean De Smet ("Black Robe") and the Reverend Samuel D. Hinman, who were once described as "specialists in the art of talking Sioux chiefs into signing papers," were recruited to lend moral authority to the proceedings. One crack interpreter, Francis LeFramboise, was invited to communicate the good faith represented by these two clergymen. All these feverish preparations came to naught, however, when Red Cloud sent word that he would not appear until enough meat had been gathered by his people for the coming winter.

Red Cloud's controversial decision to wait until after the Lakotas' fall hunt greatly increased tensions throughout the Northern Plains. Many people began to doubt whether he would ever come in and settle his differences in good faith. More ominous, fear of a new war began to grow. Colonel Augur sent a circular to all his troops on August 29, warning them to take exceptional precautions because of the uncertain state of Indian affairs.

Even members of the once optimistic Indian Peace Commission were starting to feel despair. Many of the treaties they had drawn up with the southern tribes at Medicine Lodge Creek were being violated or ignored. And now they had to cope with Red Cloud's most recent example of obstructionism. As a consequence, when the commissioners arrived in Chicago for a meeting on October 9, an angry showdown appeared likely.

Sherman quickly dominated the proceedings, tongue-lashing the tribunal's more pacifistic members, such as Tappan, who had the temerity to suggest that the government, not the Sioux, were the aggressors in this unfortunate conflict.

But Sherman's harsh words were not as important as the resolutions he aggressively pushed through the commission. Although the commissioners agreed to abide by those treaties already negotiated and agreed to help those Indians who would obey them, the new resolutions could not have been reassuring to Lakotas such as Red Cloud. One resolution dissolved the commission itself, which for all its weaknesses had tried to achieve some kind of fair settlement. Another transferred the Bureau of Indian Affairs from the Department of the Interior to the less friendly War Department, a definite triumph for those who saw force as the final arbiter. Most radical, however, was the commission's new position that the Lakotas and the other Indian tribes should no longer be treated as "domestic dependent nations" capable of negotiating treaties with the U.S. government. Rather, tribal members should be treated as individuals who must obey laws just as U.S. citizens did.

Sherman's new aggressiveness was also reflected in his position as commander of the Division of the Missouri, a vast area which incorporated much of the Plains country. Earlier, before the Chicago meeting, he issued an order in mid-August creating two military districts in the West: one was for the Sioux and the other for such Plains tribes as the Cheyennes, Arapahoes, Comanches, and Kiowas. The man put in charge of the Lakotas was General Harney—old Mad Bear, as the Sioux called him—a longtime nemesis of the Lakota tribes. The Sioux agency created under Sherman's new plans would be at Fort Randall on the Missouri, inconveniently located many miles east of Red Cloud country.

The army's hand was strengthened throughout in Sherman's reorganization. Military commanders were to act as agents for any Indians not on reservations. Moreover, these commanders were authorized to report any irregularities on the part of civilian Indian agents once the tribal members became reservation

Indians. The extent of the military's new supremacy over Indian affairs was underscored when Congress, in appropriations to implement the recent Indian treaties, stipulated that all funds should be distributed under General Sherman's direction.

Colonel Slemmer's strict interpretations of Sherman's August 10 order did not bode well for most Sioux. Inasmuch as Red Cloud and his people remained outside the jurisdiction of their proposed reservation, Slemmer decided to act as their agent. In that capacity he promptly barred the Indian Bureau's special agent to the Sioux, J. P. Cooper, from dealing with Red Cloud's people. Colonel Slemmer also told Cooper that when Red Cloud did come in to sign the treaty the Peace Commission had left him, his Lakotas would no longer be allowed to linger at the fort; Fort Randall would be their new place to trade and congregate. Whether or not Slemmer knew about Red Cloud's long and happy association with Fort Laramie, he seemed determined to prevail in this matter.

Red Cloud's weeks of delay had probably become counterproductive. Yet even after the autumn leaves had shriveled and fallen, there was still no positive word from Red Cloud's remote Powder River stronghold. But in late October of 1868 exciting news reached Fort Laramie that Red Cloud had decided that his people had finally stored enough meat for the cold months. He was now ready to come to the fort and parley with the representatives of the Great White Father. The decision caught the garrison at Fort Laramie by surprise. On November 2, Major William Dye, who had replaced Slemmer as the new commandant at the fort, anxiously telegraphed Colonel Augur for instructions. But Augur's advice did not prove helpful; he reminded Dye that the Peace Commission had been dissolved the previous month and directed Dye to tell Red Cloud that he should now go to General Harney to settle all of his differences with the federal government.

On November 4, in the middle of the morning, Red Cloud arrived for a peace conference with a large delegation of seasoned warriors. There were approximately 125 chiefs and headmen in the party, including Red Cloud's one-time rival for tribal leadership, Old-Man-Afraid-of-His-Horses. Besides the expected Oglalas, there were also prominent Hunkpapas, Blackfeet Sioux, Sans Arcs, and Brulés present. Red Cloud quickly dispelled any doubts about who was the leader; he promptly made himself the center of attention. During the introduction, for example, while the other chiefs rose to extend their hands in friendship, Red Cloud sulked and remained seated, offering only the tips of his fingers to those who insisted on a handshake. He challenged Major Dye's authority at the very beginning of the conference. He told the surprised officer that the proceedings at the conference could have little effect because none of the peace commissioners were present nor were any people of high authority on hand to replace them. But Dye was apparently more flexible and diplomatic than either Augur or Slemmer. He confidently informed Red Cloud that many of his fellow Sioux had already signed the peace treaty and that he, Dye, was authorized to represent the Peace Commission, which had left him the treaty for that purpose.

For three days Red Cloud engaged in a series of diplomatic maneuvers, which would become his trademark in future negotiations. Although Clarence Three Stars would later insist that Red Cloud never became a skilled orator, he certainly made the most of this occasion. He was aggressive. His questions were sharp, often accusatory in nature. The issues he raised were at times incidental, if not irrelevant. In short, he succeeded in keeping Major Dye and his negotiators off balance much of the time. Like Clausewitz, he seemed to feel that war and politics were part of the same process, and he often pursued his diplomacy in a manner more belligerent than accommodating.

Dye, according to his own account, tried to be patient, answering all of Red Cloud's questions as carefully as he could. He went through the provisions of the treaty with him on an item-by-item basis, a procedure that Red Cloud would either forget or deny; the domineering chief would later insist that no one had ever explained the treaty to him. Overall, the major was not encouraged by Red Cloud's unpredictable responses. When Dye discussed the treaty provisions dealing with farming and reservation life, Red Cloud's reaction was almost flippant. He

told Dye that he had already learned all he wanted to know about
such matters; his people were simply not interested in farming,
at least not at the present time. His only reason for being at
the conference, Red Cloud insisted, was to receive powder and
lead from the federal government. The whites had provided
ammunition to the Crows, it was only fair that they do so for
the Sioux. As for going to Fort Randall to get rations from
General Harney, Red Cloud absolutely refused, expressing an
obvious dislike for the old Indian fighter.

Major Dye developed his own conference strategies during
the three-day meeting. He provided a handsome feast for all
negotiators on the first night to soften Red Cloud's rigid
stance. When proceedings tended to drag, he would ask for
an adjournment. As for Red Cloud, he continued to show that
persistence for which he would later become famous. On the
final day he reintroduced the request so strongly emphasized at
the beginning of the conference: he wanted lead and powder for
his people. Dye should telegraph Augur, he insisted, if this was
the only way to get these vital items. Dye's retort showed how
resourceful he could be. He read Augur's intransigent telegram
to the Indian conferees, who looked distressed when it was
translated into Lakota. He also played upon the Sioux leader's
vanity; Red Cloud was the one chief who could make peace
possible. In the end, Red Cloud concurred with this second
Fort Laramie treaty, symbolically washing "his hands with the
dust on the floor" and putting his mark on the agreement.

Red Cloud concluded the conference proceedings with a long
oration; it seemed as though he always had to have the last
word. The thrust of his message was that, while the Lakotas
were willing to make peace, they were not ready to move
to their reservation yet. Moreover, the Sioux were absolutely
determined to resume trade relations at Fort Laramie with those
white traders who had remained friendly to them throughout
the war.

Perhaps the most alarming part of Red Cloud's parting
address, however, was his frank admission that he would have a
difficult time selling the treaty to some of his younger warriors.

Although some of his critics would insist that Red Cloud was once again equivocating, a number of young warriors, including Crazy Horse, were honestly concerned that Red Cloud might negotiate away those advantages the Lakotas and their allies had gained by the closing of the Bozeman Trail. Unfortunately, it would take the federal government a long time to realize that no leader, not even Red Cloud, could commit all the Lakotas to one unified position, especially in light of the controversial provisions of the treaty.

Following their departure from Fort Laramie in November of 1868, Red Cloud and his people were not seen for months. Even so, the federal government went ahead with its efforts to implement the treaty, the U.S. Senate ratifying it on February 16, 1869. The government's determination to move the Sioux tribes closer to Fort Randall on the Missouri River also continued, despite a distinct lack of enthusiasm among most Lakotas for such a move. Not only was the site regarded as being too far to the east, but the lands around it were also considered devoid of game. The government was able, nevertheless, to locate the helpless Laramie Loafers closer to Fort Randall, while Spotted Tail's Brulés were moved to the forks of the White River about a hundred miles from the fort.

But most Sioux stubbornly resisted efforts to move them closer to the Missouri, where they would be under the watchful eye of General Harney. Red Cloud's opposition was already on record, while some Sioux leaders were causing dangerous distractions. The resistance of such Lakotas as Pawnee Killer and Whistler, who still hunted on the buffalo-rich grasslands between the Platte and Republican rivers, was so formidable that it led to Major Eugene A. Carr's successful 1869 expedition to oust these Sioux and their Cheyenne allies from their familiar haunts in the Republican River valley. Moreover, one Sioux Indian, Grass, who signed the Fort Laramie treaty along with Red Cloud, insisted during a later visit to Fort Fetterman that Red Cloud believed that this fort, too, was in violation of the treaty and should be vacated as Forts Kearny and Smith had been.

Red Cloud's long absence was finally broken when he appeared in his usual unexpected fashion across the river from Fort Laramie on March 22, 1869. The force of approximately a thousand under him might have given Major Dye reason for pause, except that Red Cloud was not there to menace Dye but to beg for food. The previous winter had been very severe, and game was scarce. Dye once again urged Red Cloud to go to the Missouri, even offering him provisions for the trip, but the shrewd Sioux leader, who was not too proud to take the provisions, departed for the Wind River country instead.

Yet Red Cloud and his band left some effective lobbyists behind to agitate for their cause. These people were primarily white traders who had been working to reestablish Fort Laramie as a Sioux trading post. The most conspicuous member of the group was John Richard, Jr., the veteran mixed-blood trader who had known Red Cloud for years. Richard, who had acquired a license from the commissioner of Indian affairs to trade in the Powder River country, enjoyed the backing of some powerful people, including the influential Sanborn of the Indian Peace Commission, who was convinced that Richard had saved the garrison at Fort C. F. Smith from starvation and capture after the disastrous Fetterman Fight. Richard was also very controversial, however; as a matter of fact, he had been indicted for killing a corporal at Fort Fetterman in a quarrel over a woman. Nevertheless, Richard still enjoyed the confidence of Red Cloud, whom he kept in a state of turmoil by stressing the government's refusal to allow the Sioux to trade at Fort Laramie.

Early in 1870, Richard sent word through his father that Red Cloud and Man-Afraid intended to visit Fort Laramie in late March with some fifteen hundred to two thousand Lakotas. They were coming to trade, according to this report, but would fight if denied the privilege. Although the message caused pandemonium (a number of settlers sought refuge in the fort's large compound), Red Cloud's true intentions were quite different. His people were once again on another begging expedition, just as they had been the year before. But they still wanted to trade; this time they were asking for trading privileges to benefit small Lakota parties at both Fort Laramie and Fort Fetterman.

Solution of this prickly trade question was inextricably tied to getting Red Cloud and his people on the reservation. Lieutenant General Philip Sheridan, the famous Civil War cavalry officer who replaced Sherman as commander of the Military Division of the Missouri, initially opposed any trade concessions to the Sioux at Forts Laramie and Fetterman. He was inclined, however, to leave this decision to Augur, his major subordinate, who was now a brigadier general. President Grant's cabinet, on the other hand, took a firmer stand; it called for removing Red Cloud's people to their new reservation in order to avoid a disastrous conflict between the Lakota tribes and the white settlers from the Dakota and Wyoming territories. In a timely move the commissioner of Indian affairs provided the first break in this dangerous trade stalemate; he recommended that, while Red Cloud should now trade on the Missouri River, the government should provide the Lakotas with trading posts close to any encampment site they might select on their new reservation.

Because of this crisis, persuading Red Cloud to move to the Missouri River took on a new urgency; the arduous settlement worked out in the Fort Laramie treaty now appeared to rest on a solution to this problem. Much was at stake; the security of the Union Pacific was just one of the issues. The influx of Dakota settlers into Montana and the influx of Wyoming settlers northward into Sioux hunting lands east of the Bighorns was another. Although Custer would not confirm the existence of gold in the Black Hills until 1874, enticing rumors of deposits there were rampant by 1870; in fact, Dakota Governor Andrew J. Faulk shrewdly suggested that the Sioux reservation be relocated north of the forty-fifth parallel in an area embracing the game-rich Yellowstone and Little Missouri valleys.

The situation in Wyoming was probably the most urgent of all. Citizens in the territorial capital at Cheyenne had organized the Big Horn Mining Association during the winter of 1869–70 for the purpose of sending an expedition into "the unceded

Indian territory" granted to the Sioux in the Treaty of Fort Laramie; Wyoming citizens had been resentful for months over losing the northern third of their territory, a region allegedly rich in gold deposits.

In April 1870, in the midst of this looming crisis, word came that Red Cloud wanted to visit the Great White Father in Washington to discuss the Fort Laramie treaty. Major Alexander Chambers, the commandant at Fort Fetterman who received this news, was excited, believing that such a visit could reduce the Indian depredations being committed in his uneasy jurisdiction. The reasons for Red Cloud's request are still clouded in mystery. Much of the speculation revolves around Richard, who had visited Fort Fetterman several times during the previous winter and spring. Historian James C. Olson has speculated that Richard's visits to that rather isolated fort were part of his campaign to win a pardon for the death of the soldier at Fort Fetterman; if Richard could get Red Cloud to come to Washington to talk peace, then he might receive a governmental pardon in return. For whatever reason, Richard enjoyed wide support in his maneuvering; Spotted Tail, for example, addressed a petition on Richard's behalf, and it was signed by a number of army officers. More indicative of Richard's influence, however, was the fact that Red Cloud wanted Richard to come to Washington with him.

General Sherman, who replaced President Grant as general of the army, gave little encouragement to such a visit; Red Cloud should be told "plainly and emphatically" that he must go to his reservation north of Nebraska without further equivocation. But the seasoned soldier, now fifty years old, had misjudged the attitude of his old commander. Even before he assumed the presidency, Grant had proclaimed to a delegation of Quakers on January 25, 1869, a new approach toward the Indians, which historians since have dubbed Grant's Peace Policy. As a consequence, Grant and his secretary of the interior, Joseph P. Cox, decided on May 3, in consultation with the cabinet, that Red Cloud should be allowed to come to Washington to discuss the treaty. Furthermore, Richard could accompany the Sioux leader with the understanding that he must abide by the War

Department's decision regarding his involvement in the Fort Fetterman murder. Red Cloud could also choose twelve Lakotas to accompany him, including the venerable Man-Afraid-of-His Horses. Moreover, Spotted Tail was to be a part of any Sioux delegation.

Once these arrangements were made, the whole environment seemed to change. President Grant, alarmed by the Wyoming fire-eaters who wanted to invade the Bighorn country to prospect for gold, directed that any party organized for that purpose be prevented from leaving Cheyenne. General Sherman, falling into line, warned Augur to take every precaution to avoid any unnecessary incidents. Young-Man-Afraid-of-His-Horses, who was at Fort Fetterman when Red Cloud's invitation arrived, made a fast trip northward to inform Red Cloud and his father of the good news. On May 16 the man who symbolized Sioux resistance reached Fort Fetterman prepared for his long trip to meet the Great White Father; five hundred enthusiastic Lakotas were there to give him a proper sendoff.

Red Cloud's first trip to Washington was one of the best publicized visits ever made by a major Indian leader. It was a carefully orchestrated event meant to impress the visiting Lakotas with the wealth and power of their white adversaries. But the federal government also wanted to enhance Red Cloud's image; the government needed to believe that there was one Lakota leader who could speak for all of his people and deliver on all their treaty pledges. In short, federal authorities needed a "head chief" with powers not customarily granted to him by his people. The *New York Times* commented on June 1, 1870, that Red Cloud was "undoubtedly the most celebrated warrior now living on the American Continent . . . a man of brains, a good ruler, an eloquent speaker, an able general and fair diplomat." The *Times*, reflecting a bias that was in sharp contrast with the opinion of the frontier West, stressed the significance of winning Red Cloud's good will. "The friendship of Red Cloud is of more importance to the whites than that of any other ten chiefs on the plains."

Colonel John E. Smith, a patient, diplomatic officer whom Red Cloud eventually grew to trust, was given the responsibility of gaining the chief's good will. Smith, often addressed as general because of his brevet rank, was compelled to negotiate with Red Cloud on a number of things. Red Cloud, for example, wanted to bring twenty chiefs or head men on the trip rather than twelve. Smith felt he could not allow that because seven of the men chosen wanted to bring their wives; if this was allowed, there would be twenty-seven people in the delegation. Ultimately, the party's size was set at twenty-one, including four wives. As fate would have it, Red Cloud's only serious rival for power, Old-Man-Afraid-of-His Horses, got sick at Fort Fetterman and could not make the trip. Red Cloud throughout these difficult negotiations proved to be a quick study; because congressmen and others in high authority ordinarily did not take their wives on governmental missions, Red Cloud would not take his.

The Lakotas' Washington-bound delegation boarded the Union Pacific at Pine Bluffs, a small railhead forty miles east of Cheyenne. The Wyoming capital was considered too hostile for Red Cloud's departure. The party arrived in Washington at six o'clock in the morning on June 1. They were taken immediately to a hotel on Pennsylvania Avenue, where they met Spotted Tail and a group of his Brulés. Because of the rivalry between Red Cloud and Spotted Tail, federal authorities were very apprehensive about this meeting. But Spotted Tail was a quick study, too; if there was any bad blood between the two men, neither of them intended to show it during these Washington meetings.

Red Cloud's first conference with high government officials occurred on Friday, June 3; it was hastily convened because Red Cloud insisted on having it that way. Secretary of the Interior Cox and Commissioner of Indian Affairs Ely S. Parker tried to limit the agenda to friendly greetings and innocuous generalities. But Red Cloud, who refused to be manipulated, disrupted the cautious format with a forceful demand to be heard. Red Cloud then made three requests which caused Cox and Parker, a full-blood Seneca Indian and personal friend of Grant, considerable discomfort. He wanted more rations for the women and children he had left behind, ammunition so his people could kill enough game to survive, and a telegram sent to his people telling them that he had arrived in Washington. While Cox and Parker could promptly dispatch the telegram without embarrassment, they were not prepared to deal with the first two requests.

After this meeting the Sioux delegation was taken to the Senate gallery, where they viewed the legislative proceedings of the body that had ratified the Treaty of Fort Laramie sixteen months earlier. Most of the delegates seemed genuinely indifferent to the activities on the floor, fanning themselves to counteract the uncomfortable June humidity. On the following day, they were taken to the Arsenal and the Navy Yard, where Red Cloud measured the diameter of a fifteen-inch coastal gun. He and his party gave little indication of being impressed; although the awesome weapon could lob shells four or five miles down the Potomac, those shells could easily be eluded by Red Cloud and his warriors. The Lakota delegation, while polite, also showed scant interest in the howitzers being manufactured at the Navy Yard. But they were delighted to receive as gifts the bright ringlets of brass which fell from a lathe used in making the short-barreled cannons.

The Lakotas' passive response to this flashy show of strength, which also included a full-dress parade by a regiment of smart Marines, was matched by an equally passive response to a dazzling state banquet in the East Room of the White House, hosted by the diminutive president and his wife. Perhaps the attitude of the bewildered dinner guests, who enjoyed the strawberries and ice cream more than the wine and fine foods, was best summed up by Spotted Tail, who observed that their white hosts evidently ate far more elaborate foods than they sent to the Indians as rations.

Probably the high point of Red Cloud's Washington visit occurred on June 7 in another meeting Secretary Cox tried to control. On this occasion Cox, again stressing the positive aspects of Indian-white relations, praised the reservation approach. This system gave the Sioux their own lands so "they could be alone." The interior secretary reminded his passive guests, impressively arrayed in feathered regalia, that the Great White Father had already prevented determined gold seekers from Cheyenne from intruding on their hunting grounds east of the Bighorns. He also defended Grant's denial of the lead and powder Red Cloud had requested, insisting that this policy would remain in effect as long as the Sioux stayed on the warpath. As for the question of rations, the secretary promised the delegation that the Lakotas would continue to get plenty to eat. Cox, who was a couple of notches above most of Grant's appointees, concluded his reassuring remarks by introducing Felix R. Brunot, a Pittsburgh steel mogul who chaired the year-old Board of Indian Commissioners, a body Congress had created to counteract the public's loss of confidence in the government's Indian policy.

After Cox had completed his remarks, Red Cloud got up and slowly approached Cox's table. He was ready to give the Indian perspective to all of those developments lauded by the Interior Secretary. Shaking hands with Cox and his colleagues in a solemn and deliberate manner, Red Cloud refused to sit on a chair, reminding his hosts that, while they were raised on chairs, the Sioux were not. Crouched on the floor, the imposing chief gave the kind of long oration that a generation of government negotiators would come to know. It was a combination of lofty idealism and tough specifics. For example, he insisted that all the Lakotas wanted was to raise their families in peace. Aggressive whites, however, had surrounded them and reduced their lands, leaving the Sioux "nothing but an island." He bemoaned the loss of Lakota strength in the face of this ceaseless influx of settlers: "Now we are melting like snow on the hillside, while you are growing like spring grass."

Red Cloud's shift to the specifics of the Indian problem made the government's conferees even more uncomfortable. The army should evacuate Fort Fetterman, he insisted, a demand he would personally convey to Grant. But on this score he was to meet with disappointment. In an interview with Red Cloud two days later, Grant delivered the government's disappointing response: the fort was necessary for the protection of both whites and Indians, given the unstable situation in northern Wyoming. Red Cloud's other demands at the June meeting were also very direct. He wanted no more roads through the two Lakota mountain ranges, the Bighorns and the Black Hills. He was against locating the new Sioux reservation on the Missouri. He wanted access for those traders he trusted (he no doubt had the questionable John Richard in mind), claiming that much of the government material already sent to his people had been stolen along the way. The *New York Times* shrewdly picked up on this point, asserting a day later that the "gross swindling" of government agents and contractors was "at the bottom of all this Indian trouble."

Red Cloud must have sensed that his gruff remarks were winning him support, for on June 10 he stunned all the conferees by insisting that he had absolutely no knowledge of the Treaty of Fort Laramie. Contradicting the testimony of the conscientious Major Dye, who claimed that he had explained the treaty to Red Cloud point by point, Red Cloud professed complete ignorance of the entire accord. "I never heard of it and I do not mean to follow it." Red Cloud's perception of his role as a peacemaker was really quite simple: because the hated Powder River forts were destroyed, he was willing to make peace, and that was the extent of his obligation. Although Red Cloud backed down to the point of blaming the interpreters rather than the peace commissioners for all the confusion over the treaty, he remained adamant, even refusing Cox's offer to give him a copy of the treaty for study. "It is all lies," he continued to insist.

Cox, concerned that Red Cloud's visit could end on a bitter note, managed to arrange another meeting. The Sioux leader had really aroused some dangerous anxieties; in fact, a few members of Red Cloud's delegation were threatening suicide. Hoping to salvage the conference—indeed, hoping to salvage President Grant's much-heralded peace policy—Cox finally agreed to some meaningful concessions. The Sioux would not have to go to Fort Randall on the Missouri to receive their goods. They would be permitted to live in Wyoming on the

headwaters of the Big Cheyenne River, just northeast of Fort
Fetterman. Red Cloud and the Sioux delegation were even
permitted to provide Cox with the names of preferred agents
or traders so that the government could determine if they were
truly "good men."

Although Cox's concessions improved Red Cloud's mood,
the suspicious chief was reluctant to accept Cox's invitation for
a shopping trip to New York City. It took the intervention of
Senator Lot M. Morrill of Maine to convince Red Cloud that
he had a good many friends up north who desperately wanted
to see him. Still, Red Cloud remained morose. One reason for
his pessimism was that the government had made no decision
on Ben Mills, Red Cloud's choice for tribal agent, nor had it
made a decision on his choice for a reservation trader. Even
more disconcerting to the Oglala leader was the fact that the
government had taken no action on seventeen horses he had
earlier requested for his delegation's journey from the Pine Bluff
railhead at the end of their trip. This failure was especially serious
because Spotted Tail had already received horses for his people.

When Red Cloud arrived in New York City on June 14, he
was discouraged to the point of refusing to meet that staunch
Indian friend, Peter Cooper, a well-known New York inventor
and philanthropist who was also a member of the Indian Peace
Commission. This group had come to Red Cloud's hotel in
friendship on the night of his arrival. But the Sioux leader's
attitude was still negative; if he could not persuade the Great
White Father in Washington, there was no point in trying to
persuade anyone else.

On the morning after, however, Red Cloud mellowed and
agreed to see Cooper and the commissioners. At this rather
awkward gathering, a better-natured Red Cloud revealed his
sure sense of showmanship; although his fellow delegates were
lavishly adorned, Red Cloud stood in sharp contrast in his
utterly simple attire. In carefully chosen remarks, he emphasized
the importance of gifts to Indians; they were the symbols of
generosity and good faith necessary for the achievement of
peace. Cooper, sensing the high priority that Red Cloud placed

on those seventeen horses, pledged that if the government would not give the Sioux these horses, he would. This gesture so thoroughly changed Red Cloud's attitude that he agreed to meet in some public forum with the people of New York City, many of whom were curious to see the now famous chief who, along with his comrades, had stopped the Fetterman column. Thus, on the following day thousands of New Yorkers lined the delegation's travel route along Fifth Avenue and through Central Park to get a glimpse of the man who had forced their government to close the Powder River Road.

Red Cloud matched his triumphant reception with a well-received address a day later at Peter Cooper's famous institute. Cooper warmed up the audience in his introduction of Red Cloud by insisting that the Sioux people did not question the government's right to eminent domain as long as they received just compensation. But Red Cloud was the real center of attention. He attracted immediate favorable notice when, standing erect, his blanket wrapped around him, he pointed to the ceiling and said that, as different as people might be, God Almighty had made them all. Even though whites were clothed and ate "tame meat" and Indians were naked and ate "wild game," the Great Spirit, Red Cloud insisted, wanted them both to live in peace and tranquility.

The charismatic leader with his high pitched voice delivered his remarks in rapid fashion. He would stop after each sentence to allow his interpreter to translate his thoughts to the Reverend Howard Crosby, who in turn would pass them along to the audience. How much of the wording was Red Cloud's and how much was Crosby's, an impressive orator in his own right, will never be known. But the impact of his talk was telling; there was exuberant applause after each of his sentences, matched by sustained applause at the end.

Red Cloud, in his message at the Cooper Institute, reiterated many of the positions he had taken in Washington. But keen observers could detect at least two helpful insights from this speech. First, Red Cloud's relations with whites during the first half-century of his life had been friendly and close: "I was brought up among the traders, and those who came out there in early times treated me well and I had a good time with them. They taught us to wear clothes and to use tobacco and ammunition." In contrast, those whites sent to the Sioux more recently by the Great White Father "cheated and drank whiskey." Second, Red Cloud revealed a character trait that had become quite consistent. Although at times he could be exceedingly difficult to deal with, he tended to keep his commitments (at least according to his own interpretation). "I am no Spotted Tail," he told his enthusiastic listeners, "to say one thing one day and be bought for a pin the next."

Following Red Cloud's well-publicized eastern visit, he and his delegation headed west in their own special railroad car. When they reached Pine Bluff, much to their delight those seventeen horses were waiting for them. Another event at Pine Bluff that seemed to augur well for future peace was the attitude of the other passengers on Red Cloud's train. When Red Cloud's coach was switched off the main track, these people could finally view their fellow travelers. Their attitude was an especially warm one characterized by enthusiastic waves and other gestures of friendship.

But the warm attitude of the train passengers was in sharp contrast to the editorial opinion expressed by many western newspapers. One Dakota journal, for example, condemned the entire visit, insisting that what Red Cloud needed was "a dose of terrible war." The *Cheyenne Daily Leader*, which insinuated that the reason behind this much ballyhooed trip was to clear John Richard's odious name, proclaimed Red Cloud's return in its June 22 issue with the sarcastic words, "Lo! the conquering hero comes!" But the most important question raised by this visit was whether Red Cloud could convince those Lakotas who did not make the trip that the proceedings were in their best interest.

CHAPTER 6

Turbulence on the Reservation

ALTHOUGH Red Cloud signed the Treaty of Fort Laramie in 1868, his long career as a reservation Indian did not truly begin until after his trip to Washington two years later. For most of the nomadic Sioux the months between these two momentous events differed little from those that characterized the first five decades of Red Cloud's life. There was, however, one decidedly disturbing development they had to face. The not uncommon scarcity of game that plagued the Lakotas and the destitution that invariably accompanied it seemed worse than ever. Although hard times were not unfamiliar to the Lakotas, whose hunting economy had often forced them to face severe adversities, the gradual reduction of buffalo herds during the past two or three decades was finally having its effect. Moreover, these conditions of scarcity were compelling them to become more dependent on whites at the same time their leader was in Washington trying to represent them.

While visiting the capital, Red Cloud never gave any indication that he was impressed with the power and scope of the white man's land, the place "where the sun rises." Yet he was far too perceptive not to realize that his people faced a most formidable foe. Colonel John E. Smith, who had established excellent rapport with Red Cloud during his eastern trip, insisted that this visit to Washington had convinced Red Cloud that it was "useless to contend with the whites with any chance of success." Overawing the great Lakota chief, of course, was exactly what the U.S. government wanted to do; for years officials at Washington had been bringing Indian chiefs to the capital for that purpose in much the same way that leaders from the ancient Byzantine capital of Constantinople had done centuries ago with their nomadic "barbarians."

But the government also hoped to build Red Cloud's stature among his own people. Federal authorities needed an Indian spokesman who could command the respect of the Sioux and insure their adherence to all new treaty commitments. Many in Washington argued that Red Cloud was that person. Although a number of the chief's newly acquired friends in the East also felt that way, many westerners did not share that opinion. Among these detractors were a few prominent army officers, of whom Brigadier General Christopher Augur was a very important one.

In a letter penned to a colleague just before Red Cloud's Washington trip, Augur scoffed at the widely held impression in the East that Red Cloud was the "head and front of all hostile bands." Red Cloud's band was not a large one, he insisted, nor had it been a particularly troublesome one in recent months. The Miniconjous and the Northern Cheyennes, along with Pawnee Killer's Sioux to the south and the Northern Arapahoes and Hunkpapas to the north, had caused far more complex problems during the past two years. Augur was dubious about Red Cloud's ability to speak for those tribes: "Red Cloud cannot control any of these bands and his influence with them will be no greater than that of Spotted Tail." Moreover, the general believed that Red Cloud had already compromised himself by becoming a treaty Indian. "I think it will be found that any chief or head man who becomes friendly to the whites will cease to exert any influence over the hostiles."

Colonel Augur's insightful letter perfectly described Red Cloud's plight during these crucial months in 1870. The Lakota leader, who was probably only a shirtwearer when he assumed the direction of his people, knew it would be difficult to convince his fellow Lakotas that the Treaty of Fort Laramie was of benefit to them. Nevertheless, a few weeks after his return from the East, he traveled to the Powder River country in an attempt to organize a great council of the various Sioux tribes (a gathering that was presumably held during the last week of July). Yellow Bear, one of the chiefs who accompanied

Red Cloud to Washington, told Colonel Franklin F. Flint, the new commandant of Fort Laramie, that Red Cloud was using his influence for peace not only among the Lakota peoples but among the Cheyennes and Arapahoes as well.

But there was evidence that these well-intentioned efforts were meeting with both opposition and indifference. Red Cloud told Colonel Flint in January 1871, for example, that he could not pressure his people too vigorously on the question of a location for their new agency without appearing to be a tool of the whites. In fact, some Lakotas resented his descriptions of the immense power and wealth he saw in Washington. Some even refused to listen to him. "Red Cloud saw too much," one Sioux leader insisted during the spring of that year.

As for the indifference that Red Cloud encountered, it took the form of a return to the old ways by many Lakotas. When Red Cloud reached Fort Laramie on June 26, 1870, after his Washington trip, he was greeted by an impatient throng of Lakota tribesmen who had been there for days with robes to trade and hopes that the Sioux could once again conduct business there. Also, in the weeks that followed there were reports that the Sioux were again waging war on their perennial Crow enemies, notwithstanding the fact that Red Cloud had announced on his return trip from Washington a willingness to deal more amicably with such tribes as the Pawnees as part of his contribution to the new order established by the Treaty of Fort Laramie.

The federal government, anxious to stabilize conditions in the West, was willing to match Red Cloud in his efforts for peace. In August 1870, Washington sent to the Platte country the chairman of the Board of Indian Commissioners, Felix Brunot, whom Red Cloud had met in Washington two months earlier. Brunot was accompanied by another board member, Robert Campbell, whose name had long been associated with the early fur business; in 1834 Campbell, along with William Sublette, had founded the Sioux's favorite symbol of white culture, Fort Laramie.

When Brunot and Campbell arrived in Omaha in late August,

they learned, to their disappointment, that Red Cloud had not been heard from for some time. Responses to telegrams sent to the commandants at Forts Laramie and Fetterman informed them that a messenger sent north by Colonel Flint twelve days earlier to contact Red Cloud had never reported back. Major Chambers at Fort Fetterman did pass along an apparently reliable report that, although Red Cloud was at the sacred Sioux site of Bear Butte, northeast of the Black Hills, he did plan to return to Fort Laramie soon.

When the two Washington commissioners reached Cheyenne on August 27, however, they were told that Red Cloud would not be in until mid-September. To fill their spare time, Campbell and Brunot, a successful eastern industrialist who was not accustomed to being trifled with, decided that they would travel to Colorado to settle a serious problem with the Utes. When the pair returned to Cheyenne on September 10, they had to wait three more weeks before they could meet Red Cloud at Fort Laramie. Their patience was just about exhausted. But the impressive gathering of Lakota warriors at the fort, reported to be as high as seven thousand by the *Omaha Weekly Herald*, convinced them that this long-delayed conference could provide a real opportunity to reach some kind of settlement.

Before this much anticipated council, Red Cloud, whose actions had already dictated the time of the meeting, also gained control of its ground rules and much of its agenda. Before the proceedings could commence, for example, Red Cloud had the conference site moved from a large tent erected by the quartermaster to a place where more Indians could be present. The new location was the commandant's front porch, where the Lakota leaders could assemble while their warriors could sit on the spacious grounds in front of the porch.

When the meeting finally got started, Brunot, a take-charge kind of businessman, tried in vain to control its agenda. He opened the conference with a sanctimonious prayer in which he beseeched God that both white and Indian peoples be guided by the highest motives so that the "savage warfare" that had previously characterized their relations could come to an end. Brunot expressed particular concern about the spiritual welfare of the Sioux: "May these heathens be claimed for the inheritance of our Lord and Savior." When Red Cloud was given his opportunity to speak, he proved he could not be outdone. He rose to his feet and touched his hand to the ground, and all the Indians present stood up. Then, with one hand pointing to the sky, Red Cloud beseeched the Great Spirit, using those ecumenical terms reminiscent of his New York speech, to bless this important gathering: "You are the protector of the people who use the bow and arrow, as well as the people who wear hats and garments and I hope we don't pray to you in vain."

After Red Cloud's prayer, which was just as self-serving as Brunot's, both parties got down to business. Red Cloud again insisted on a trading post on the North Platte near Fort Laramie. He put on the conference agenda a not unexpected inquiry about presents as well as his oft-refused request for ammunition. Red Cloud also injected a host of new issues that caught Brunot and Campbell off guard. He complained about the fifty-year annuity payment promised at the 1851 conference at Horse Creek; these payments had been suspended after only a decade. He objected to the use by white travelers of a small section of the Emigrant Road above the North Platte and to a work detail from Fort Laramie that had recently cut hay in that same region; both developments were regarded as serious treaty violations by Red Cloud.

Although the government's position had not changed on the question of supplying ammunition, Brunot and Campbell did surprise the Lakotas by backing down on naming the Missouri River as the main trading site for the Oglalas. They suggested instead that the area around Raw Hide Buttes, forty miles north of Fort Laramie, be considered the new site. When Brunot tried to sweeten this offer by promising teachers for this new location in order to train Sioux children to farm instead of hunt, Red Cloud really became adamant that his people be allowed to trade somewhere on the Platte. Although he did admit that the bison population was in decline, he insisted that there was enough game to hunt if the whites would stay out of Lakota country.

Moreover, as long as buffalo remained, he would not tolerate schools for his young people.

The conference lasted about three days and featured the always popular distribution of presents on the second day. This ceremony involved approximately five thousand Indians, who formed a great circle around wagons laden with boxes and bales of eagerly anticipated goods. Remembering Red Cloud's assertion that very few of the goods sent from Washington ever reached his people, Brunot and Campbell made a point of carefully checking all the trade items to make certain that the Sioux were not being cheated. This procedure greatly impressed Red Cloud. Some of the chiefs involved in this distribution, however, would have preferred heavy kettles to tinned ones and black blankets to white ones. But, on the whole, they were pleased with their new possessions.

Just before adjournment of the conference the commissioners, who were anxious to have Red Cloud agree to Raw Hide Buttes as the Oglalas' new agency, sent John Richard to Red Cloud's encampment to bring the chief to the fort for a private consultation. During this hastily called meeting, which also included Old-Man-Afraid-of-His-Horses, American Horse, and Red Dog, Red Cloud was once again successful in postponing a decision on the Raw Hide Buttes location. But he did continue to lobby for those things he wanted. For example, he argued persuasively that Ben Mills should be his agent and that old friends such as Bullock and Richard should be his traders. He again expressed his hope that when his people came to visit Fort Laramie, they would be given rations. Brunot, miffed by Red Cloud's stubbornness, took a hard line; he insisted that the Sioux would have to go to the Missouri River for their rations unless Red Cloud agreed to locate his agency at Raw Hide Buttes.

Although a largely uncommitted Red Cloud left for the Powder River country in October, by mid-December many of his people were drifting back to the fort, hungry and in need of clothing. One band, under Red Leaf, that had not been to Fort Laramie since the summer of 1869, complained about the dearth of buffalo in all the river valleys of northern Wyoming and southern Montana. Red Leaf wanted permission to hunt in the Republican Valley, where game was allegedly bountiful. The situation got so serious that the army was given one hundred thousand dollars to feed and clothe these hungry Indians. By mid-February, almost three thousand Lakotas, Cheyennes, and Arapahoes, including the seventy-eight lodges of Red Cloud's followers, had gathered around the fort; by mid-May 1871 that number had swollen to more than six thousand.

Brunot, who categorically told Red Cloud in October that his people would have to go to the Missouri for their rations, was unhappy about the government's new policy of feeding the Indians. He felt that it significantly undercut his authority. Embracing the same conviction was John M. Wham, the man finally appointed as Red Cloud's Indian agent. Wham, too, felt that his position would be diminished if the army continued its large-scale feeding program. But despite Wham's negative attitude on this issue, his selection was more positive than negative for Red Cloud. Wham honestly believed, for example, that Red Cloud had the best interests of the government at heart. Moreover, he came to the conclusion, along with Red Cloud's old friend Colonel Smith, who had replaced Flint as the commandant at Fort Laramie, that Red Cloud's people should be given at least a temporary agency near the fort.

In the meantime, Wham, who was not a very tactful person, was having serious troubles with his new charges. Colonel Smith, who was called to Washington for consultation largely because of Wham's difficulties, recommended that the government should send Felix Brunot back to Fort Laramie so that the Grant administration could finally choose a site for the new Oglala agency. A reluctant Brunot agreed, eventually arriving at the fort on June 9, 1871. At this new conference, he vigorously pressured Red Cloud to choose a location. Red Cloud characteristically responded with another diversion: he demanded that his people be compensated for the land taken by the Union Pacific to build the transcontinental railroad. But the embattled Lakota chief could not win this argument. He finally persuaded

Brunot, Smith, and Wham to postpone any decisive action until he could travel north and consult with Black Twin, a powerful Oglala with whom he shared power.

Although the three negotiators agreed to wait, Brunot warned Red Cloud that he would confer with those Sioux who remained at the fort regarding the new location if he did not hear from Red Cloud in fifteen days. The canny chief agreed to this stipulation, even though it bordered on an ultimatum, promising Brunot that he would send messengers "every few days" to keep the board chairman informed about his progress. Feeling confident, Brunot left the fort about the same time that Red Cloud did; he was certain that the Sioux leader would be back in time for a final settlement of the issue.

When Red Cloud failed to return at the agreed time, however, Colonel Smith and Agent Wham convened talks with those Indians who still remained at the post; it was a large gathering that included virtually all the Indians there except those who comprised Red Cloud's loyal camp, which had dwindled to forty lodges. Although the Lakotas who attended the gathering were agreeable on many points, they refused to leave the Platte and relocate in the interior because of the parched conditions that characterized much of Sioux country during the summer months. They argued persuasively for a place on the North Platte, recommending a site eighteen miles below Fort Laramie. On June 30, Wham and Colonel Smith telegraphed Commissioner of Indian Affairs Parker, endorsing this new location. Wham also suggested that the issuance of rations, terminated earlier, be resumed, as the number of Indians at Fort Laramie now totaled seven thousand and constituted a potentially dangerous threat. Although Parker refused to cooperate at first, he changed his position a week later and approved of the new site; he also agreed to Wham's proposal for new rations.

The site selected by the conferees, without Red Cloud's participation, was thirty-two miles downriver from Fort Laramie. It was on the upper bank of the North Platte about a mile west of the Nebraska-Wyoming border. Wham took a leading role in the agency's construction; the new compound included three storehouses, quarters for several employees, corrals, stables, and a blacksmith's shop. Although the new station was often called the Sod Agency, its major buildings were constructed of logs. It was even surrounded by a log stockade, indicating that the protection of agency employees was an early concern. Wham was pleased that the Oglalas had agreed to locate their agency on the north rather than the south bank of the river, where the Oregon Trail still served as an important route. He was even prompted to recommend that the arms and ammunition that Red Cloud had often pleaded for be granted.

Although most of the buildings of the new Red Cloud Agency were completed and in operation by the fall of 1871, affairs at the site were still not going well for Wham. For one thing, Red Cloud remained outside the agency, enjoying the free and nomadic life that had characterized his entire existence. Second, Wham was having problems with Spotted Tail, who was then living with his Brulés at the Whetstone Agency on the White River. Wham's efforts to tell Spotted Tail what to do were causing resentment. Even the Brulé agent, James W. Washburn, believed that Wham's actions were undercutting Washburn's authority. Third, the Territory of Wyoming bitterly opposed having a Sioux agency located within its boundaries; Wyoming Governor J. A. Campbell was openly critical of this arrangement. Finally, Felix Brunot, who had worked hard to locate Red Cloud's agency at Raw Hide Buttes, was decidedly unfriendly toward the new site. Even Colonel Smith had a change of heart; he now opposed the agency's precise location.

When the respected Francis A. Walker, former superintendent of the ninth U.S. census, was named a special commissioner to investigate conditions at both the Red Cloud and Spotted Tail agencies, Wham's job was in peril. Walker's discussion with Spotted Tail had convinced him that Wham was alienating the Indian leader whom Walker regarded as the government's most valuable ally among the Sioux: "He is not only the best Indian in this part of the country, but his power is manifestly on the increase while Red Cloud's influence is somewhat waning."

Walker also submitted evidence that, because of Wham, the government had been swindled by beef contractors and that flour sent to the Sod Agency had been diverted to Cheyenne, Wyoming, by Red Cloud's old friend, John Richard. While Wham was probably a victim of circumstances—there were no scales to weigh the beeves at either the agency or Fort Laramie, and the Sioux clearly had no taste for flour—his days were numbered. On October 31 he was replaced by Dr. J. W. Daniels, another Episcopalian like Wham, who was currently serving as an Indian agent in Minnesota. Colonel Smith was given the responsibility of controlling the agency until Daniels could arrive the following year.

Wham might have survived all of the criticism if it had not been the underlying policy of the U.S. government to locate the Lakotas as far north of the vital Platte corridor as possible. Even though Commissioner Parker and Colonel Smith had also approved of the present North Platte site, it was Wham who was blamed for the decision; indeed, he ultimately became the scapegoat. It was no surprise, then, that Dr. Daniels, the new agent, was determined to remove the Oglalas to a new agency on the White River, approximately seventy miles above the North Platte.

When Dr. Daniels finally arrived at the Sod Agency, conditions were in disarray. Many Lakotas were hunting on the Republican River to the south or on the Powder River to the north. Every fifth day the Indians who lived near the agency would come in for their rations. Because Wham and his employees were very solicitous toward them, having those whites married to Lakota women cut and haul their wood, these Sioux warriors, regarding such duties as servile, had little respect for most of the agency's personnel. It was a sad time. The fur trade was dead and even buffalo robes were becoming scarce. Whiskey was being traded at the agency for clothing, flour, and bacon; not surprisingly, drunkenness was rampant. The preponderance of those Lakotas residing near the agency were of mixed blood, placing many of them in the same category as the old, discredited Laramie Loafers, in the opinion of less tractable Sioux.

Daniels was determined to change these conditions and was willing to work to win the support of Red Dog, a leader of Man-Afraid's band. When Red Dog's son died, Daniels was kind to him, having the agency carpenter build a coffin for the young warrior's body. Through the strong-willed Red Dog, who could not be intimidated by those Lakotas who opposed all aspects of reservation life, Daniels gradually began to make headway in changing the atmosphere at the turbulent agency.

Daniels's efforts as a reformer were complicated by the arrival of Red Cloud at Fort Laramie in March 1872. The still influential chief, who had been gone since June of the previous year, had apparently not spent the fall and winter of 1871–72 with his Bad Faces on the Powder River, but rather had lived in the Republican River valley with a band of Sioux known as the True Oglalas (once the head band of the Oglala people). Colonel Smith, whom Red Cloud first contacted, described his old friend, still vigorous in his early fifties, as being noticeably reserved, even "insolent." Smith surmised that Red Cloud was not entirely happy that the decision to move to the new agency was made without him. Moreover, the unhappy chief was openly critical of the new location; he wanted his share of government rations to be delivered at Fort Laramie rather than at the Sod Agency.

When Red Cloud finally visited the agency on March 21, he tried to pressure Agent Daniels into sending his goods to Raw Hide Creek near Fort Laramie. Daniels, after some negotiations, gave in on this point with the understanding that Red Cloud would choose a new site for the Oglala agency on the White River. Recognizing Red Cloud's skills in stalling on a difficult decision, Daniels gave him two weeks to make up his mind. When a meeting for this purpose was finally called on April 10, Colonel Smith and Brigadier General E. O. C. Ord, who succeeded Augur as the commandant of the Department of the Platte, joined Red Cloud and all the important Oglala chiefs in the hopes of reaching some decision. Red Dog, still grateful to Daniels for many past kindnesses, spoke for those Lakotas who wanted to move the agency. Red Cloud, sensing that there was strong support among his people in favor of a new location, agreed that the time to make a decision had arrived; he did suggest, however, that a number of Lakotas and a few of their Cheyenne and Arapaho allies should also be heard.

But the Sioux chiefs clearly wanted concessions for moving from the Platte Valley; the Oglalas, after all, had lived along the Platte and North Platte for more than a generation. One possible concession considered at the conference was the government's willingness to let the Oglalas use their own people to haul those government goods destined for any new northern location. But Colonel Smith, tired of what he perceived as constant bickering and stalling on the part of the Sioux, was adamant in his opposition to this arrangement. To put the Sioux on the defensive, he brought up a recent incident, the theft of some horses and mules near Fort Fetterman. Although Red Cloud admitted Sioux participation in this incident, he refused to accept responsibility, because no one from his band was involved. Smith also discussed the robbery and murder of a rancher named Powell near the agency, an event that had prompted Daniels to call in troops for protection. Although Red Cloud admitted that incidents like the latter one illustrated why it was dangerous to locate a Sioux agency too close to white settlement, he refused to accept responsibility for it, too.

Smith's remarks angered the Sioux and postponed meaningful action on a new agency site for about a month. But the die was apparently cast. During the delay, for example, Daniels took Red Dog and a few other friendly Lakotas to the White River to select a new site. After carefully exploring the area, they decided that the best location for a new agency was a site about a mile from where the Little White Clay emptied into the White River. It was a beautiful, partially wooded spot located a little more than seventy-five miles northeast of the Sod Agency. It was marked by lofty bluffs that commanded the green and rolling prairie below.

Although Red Cloud did not accompany Daniels and his party on this trip, he approved of their new selection; in fact, he eventually took credit for it. But any implementation of the proposal had to await a decision on Red Cloud's latest project; the unpredictable chief had insisted on going to Washington to see the Great White Father again. Daniels, anxious to placate the strongest voice among his Lakota charges, supported Red Cloud's request. As a consequence, Red Cloud was allowed in May to take to the capital a delegation of twenty-seven of his people, none of whom, except for Red Dog, had made the trip before.

When this second major Sioux delegation reached Washington, Red Cloud, anxious to bolster the authority he had lost by being away from his people for almost a year, confidently told Secretary of the Interior Columbus Delano, who had replaced Cox in 1870, of his decision to move the agency that bore his name to the White River. But his people wanted something in return for this concession. For example, the government should give the Sioux guns and ammunition so that they could hunt game more successfully. Also, recalling his trip two years earlier, Red Cloud again asked that a horse be given to each member of his party when they reached Pine Bluffs, Wyoming, on their return trip from Washington.

Official Washington was conciliatory toward Red Cloud on this trip. Secretary Delano, who claimed that ammunition was currently being withheld because of the murder Colonel Smith had alluded to, promised that he would allow Daniels to give Red Cloud's people some ammunition for hunting purposes. When the temporarily elated Indian delegation met President Grant on the following day, May 28, however, a new doubt regarding their ultimate fate was introduced. Grant suggested to the hopeful Lakotas that the Cherokee country in present-day Oklahoma might be a better place for them to live as reservation Indians. The climate was good and they could have a large and pleasant tract of land. Moreover, Washington would even build houses for the Lakota leaders and supply them with herds of cattle and flocks of sheep. Red Cloud resisted the president's tempting lures, insisting that the White River was the only place for him and his people. But Grant persisted, reminding the Sioux delegates that the new White River site was within the boundaries of Nebraska and that one day the citizens of that state might demand that the Oglalas be moved elsewhere.

Despite the doubts cast by the Great Father, Red Cloud remained enthusiastic upon his return from Washington. In fact, he was so busy promoting the virtues of the new White River site that he declined an invitation from Daniels to accompany him to Fort Peck for a meeting with a group of northern Lakotas agitated over the growing presence of the Northern Pacific Railroad in their region. Red Cloud, however, did give Daniels a message in early July to pass along to the leaders of this unhappy delegation, which included the powerful Hunkpapa medicine man, Sitting Bull. It was the Oglala leader's most forthright statement in behalf of accommodation to date. "I shall not go to war any more with whites," he declared. "I shall do as my Great Father says and make my people listen." Red Cloud also expressed a previously undetected faith in the federal government's word: "Make no trouble for our Great Father. His heart is good. Be friends to him and he will provide for you."

Red Cloud's message to his northern brethren apparently had little impact. Indeed, the ubiquitous Daniels returned from Fort Peck disappointed, a mood made more distressing by a new set of problems at the Sod Agency. During the month of August, while Daniels was still in the north, troops from Fort Laramie almost clashed with some young Lakotas who had grazed their ponies below the North Platte in violation of an understanding that the area was closed to all Sioux. The incensed Lakotas, in response to this military intervention, threatened to kill not only the soldiers but all the other whites at the agency, too. Fortunately, Red Cloud intervened, but he had to use all of his powers of persuasion to get the irate herders to move their animals back across the river.

Notwithstanding this dangerous unrest, many Indians at the Sod Agency were ready to move to their new homes in the north. But there were problems connected with this phase of reservation life, too. For example, preparations for the move came to an abrupt halt on September 11, 1872, when Red

Cloud, reversing his position, now opposed relocation. Eleven days after his announcement of the move, when all the agency wagons were loaded, ready for the seventy-mile trip through the sand hills to the White River site, Red Cloud and Little Wound, another powerful Oglala leader, told Daniels that it was their understanding that the Treaty of Fort Laramie did not require the Sioux to move from the Platte Valley for another thirty years.

Although the reasons for Red Cloud's surprise reversal cannot be ascertained with any degree of certainty, Daniels bitterly credited it to the chief's "natural duplicity." But Red Cloud's real reason probably had more to do with his desire to maintain strong leadership over his people. Ever since he agreed to the 1868 treaty, he had been accused by some Lakotas of selling out, a charge that made him cautious about being too pliable in any of his dealings with whites. Another reason for Red Cloud's change of heart was his reluctance to locate too close to Spotted Tail's new agency, which had been established a year or so ago in the White River area. Despite their show of unity during the Lakotas' 1870 Washington visit, both men were still jealous of each other.

Red Cloud's refusal to move provoked new hostilities at the Sod Agency. In October, a number of young Lakotas, intoxicated with liquor sold by white traders from across the North Platte, threatened to kill Daniels and all his agency employees. For twenty-four hours Red Cloud, Little Wound, and a few other leaders kept these reckless and drunken Sioux at bay until troops from Fort Laramie arrived to secure the situation.

Curiously, a short time after this incident Red Cloud and a group of his followers moved to Hat Creek, near the spot already selected for the new Red Cloud Agency. This action triggered anew the painful debate over relocation. Yet, by November 1, almost all the Sioux had left the Sod Agency and were preparing to winter along the White River. Although Red Cloud still returned to the North Platte for supplies, Daniels decided to make Red Cloud's unofficial northward migration an official one. Figuring that the cost of sending fifty thousand pounds of food a month was not excessive, the resourceful Indian agent began feeding Red Cloud's Lakotas in the White River country as if they were living there on some official basis.

Although Red Cloud expressed no objection over being fed and supplied at the White River site, he continued to send mixed messages to the government regarding his feelings. At first he insisted that his people should stay in the Platte River valley. Then he insisted that Hat Creek should be the site for the new Oglala agency, despite the scarcity of water at that location.

When Edward P. Smith became the new commissioner of Indian affairs, he decided to appoint a commission to settle this perplexing question once and for all. Its members included the now familiar Felix Brunot, who was asked to chair the group, plus E. C. Kemble, Henry Atwood, and Wyoming Territory's Governor J. A. Campbell. On June 20, 1873, the new commission met with thirty-five Oglala, Brulé, Arapaho, and Cheyenne chiefs. After two days of bargaining, Red Cloud and Little Wound, who had also caused the government problems by insisting that his people had a right to hunt buffalo in the Republican River valley, agreed to move their agency to the White River. But they continued to insist that the government supply them with guns, ammunition, and food in return for this concession. Although the commissioners refused to make such a promise, there was enough equivocation in their response to convince the Indian leaders that their demands would eventually be met.

On July 25, agency wagons were on their way to the White River again when Red Cloud came up with another objection. On this occasion he wanted to postpone the move until the new Indian agent arrived; Daniels, tired of the hazards and frustrations of his position, resigned, and another Episcopalian doctor, J. J. Saville, was appointed as his successor. This newest crisis, however, was promptly resolved. Jules Ecoffey, the agency trader, distributed enough presents to the right chiefs to allow the wagon train, loaded with all the worldly possessions of most of Red Cloud's people, to leave the Sod Agency by July 27.

The removal of the Red Cloud Agency to the White River was a success for Grant's sometimes disappointing policy toward western Indians. As historian James C. Olson has observed, the move was accomplished through patient but tedious negotiations. Moreover, the choice of the site was largely made by those Lakotas involved in the process. It was also a triumph for the persistent Daniels, who had planned to relocate the Red Cloud Agency at the beginning of his tenure. Yet Daniels's satisfaction over the move was tempered by a belief that the new site could never be successfully maintained without military protection.

That there would be problems for Daniels's successor was a foregone conclusion. Dr. Saville, in his first council with the Oglala leaders on August 14, 1873, was told by Red Cloud that the Sioux expected the guns and ammunition the commission promised them. The well-meaning physician, chosen by well-meaning church leaders, must have been astounded when Red Cloud demanded ten guns for each of his eleven bands. His enthusiasm must have waned significantly when he heard Red Cloud say that no white man should ever stray north of the White River, nor should supply wagons destined for Spotted Tail's agency, less than fifty miles to the east, ever be permitted to travel through the new Oglala agency, which many would later call the White Rock Agency.

While Wham and Daniels had rough moments during their tenures, Dr. Saville would have an especially difficult time during his. For one thing, the new agency was much farther from the protection that Fort Laramie had provided at the first agency, making Saville's employees more vulnerable to the violence and misunderstandings that often resulted. Then there was the fluid nature of many of the Sioux living on this remote reservation. One very disturbing development was the arrival of a large number of Miniconjous about the time the agency opened. Many of them had never been to an agency before and were, as Daniels once described them to the commissioner of Indian affairs, "impudent and saucy." They would be joined later by other northern Lakota bands, such as the Hunkpapas and Sans Arcs, who would often camp in the badlands north of the White River; these largely unreconstructed Lakotas wanted to be close enough to the government rations provided at the agency yet far enough from agency personnel to still enjoy their old freedoms.

Another problem that plagued Saville was Little Wound's insistence that his people had a right to hunt along the Republican River. The seriousness of this problem was compounded when Little Wound's followers during their hunt massacred a party of Pawnees they encountered at a place now called Massacre Canyon, west of present-day McCook. This incident particularly enraged General Sherman because the Pawnees had been authorized by the government to hunt in that area. But the problems created by the disastrous episode were not as persistent as those created by Red Cloud's stubborn belief that the government was committed to give his people guns and ammunition because they had finally settled on the White River.

But the most immediate dilemma facing Dr. Saville was the construction of a sturdy compound to headquarter Red Cloud's new agency. The site he ultimately selected for its location was much more picturesque than that provided for the first agency. It was a large grassy area with tall, tawny bluffs in the background; the slopes of these bluffs were graced by a scattering of pine trees that gave them the aura of a Bierstadt landscape. When construction on the agency started, its rapid completion seemed most unlikely. Saville, small in stature but willful in nature, became involved in a heated dispute with Jules Ecoffey, the agency trader who had been given the contract to supply logs for the new compound. When Saville revoked Ecoffey's trading license, he not only slowed progress on the project but he also alienated Red Cloud, who was a good friend of Ecoffey. Nevertheless, the feisty agent persevered in cooperation with the new trader, J. W. Dear, and by mid-September a warehouse for all Indian supplies had been built, and substantial progress had been made on a barn, stockade, employee living quarters, agency office, and Saville's own residence. In time a high fence, which was especially reassuring to the agency's staff during times of tension, was built around these buildings.

As far as most Sioux were concerned, the site of this new agency was good. However, when a subsequent land survey found that it was located in Nebraska, just south of the Dakota Territory, there were cries of outrage from Nebraska citizens, who demanded that the Lakotas be moved from their state. Even so, a number of Nebraskans would soon profit from this new location, notwithstanding the controversy. The agency's beef contractor, for example, could graze vast herds of cattle on the Platte, while Nebraska cowboys could drive the animals northward to the Red Cloud and Spotted Tail agencies for the big beef issue at both places. While beef was not buffalo meat, there was plenty of it, and soon the Sioux were feasting along the wooded streams of their new home. By winter the nontreaty Indians, called Northern Indians by those at the Red Cloud Agency, started to arrive in large numbers from the Powder River country to winter along the White River and consume some of this new beef. Nebraskans also benefited from the three new roads built to service the agency and from another one being planned.

In some respects it was this new prosperity that created most of Dr. Saville's problems. According to Article 10 of the Treaty of Fort Laramie, the government was only committed to feed those Indians who complied with the treaty by living on a reservation. Yet with the arrival of the staunchly independent Northern Indians during the winter of 1873, Agent Saville had to confess to his Washington superiors that his beef supply was nearly exhausted. Feeding thirteen thousand Indians—Saville's own estimate—required eight hundred thousand pounds of beef per month, which was double the original calculation. The influx of nontreaty Indians not only swamped the Red Cloud and Spotted Tail agencies, but two other Sioux reservations on the Missouri as well. It caused serious logistical problems, which were compounded by the frequent movement of the Northern Indians between reservation sites. A similar dilemma had been noted at the Sod Agency, but the new location along the White River, being closer to the free camps of the obstreperous winter visitors, made this new dilemma even more serious. In fact, these restless migrations would remain a headache for Dr. Saville throughout the four years of his difficult tenure.

What was needed was a census so that the government would know how many legitimate treaty Indians there were to feed. Saville, in order to get some action on this issue, gave a feast on Christmas Day for all the chiefs and head men to discuss the possibility of a census, hoping that Red Cloud would support him on this question. Red Cloud, however, still smarting from Saville's feud with Ecoffey, announced at the feast that there would be no serious talks about a census until the Great White Father sent the guns and ammunition that Brunot and the other commissioners had promised.

Actually, Sioux opposition to the census was based largely on superstition; they had never been counted before and they did not intend to be counted now. When Saville decided to take a census regardless of the consequences, he was surrounded on all sides by sullen warriors at the beginning of his trip. When he reached his first camp, he was promptly escorted back to the agency stockade. There, Little Big Man and Pretty Bear, two Oglalas from Crazy Horse's sulking camp, began to conduct proceedings not unlike an army court-martial. Probably only the arrival of Red Cloud and Little Wound saved Saville's life on this occasion.

On January 14, 1874, an intimidated but not entirely cowed Saville requested that a military post be established at the Red Cloud Agency. Although the Department of the Interior willingly concurred, the War Department was curiously reticent. General Sheridan, still clinging to the idea that Red Cloud's people should be located along the Missouri rather than the White River, did not agree to send troops until sometime in late April or early May. Only a series of dangerous developments forced him to reverse his position. One of them occurred at the agency stockade. At two o'clock on the morning of February 9, a band of vengeful Miniconjous climbed over the stockade fence by leaning boards against it and shot to death Saville's clerk Frank Appleton, who stood with a lamp in his hand at the door of an office ordinarily occupied by Saville. Ironically, on that same day Lieutenant Levi H. Robinson and Corporal James Coleman, who had separated themselves from a wood train twelve miles east of Laramie Peak, were fatally ambushed by another party of hostile Indians.

These two incidents in particular finally brought decisive military action. On February 18, General Ord dispatched a force from Fort Laramie under the command of Colonel John E. Smith to provide protection for agency employees and friendly Indians at both the Red Cloud and Spotted Tail agencies. With eight companies of cavalry and eight companies of infantry, Colonel Smith marched northward, arriving at the two trouble spots in March. One of his first actions was to request that Dr. Saville gather Red Cloud and approximately a dozen chiefs and headmen for an important meeting. Despite Saville's pleas to Smith to proceed with caution, the seasoned officer, whose four-year relationship with Red Cloud undoubtedly gave him a great deal of leverage, tongue-lashed the ordinarily cooperative agency Indians, telling them that if they could not make their northern cousins behave, he would do it for them. Although an angry Red Cloud refused to reply, he later apologized to Saville for his opposition to the agent's hopeful census proposal. Surprisingly, while Saville's relationship with Red Cloud improved as a result of Smith's forceful words, the prickly agent's once warm relationship with Colonel Smith and the army was starting to show some signs of serious deterioration.

As a result of Saville's disagreements with Smith, Episcopal Bishop William H. Hare, who headed another presidential investigating committee that was at the agency at the time, telegraphed Interior Secretary Delano, inquiring whether the "authority of Agent or Commanding Officer . . . [was] superior on this reservation." The army, although nervous about Hare's irritatingly nosy commission, had hoped that body would at least recommend the removal of the Red Cloud Agency to another location to stem the growing unhappiness of Nebraskans. The failure of the Hare commission to deal with this issue, along with the increased restlessness at the agency, however, compelled the federal government to make the difficult decision to build an army post at the new White River agency.

In the spring of 1874, Colonel Smith implemented this change of policy by starting construction on a new post at the confluence of the White River and Soldier Creek, a mile and a half from Saville's agency headquarters. After a few months, on July 21, Smith announced completion of Camp Robinson, named in honor of the luckless lieutenant killed near Laramie Peak on February 9; its name was not changed to Fort Robinson until 1878. Red Cloud, who at the time was being severely criticized by his opponents for supporting the troublesome northern bands at the agency, was not happy with this new arrangement. He did, however, approve of a new wagon road from Sidney to supply the growing activity at the agency. It was a shorter route, he argued, making it more difficult for "two-legged mice" to devour the dwindling supplies.

But Red Cloud's attitude remained negative, notwithstanding his eventual acceptance of the new military post along the White River. Indeed, his on-again, off-again relationship with Saville only worsened with the passage of time. Nevertheless, to stay on the good side of the government, he would often intervene on the unpredictable agent's behalf. But this cooperation did not extend to Saville during the disruptive flagpole incident of October 1874, even though Red Cloud's brother, Big Spider, and other treaty Indians, such as Young-Man-Afraid-of-His-Horses, were willing to support the embattled agent.

This brouhaha started because Saville was determined to build a flagstaff over the agency stockade. The Lakotas, who long associated the American flag with the U.S. Army and therefore saw it as a symbol of war, strenuously objected. According to William Garnett, an interpreter at the agency, the most vociferous opponents of this flagpole idea were the followers of old Conquering Bear, the chief killed in 1854 during the Grattan affair. His son led some dangerously discontented critics in an agitation that eventually resulted in the destruction of one of the sturdy logs brought to the stockade to serve as a flagpole. During this potentially violent episode, when logs were being chopped and cut with a vengeance, Saville asked Red Cloud, who was stoically sitting in his office at the time of the incident, to intervene. But Red Cloud absolutely refused, compelling the harried agent to call upon soldiers from nearby Camp Robinson for help. A confident Lieutenant Emmet Crawford was sent. When Crawford arrived with only twenty-two men, however, he was chagrined to see several hundred angry Lakotas there, smarting for a fight. Perhaps only the arrival of a picked body of agency warriors under Young-Man-Afraid and Little Wound's nephew, Sitting Bull, avoided what could have been the bloodiest incident up to that time. The result of the flagpole affair was to alienate Saville even further from the military, which felt that Crawford had not been properly forewarned of the dangers he faced; the incident also worsened the serious schism between Dr. Saville and Red Cloud.

Curiously, though, this incident did allow Saville to go ahead with his controversial census. Despite Red Cloud's continued opposition, the willful little doctor, who almost gleefully proclaimed the government's new policy of withholding annuities until the Sioux were counted, received the support of Young-Man-Afraid and Red Cloud's nephew, Sword, to proceed with the disputed census. During early November a group of young employees, so-called squaw men, and government interpreters went from camp to camp to count the reluctant Indians. The results were surprising: there were 9,339 Sioux at Red Cloud, not counting approximately eight hundred Kiyuksas, Oglalas from the Platte country who had broken from the rest of the tribe many years before as a result of Bull Bear's death. There were also 1,202 Cheyennes and 1,092 Arapahoes living at the agency. The number obviously would have been higher if the hordes of nontreaty Indians, who viewed a census count as being just short of a plague, had not abandoned the agency and sought refuge in the badlands north of Pine Ridge.

The flagpole incident seemed to distort Red Cloud's ordinarily intelligent perspective of events and conditions at the reservation. He appeared willing to jeopardize much of his support in this battle of wills with Saville, a real risk given the fact that he had already been overruled by many of his own people on the census question. More important, his angry quarrel with Saville made him less sensitive to a far greater danger to his people: the loss of the Black Hills. The threat to the Lakota mountains was very real. During the summer of 1874, a few months before the flagpole affair, the flamboyant Lieutenant Colonel George Armstrong Custer led a party of soldiers into the Paha Sapa on a scientific and military expedition; ironically, one of the purposes of the expedition, as far as the army was concerned, was to quell persistent rumors that there were great deposits of gold in those sprawling, pine-covered hills.

Protests over this important expedition, the findings of which launched a full-scale gold rush into Sioux territory, had even preceded Custer's departure for the hills from Fort Abraham Lincoln on July 2. The respected Bishop Hare wrote President Grant that this expedition "would be a violation of national honor." Red Cloud's long-anticipated dissent over the Custer excursion, however, occurred six weeks after the expedition had started, when Red Cloud put his protest at the head of a list of grievances given to a *New York Herald* reporter in mid-August. But this objection, which had been provoked by the death of one Lakota warrior and the capture of another by Custer's party, was almost an afterthought, given the fact that Red Cloud's charges against Saville largely dominated his list.

Red Cloud's concern over the Black Hills expedition was distracted even more by the arrival at his agency of a noted eastern scholar, Othniel C. Marsh. Marsh was a nationally famous professor of paleontology from Yale University who reached the banks of the White River about the time of Saville's disruptive census. The man was determined to dig for prehistoric fossils in the badlands north of the river, despite warnings that people at the agency, already rocked by the flagpole incident, were never more tense. At Fort Laramie he had already been given a military escort for his expedition, and to ensure the success of his mission he had also sought permission to cross the White River from the Sioux council at the agency. But his request at the council stirred up a bitter debate; some Lakota leaders honestly believed that it was gold, not fossils, that this curious white man was after. The unhappy result of this heated conference was an escort for Marsh and his party by unfriendly Indians to nearby Camp Robinson, a not so subtle message that Marsh's request to dig for fossils had been rejected.

But the professor, not to be denied, slipped across the river at night in order to reach the site of his diggings, passing the encampments of about three thousand Miniconjous, Hunkpapas, and Sans Arcs, who were still smarting over their rebuff at the hands of the agency Indians during the flagpole incident. During Marsh's brief stay at the site, several parties of curious Indians visited the fossil beds to watch the remarkable display of vigor generated by this daring expedition. In fact, the day after Marsh had completed his work, a party of Miniconjous, determined to attack the foolhardy intruders, arrived at the scene only to find that Marsh had already left.

After Marsh's party returned to the agency with two tons of fossils packed in its wagons, he was approached by Red Cloud, who had earlier tried to discourage him from this controversial project. The Lakota leader, however, did not come to harangue Marsh this time. Rather, he wanted to use him to discredit Saville; he had already lobbied those officers and men at Camp Robinson who were unhappy over the way Saville had jeopardized the lives of Crawford and his men during the flagpole affair. Red Cloud, using all his persuasiveness, told the professor that the Indians at the agency were hungry, that their rations were bad, and that Saville, in the discharge of his duties, had cheated both the government and the Sioux.

When Marsh asked Red Cloud to substantiate these accusations, the Oglala chief returned later with samples of inferior food guaranteed to increase the skeptical professor's interest. He brought Marsh such items as substandard flour, gritty with the clay dust so common along the White River; discarded mess fare that had soured; moldy plug tobacco; and bitter tasting coffee. How typical these specimens were has been subject to much dispute ever since. Historian George E. Hyde speculated that Saville's white enemies at the agency deliberately picked this sorry selection of rations to make Saville look as bad as Red Cloud wanted him to look; the Oglala chief, now fifty-four years of age, had always been influenced by certain white traders and interpreters who were close to the Sioux.

Marsh preserved the samples until he returned home. Then, five months later, he showed them to curious members of the Board of Indian Commissioners at a highly publicized hearing in New York City on April 28, 1875. This meeting, called to consider charges made by Marsh that had been widely circulated in the New York press, led to a three-month investigation of the government's handling of affairs at the Red Cloud Agency, an important issue in that the operation of the agency had been considered one of the successes of Grant's much lauded peace policy. Starting on July 16, a special commission selected by the Indian Board held a series of intensive hearings at such eastern sites as New York City and Washington and at such western sites as Cheyenne, Omaha, Fort Laramie, and both the Red Cloud and Spotted Tail agencies. Eighty-seven witnesses were called, and when the well-traveled commission submitted its official report on October 16, it required 841 pages to include all of its findings. Throughout this carefully watched procedure, Marsh took an uncommonly keen interest; indeed, he was so convinced that Red Cloud's allegations against Saville were valid that he sat with the commission during its hearings in New York and Washington.

Although the distinguished-looking Marsh was a good vessel through whom Red Cloud could reach Saville's bewildered superiors, the chief desperately wanted to go to Washington himself and personally present his case to President Grant. Saville was uncomfortably aware of this threat. In December 1874 he wrote to Commissioner of Indian Affairs Edward P. Smith about Red Cloud's constant agitation for a Washington visit. In desperation, Saville even stirred up the perennial military-civilian conflict by relating Red Cloud's claim that Captain W. H. Jordan, the commander at Camp Robinson, had agreed to go to Washington with Red Cloud if Saville would not. Although Jordan denied he had made such an agreement, Red Cloud remained determined to go over Saville's head and present his grievances personally. Indeed, in collaboration with Spotted Tail, he persuaded Lieutenant Colonel L. P. Bradley, the commandant at Fort Laramie, to endorse his trip. As a consequence, in the spring of 1875 a delegation of thirteen Lakotas from the Red Cloud Agency and six from the Spotted Tail Agency were selected for a visit to Washington in late May. They were to be joined by a party headed by Lone Horn, a Miniconjou from the Cheyenne River Agency, which included Standing Rock representatives as well, making Red Cloud's third Washington visit a potentially significant one.

Newspapers throughout the country, especially in the West, interpreted this proposed meeting as a great opportunity for Washington to persuade the Lakotas to cede the Black Hills. A clarification of the status of the hills, whose tempting dark slopes were visible from the northern fringes of the Red Cloud Agency, had become crucial. Gold seekers were already flocking to them, notwithstanding the government's position that such activities were illegal. Nevertheless, as early as March 25 the *Yankton Press and Dakotaian* heralded the trip as proof that, after a decade of inaction, Washington was finally ready to negotiate for the Black Hills. But the truth of the matter was that while Red Cloud and Spotted Tail were willing to discuss the Black Hills, it was the resolution of his dispute with Saville that motivated Red Cloud to lobby for this Washington trip.

Red Cloud would have to wade through a host of problems, however, before he could get Washington authorities to listen to his complaints against Agent Saville. Even before his departure from the West, he and Spotted Tail became involved in a dispute over which interpreters they were to take to the conference. Both chiefs accused federal officials of trying to pack their delegations with selected interpreters "to the exclusion of those whom the Indians wanted." Ultimately Todd Randall, a trader whom Red Cloud's first agent, John Wham, once called "disreputable," was selected to serve as the Sioux interpreter;

accusations about his characteristically "loose translations" indicate that he was probably not the best choice.

When the anxious delegates finally reached Washington, they found it difficult to communicate with Grant. More concerned about the Black Hills issue and beset by the damaging scandals of his administration, the troubled president announced at a White House meeting that he wanted to turn all important matters of discussion with the Indians over to his secretary of the interior and his commissioner of Indian affairs. This proposal was an insult to both Lakota chiefs, who wanted a direct dialogue with the president. The more conciliatory Spotted Tail told the aloof Grant that he had already spoken to those two officials and they had only lied to him. Red Cloud, deeply disappointed, insisted that he had come to Washington only to see the president, and when Grant was ready to talk, he should send for him.

Another problem faced by Red Cloud during his Washington visit was that the government had one agenda while the Lakotas had another. Although the Black Hills question would cast a dominant shadow over all the proceedings, other issues were vigorously pushed by the government's negotiators early in the conference. They wanted the Sioux, for example, to terminate their rights to hunt in the country between the Republican and Smoky Hill rivers along the Kansas-Nebraska border. Even though federal authorities conceded that Lakotas by treaty had a right to hunt there, they stressed the potential problems with whites if this practice were to continue.

The government used a number of good arguments to win support for its viewpoint. For one thing, the great buffalo herds along the Republican were almost gone; when several thousand Oglalas, Brulés, and Cheyennes were permitted to hunt in the Republican Valley later that year, only a hundred of the great beasts were killed by disappointed Indians. For another, Article 10 of the Fort Laramie Treaty would have to be revised. That section of the treaty provided each tribal member with one pound of meat and one pound of flour each day for four years after the Lakotas took up reservation life. As that article was about to expire, the government used its possible extension to entice the Sioux into giving up their rights to their once fabled hunting ground. Sioux cooperation on this issue was also encouraged by a congressional appropriation of twenty-five thousand dollars if they agreed to the government's terms by the end of June. Yet despite these enticements, the hesitant Lakotas waited until June 23, after they returned from Washington, to surrender those once-treasured hunting rights; Red Cloud apparently took no part in the details of this painful concession.

Another of Washington's agenda items which differed from the Lakotas' was the proposed relocation of the Sioux to Indian Territory in faraway Oklahoma. Grant had already made that suggestion during Red Cloud's 1872 Washington trip; Secretary of the Interior Delano would make it at this meeting. The determined Delano argued as persuasively as he could that the Sioux and their children would be happy there and that Congress would continue to supply them there until they could achieve self-sufficiency. Spotted Tail promptly ended Delano's agitation. Speaking for Red Cloud and the other chiefs, he claimed that such a move would require the negotiation of a new treaty, something that he and the other delegates were not authorized to do.

Red Cloud finally got an opportunity to talk about his main agenda item, Agent Saville, on May 28 when he and the other Sioux leaders were invited to a conference at the Indian Bureau. Although the president and Secretary Delano did not attend this meeting, Professor Marsh was there, reassuring Red Cloud that he had already shown Grant the inferior food samples and discussed with him Red Cloud's well-publicized frustrations. During this meeting, Marsh and Assistant Secretary of the Interior B. R. Cowen tried to ascertain exactly what bothered Red Cloud the most about Saville's handling of the Red Cloud Agency. But the Sioux leader would not be pinned down.

Even though part of the problem may have been Todd Randall's faulty interpretations, Red Cloud was not giving Marsh the support he needed at this meeting, despite the fact that the strong-willed professor had put his prestige on the line in behalf of Red Cloud. For example, Red Cloud's complaints about the small size of the cattle that had been provided as meat rations for the agency were undercut when he admitted that Saville himself had rejected those same undersized animals. Most damaging to the chief's credibility, however, was his admission that the food samples he had given to Marsh were not necessarily representative of those issued at the agency; in fact, the ones Marsh received were taken from wagons that had gotten wet on their way to the White River agency.

Although Marsh's position was undermined by Red Cloud's rather inept testimony, he insisted that there was "substantial truth" in what the ordinarily articulate chief had to say. Moreover, he argued that Red Cloud had only equivocated in his charges against Saville because he feared future prejudice against his people on the part of officials from the Department of the Interior and the Indian Bureau. But the government's negotiators had a different slant on Red Cloud's substandard performance. They insisted that Red Cloud's long and evasive discussions about Marsh's charges at this meeting were only meant to delay any substantive action on the Black Hills. Red Cloud was even accused of being under the influence of alcohol during some of these Washington proceedings. Although it is evident that some members of this Lakota delegation did imbibe, Red Cloud, who was strongly on record against liquor for his people, was usually good about avoiding excesses of this kind.

Although Red Cloud's charges against Saville had been weakened by his testimony at that May 28 meeting, the work of the Board of Indian Commissioners' special body to investigate his complaints against Saville continued for almost five months, attracting national attention and both winning and losing friends for Red Cloud. During this prolonged and often bitter process, Professor Marsh incorporated his complaints into a pamphlet addressed to Grant, which he filed on July 10 after giving advance copies to the press. Secretary Delano, who disliked Marsh as intensely as Marsh disliked him, responded with an equally critical pamphlet in which he attacked Marsh's role in the whole sordid affair. The intensity of their exchange matched that generated by many of the other scandals that beset Grant's administration at the time.

The final report, while acknowledging a host of problems at the Red Cloud Agency, did acquit Saville of the charges that he had defrauded the government and deliberately cheated the Indians. Indeed, the authors of the report conceded that he may have been quite honest, given the caliber of government service during the troubled Grant era: "He may certainly be referred to as an example of at least one Indian Agent who goes out of office a poorer man than when he entered it." Although Saville had tendered his resignation four months earlier, while still in Washington, he did not leave his agency post until December 3, 1876.

Red Cloud may have prevailed over Dr. Saville in this two-year feud, but his victory was, in many ways, a Pyrrhic one. For one thing, the special commission did not support his most serious charges; it concluded that the food samples he gave to Marsh, for example, were atypical of the rations provided at the Oglala agency. Although the commission acknowledged that much of the food was inferior in quality and that many of the suppliers, contractors, and inspectors involved in feeding the Sioux had probably defrauded the government in one way or another, Red Cloud's failure to prove his most damaging personal charges against Saville had undercut much of the eastern support he had cultivated during his two previous Washington trips. His status with these eastern friends was further undermined at one of the hearings held at the Red Cloud Agency in mid-August, when one of the Lakotas' trusted white interpreters, Leon Palladay, claimed that Red Dog told him that he and Red Cloud had chosen bad grains of coffee for Marsh to discredit the irksome agent.

Red Cloud's persistent campaign against Saville had even undercut his support among some of his younger warriors. The scrappy little agent had evidently won the admiration of several Sioux leaders whom Saville had cultivated in his struggle against Red Cloud. Little Wound's nephew Sitting Bull (not to be confused with the famous Hunkpapa medicine man) testified at one of the commission hearings that Dr. Saville had helped many of the Oglalas at the Red Cloud Agency and that he did not know where the Sioux would find a better agent. Scalp Face, another Lakota who went to Washington with Red Cloud, echoed a similar sentiment: Saville was a good agent, a "brave, true man" who could not be broken; the Sioux should take him back home with them.

But the most destructive part of Red Cloud's feud with Saville was that it was distracting the Sioux from their greatest challenge: the potential loss of the Black Hills. If there was ever a time for Lakota unity, it was during the spring and summer months of 1875. By that time the tide created by the lure of gold in those Sioux hills may have been impossible to oppose, but Red Cloud's concentration should have been on that threat almost to the exclusion of all others. Besides, his quarrel with Saville did little to help the lot of his people. Although it did attract national attention and resulted in Saville's ultimate removal, no important reform of the reservation system occurred because of it; in truth, no reform of the controversial system transpired until Grant's successor, Rutherford B. Hayes, appointed reformist Carl Schurz as secretary of the interior. But notwithstanding this aspect of the Red Cloud–Saville feud, it was the threatened loss of the Black Hills that remained the most real and immediate one.

Red Cloud's third trip to Washington was a disappointment to him even though he managed to thoroughly embarrass Dr. Saville. In fact, historian James C. Olson has characterized this trip as a "fiasco." The Lakota leader had let down Professor Marsh, who was from that well-educated, usually affluent group of easterners who were genuinely concerned about the fairness, if not the morality, of the government's Indian policy. Fortunately for Red Cloud, this steadfast new ally remained a friend; in 1883 Marsh entertained him in his New Haven home for three days. Red Cloud had also alienated many of those in government with whom he still had important business; his plea at the end of the Washington conference that the government should compensate those perennially unpopular interpreters of mixed blood that the Sioux had insisted on taking to Washington was unquestionably a self-defeating one. The influential commissioner of Indian affairs, Edward P. Smith, had characterized those people as "sources of mischief and trouble" throughout the three weeks of the meeting. "Now they have the impudence," he railed, "to come and ask me to pay for their questionable services."

The discouraging outcome of the 1875 Washington conference hurt Red Cloud at a most crucial time. The meeting was pegged as a failure even by the more friendly elements of the press. The *New York Herald*, for example, thought that the fiasco should put "an end to the foolish practice of [bringing] Indian embassies to negotiate with the government." It also marked the end of four turbulent years of reservation life for the Sioux and presaged the government's renewed determination to acquire the Black Hills, which by treaty had been granted to all the Lakota tribes "for their absolute and undisturbed use and occupation." Red Cloud's return from Washington would be marked by tense months of feverish maneuvering by both sides at the agency.

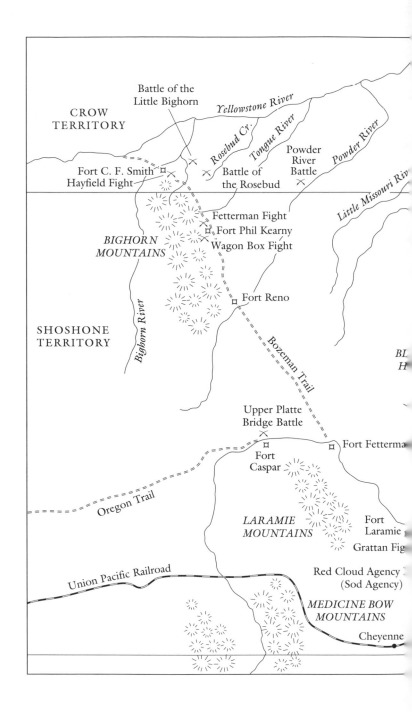

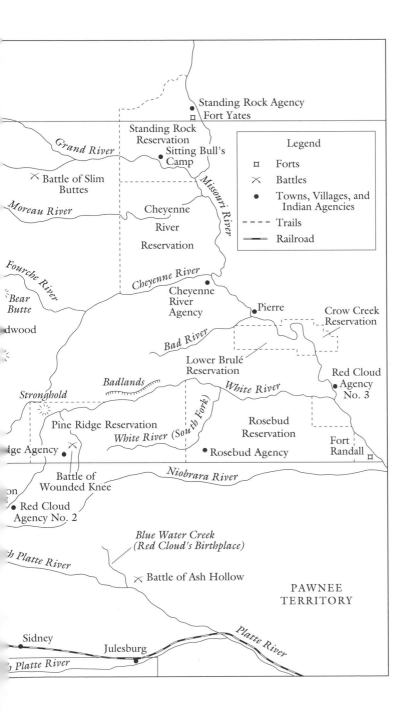

Standing Rock Agency
Fort Yates

Grand River

Standing Rock
Reservation
Sitting Bull's
Camp

Battle of Slim
Buttes

Moreau River

Cheyenne
River
Reservation

Missouri River

Legend

⌑	Forts
✕	Battles
●	Towns, Villages, and Indian Agencies
= = = =	Trails
▬▬▬	Railroad

Fourche River

Bear
Butte

dwood

Cheyenne River

Cheyenne
River
Agency

Pierre

Crow Creek
Reservation

Bad River

Lower Brulé
Reservation

Badlands

Stronghold

White River

Red Cloud
Agency
No. 3

Pine Ridge Reservation
White River (South Fork)

Rosebud
Reservation

Fort
Randall

lge Agency

Rosebud Agency

Battle of
Wounded Knee

Niobrara River

on

Red Cloud
Agency No. 2

Blue Water Creek
(Red Cloud's Birthplace)

h Platte River

Battle of Ash Hollow

PAWNEE
TERRITORY

Sidney

Julesburg

Platte River

Platte River

An aged Red Cloud in 1897 when visits to his friend Captain James H. Cook's ranch in northwestern Nebraska were important in breaking the monotony of reservation life. His fully feathered headdress is in sharp contrast to the lone eagle feather he ordinarily wore when posing for the camera. (*Photograph by David F. Barry, Denver Public Library, Western History Department*)

Although historians of the Plains tribes have tended to focus on the introduction of the horse as it affected Indian warfare and the hunt, this animal was also useful to tribal women in helping them move camp. The travois being pulled by this Sioux woman's horse on the Rosebud Reservation during the twilight of the frontier would probably have been loaded with camp equipment during the highly mobile years following the appearance of the horse on the Northern Plains. (*John A. Anderson Collection, Nebraska State Historical Society*)

Red Cloud and his wife, Pretty Owl, during their declining years. (*Photograph by Mrs. R. H. Blanchard, Eli S. Ricker Collection, Nebraska State Historical Society*)

At one time buffalo herds dotted the Great Plains providing a bountiful food commissary for the Lakota Sioux and other Plains tribes. (*Photograph by Edward S. Curtis, Denver Public Library, Western History Department*)

Jack, Red Cloud's only son, during his younger years. (*Photograph by G. Trager, Nebraska State Historical Society*)

This 1876 encampment of Red Dog and his band of Lakotas was typical of many of the Plains Indian camps of the early nineteenth century. *(Nebraska State Historical Society)*

Spotted Tail, lower right-hand corner, and Red Cloud, standing above him, were major rivals for Sioux leadership during the early struggles against the federal government. Others in this group photo are Julius Meyer, an interpreter, standing alongside Red Cloud, and Sitting Bull, not the famous Hunkpapa medicine man but a prominent Oglala leader, sitting in front of Meyer, alongside the Brulé chief Swift Bear. *(Nebraska State Historical Society)*

This illustration of the famous Fetterman Fight appeared in *Harper's Weekly* on March 23, 1867, shortly after the army's resounding defeat by Red Cloud's warriors near Fort Phil Kearny on December 21, 1866. Although the artist's depiction reveals the utter chaos, it fails to show that many of the Sioux and Cheyenne attackers were on foot.

In this photograph members of the United States Peace Commission are seated under four makeshift tipis during their 1868 peace conference with the Sioux and other Plains tribes at Fort Laramie. Seated in the middle, to the left of the white-bearded General William S. Harney, is the commission's most powerful military man, General William Tecumseh Sherman, and seated at the end is the commission's most influential civilian member, N. G. Taylor. Although the commissioners were deeply disappointed that Red Cloud was not there, the independent-minded Oglala leader did agree to the Treaty of Fort Laramie later that year. (*Nebraska State Historical Society*)

Below picturesque bluffs in northwestern Nebraska, this stockaded headquarters for the second Red Cloud Agency served the Oglala Sioux from 1873 to 1877. In 1876, when this photograph was taken, much of the country's attention was focused miles to the north where the fateful Battle of the Little Bighorn was fought. (*Nebraska State Historical Society*)

John J. Saville, the strong-willed Indian agent whose early disagreements with Red Cloud eventually led to an investigation of alleged mismanagement at the Red Cloud Agency. Judging by his white beard, this photograph was probably taken many years after Saville left the agency. *(Photograph by Keyn of Omaha, Nebraska State Historical Society)*

Cheyenne chief Two Moons on Custer Hill in 1902 during the twenty-fifth anniversary of the Battle of the Little Bighorn. On June 25, 1876, Two Moons, along with Crazy Horse, led those Cheyenne and Lakota warriors who destroyed Custer's column on this hillside. *(Hoffman Pictures, Miles City, Montana, Nebraska State Historical Society)*

The Lakotas' sacred sun dance held on the plains south of Pine Ridge in 1883. This Sioux celebration was held over the objections of Agent McGillycuddy. (*Nebraska State Historical Society*)

This May 4, 1889, gathering of Lakota Sioux at Rosebud occurred during the Crook Commission's controversial visit to persuade the Brulés to accept the Sioux bill of 1889. The tall building on the right later became the familiar reservation store of Charles B. Jordan, one of Red Cloud's friends and admirers. *(John A. Anderson Collection, Nebraska State Historical Society)*

Army troops marching on the parade ground at Fort Laramie during the late nineteenth century. This fort, which started as a trading post for Lakota and other Plains Indians in the 1830s, became an especially important place during the Great Sioux War of 1876–77. *(Photograph by D. S. Mitchell, Nebraska State Historical Society)*

Indian Agent Valentine T. McGillycuddy in Washington in 1883 with a group of Lakota supporters. Standing, left to right, are Sword (formerly Hunts the Enemy), who was a captain in McGillycuddy's Indian police force, and William Garnett, a prominent mixed-blood. Seated, left to right, are Standing Soldier, McGillycuddy, and Young-Man-Afraid-of-His-Horses, McGillycuddy's most powerful supporter at Pine Ridge. *(Nebraska State Historical Society)*

A Ghost Dance held on November 25, 1890, at Wounded Knee on the Pine Ridge Reservation. This photo is one of two Ghost Dance photographs authenticated by scholars of Sioux history. *(Photograph by G. Trager, Nebraska State Historical Society)*

The tragic aftermath of the Battle of Wounded Knee Creek. Snow which fell the following day covered much of the carnage resulting from that bloody encounter. *(Photograph by G. Trager, Nebraska State Historical Society)*

Age caught up with Red Cloud by the end of the nineteenth century. This photograph, taken during the Ghost Dance troubles of 1890, shows the Sioux chief, almost seventy, wearing sun glasses to protect his half-blind eyes. He looks small alongside Major John Burke, an associate of "Buffalo Bill" Cody, and Rocky Bear, another member of Buffalo Bill's Wild West show. *(Nebraska State Historical Society)*

Red Cloud's home, the only two-story private residence on the Pine Ridge Reservation for many years, was the chief's simple, but comfortable, abode during the last decades of his long life. *(Nebraska State Historical Society)*

CHAPTER 7

Reverberations from the Little Bighorn

BY June 1875, when Red Cloud had returned from Washington after three weeks of difficult wrangling, he found that his increasingly threatened Black Hills were the center of great publicity. Newspapers in towns such as Cheyenne, Yankton, and Sioux City reported that parties of prospectors were prepared to move into these forbidden hills, notwithstanding the government's officially proclaimed efforts to stop them. The Sioux commission, under Bishop Hare, did its best to discourage this illegal gold rush, continuing to insist, as persuasively as it could, that the Black Hills were not the new Eldorado. The commission's negative assessment of the mineral deposits in the Paha Sapa, in fact, had already received powerful support from the disappointing findings of Professor Newton H. Winchell, who, in the company of President Grant's son, Colonel Fred Grant, explored the Black Hills shortly after Custer's party had left in August 1874. But most prospectors were attuned only to the positive findings. The promising discoveries of Professor Walter P. Jenny of the New York School of Mines, who spent the summer and early fall of 1875 exploring the Black Hills, provided the kind of news they wanted to hear.

It is difficult to measure Red Cloud's concern over this growing threat to the Black Hills. Officially the government opposed any and all prospecting in the hills, and the army was ordered to turn back bands of miners whenever they approached the area. Yet during the summer of 1875 a number of mining parties got through the loose military cordon blocking most major approaches to the Black Hills, forcing the less-than-enthusiastic soldiers to eject them. But most of these single-minded intruders usually returned; in August 1875 alone, almost six hundred expelled miners were soon back at their new diggings.

The entrance of Brigadier General George Crook into this confused scene in July only exacerbated the situation. Succeeding General Ord as commander of the Department of the Platte, Crook, a seasoned Indian fighter from the Southwest, toured the area and found twelve hundred miners illegally prospecting in the Black Hills. Characteristic of most military personnel during this crisis, he ordered the prospectors to leave but made no effort to enforce his decree. Indeed, in his annual report to Washington, he took the miners' side in the controversy. Although they were violating a "treaty stipulation," he observed, "it was but natural that they should reply that the Indians themselves were violating the treaty hundreds of times every summer by predatory incursions, whereby many settlers . . . [are] utterly ruined." He showed little sympathy even for those Sioux abiding by the Fort Laramie Treaty, referring to the Lakotas and other Plains tribes as Indians "who are fed, clothed, and maintained in utter idleness by the Government they, the settlers, help to support."

To settle this potentially dangerous situation, the federal government adopted an idea that Red Cloud had suggested during his recent trip to Washington. Commissioner of Indian Affairs Edward P. Smith, whose reputation was partially tarnished by Marsh's accusations and the results of the Sioux's disappointing Washington visit, persuaded Grant that a new on-site commission should be appointed to deal with the Black Hills problem. On June 18 a new commission, headed by Senator William B. Allison of Iowa, an influential friend of Grant, was organized. Although comprised of prominent citizens, the commission's membership was not exactly peopled with knowledgeable, or even sympathetic, Sioux experts. Allison was a well-meaning man, but he had little aptitude for such a mission. Brigadier General Alfred H. Terry, although familiar with the Lakota people, looked upon them as adversaries. The Reverend S. D. Hinman, although comfortable in several Sioux dialects, had much more experience working with the Dakota or Santee Sioux; besides, neither Red Cloud nor Spotted Tail really liked the man. Nevertheless, what the Allison commission lacked in balance, it made up for in determination; by late summer most of its undeniably purposeful members had left Washington for Sioux country.

Red Cloud would again be a major factor in the Sioux negotiations once the commission reached the Northern Plains, despite the widespread criticism of his conduct in Washington. Indeed, he proved just as stubborn in the West as he had in the nation's capital. His disagreement with Spotted Tail over the location of the commission's meetings, in fact, almost derailed Allison's mission before it got started. Reverend Hinman, acting in behalf of the commission, had wanted all the negotiations held at the Red Cloud Agency after almost all Lakotas had rejected holding such meetings along the Missouri River. But when Spotted Tail objected, Hinman accepted Spotted Tail's recommendation to hold talks along Chadron Creek, halfway between the Red Cloud and Spotted Tail agencies. Red Cloud refused such a compromise, insisting that the sturdy stockade that Saville had built two years earlier should be the site. After more bickering, both sides reluctantly agreed to meet in the vicinity of the White River, eight miles east of the Red Cloud Agency. The site was described by Sioux interpreter William Garnett as a remote spot dominated by a lone tree standing apart from the other cottonwoods along the banks of the Chadron.

Despite the problems faced by the Allison commission, including the apparent reluctance of Red Cloud to deal substantively with the Black Hills issue, it did have some prospects for success. For one thing, it made an effort to bring as many Lakotas to the conference as possible, an objective which had Red Cloud's hearty approval. Young-Man-Afraid-of-His-Horses and Louis Richard were sent northward to bring in those fiercely independent bands that followed Crazy Horse, Black Twin, and Sitting Bull. The two emissaries located along the Tongue River as many as nineteen hundred lodges, which were occupied by such Lakota tribes as the Oglalas, Hunkpapas, Miniconjous, and Sans Arcs, along with their good friends, the Cheyennes.

Because game was scarce, many of those people were tempted by the customary feasts that usually accompanied such negotiations. Nevertheless, the suspicious Crazy Horse and Black Twin gave only a tentative commitment that they might participate, while Sitting Bull, speaking for his sullen Hunkpapas, refused to treat with any commission as long as there was still game to hunt, a position embraced by most of his Miniconjou and Sans Arc allies.

The commission's chances for success were also complicated by its unreasonable instructions. Although the acquisition of the Black Hills "between the North and South Forks of the Big Cheyenne" was Washington's main objective, the commissioners were also instructed to get the Sioux to surrender their rights to the Bighorn Mountains and to grant the government strategic rights of way through the unceded Indian lands east of those mountains. No price for these concessions was set for the commission; Allison and his associates were simply to assure the Indians that they would receive a "fair equivalent" for the surrender of all their rights and properties. The commission was also told to impress the Sioux that any agreement reached with the Allison commission would have to receive the approval of Congress before it could go into effect.

The arrival of the commission at Red Cloud's agency on September 4 was a precursor of some very difficult times ahead. Red Cloud issued an immediate objection to the cavalry escort that accompanied the commissioners; he insisted that it showed a lack of good faith in the Lakota people. Although General Terry, the only commissioner with any qualifications as an Indian fighter, was willing to dispense with this escort, the other members of Allison's commission were not; throughout the negotiations in late September there were 120 cavalrymen at every meeting.

With emotions running extremely high, it was up to Senator Allison and his peers to work out some sort of strategy that would bring the Lakotas around to the government's thinking. Allison was especially concerned about Article 12 of the Treaty of Fort Laramie, which stated that no part of the Sioux reservation could be ceded without the approval of three-fourths of all the adult males. To avoid any possible obstruction, the Iowa Republican, therefore, agreed that in their negotiations for the Black Hills, he and his fellow commissioners would bargain only for the mining rights. Although none of the commission members could match Allison as far as his strong presidential backing was concerned, a few of them disagreed with him; they took the position that the commissioners should go instead for the direct cession of the hills, because the Indians would never know the difference. Price was another dividing point; three of the commissioners believed that the current agreement to pay the Sioux their annual appropriation of $1,750,000 for a stated period was sufficient, while others were prepared to be more generous. The commission finally agreed with its chairman to go for the mining rights but decided to allow the dynamics of their negotiations with Red Cloud, Spotted Tail, and the other Sioux leaders determine a fair price for some kind of guaranteed access to the mineral-rich Black Hills.

The first conference, which was held on September 20, was hardly reassuring to its supporters. When the commissioners arrived at the conference site, no one was present. Finally wagons appeared burdened with canvas and poles for a grand tipi, which fifteen soldiers raised for participants under the lone cottonwood marking the council site. Spotted Tail and a few other chiefs eventually arrived. But what distressed the commissioners most was the sudden appearance of a number of wild-eyed, demonstrative warriors, who charged down from the hills as if about to attack, only to swerve abruptly to the side to form a line some distance away. Even more ominous for the success of this conference was the absence of Red Cloud, who was still miffed over the site selected for the negotiations. Indeed, many Oglalas stayed away from this first meeting either because of Red Cloud's opposition or because September 20 was a distribution day and many of them were at the agency eight miles away collecting their rations.

Notwithstanding these signs of indifference, if not hostility, Senator Allison, who presided over the meeting, rose from his chair under the tent to address the assembled chiefs sitting in a semicircle in front of him. The senator, with apparent sincerity, asked these men for the right to mine in the Black Hills "for a fair and just price," with the understanding that when the gold was played out, the hills would be returned to them. He also asked the Indians if they would sell the unceded land east of the Bighorns. "It does not seem to be of very great value or use to you, and our people think they would like the portion of it I have described." The inexperienced Allison had once again misjudged the attitude of the Sioux, who categorically refused to cede any of the Bighorn country. The disposition of the Black Hills, then, would be the only major item on the commissioner's agenda for this day.

Spotted Tail, in Red Cloud's absence, took the lead in dealing with Senator Allison's proposal for mining rights in the Paha Sapa. Given the recent influx of miners, this was an issue that undoubtedly required immediate action. The skillful Brulé negotiator, who had characterized Allison's plan as a loan from the Indians that would temporarily give whites the Black Hills, turned dramatically to Dr. Saville, who was still serving as Indian agent at Red Cloud, and sarcastically asked him if he would like to loan Spotted Tail a team of mules on the same terms proposed by Senator Allison. Clearly, all the Indian leaders sitting under the council's solitary cottonwood tree believed that once the U.S. government got hold of the Black Hills, it would never return them.

Before Senator Allison could complete his response to Spotted Tail's remarks, an excited Red Dog hastily arrived with a message from Red Cloud. In it the reluctant chief claimed that a "good many tribes" had arrived in the last few days, and these newcomers needed an extra seven days to discuss all relevant issues with the Indians at the agency before attending any conference. Red Cloud's words broke up the meeting: all the Indian conferees, except for Spotted Tail and his friends, left the conference site immediately.

But the frustrated commissioners were determined to prevent Red Cloud from postponing these urgent negotiations for an entire week. Instead they insisted on another meeting in three days. Although they got their way, the gathering on September 23 was so unruly it almost made the first meeting seem like a love feast. When this second conference convened, the commission members found themselves surrounded by thousands of restless Indians; some estimates placed the number as high as twenty thousand, although Allison himself counted less than five thousand. Again, there was a repeat of the same frightening Indian charges, which were only aborted at the last minute; this time, however, the war cries were more shrill and the war paint more menacing.

The nervous escort of soldiers, although greatly outnumbered, was about to respond militarily to this intimidation when Little Big Man, a shirtwearer representing Crazy Horse's hardline Oglala camp, broke through Indian lines on horseback, with a Winchester in one hand and a fistful of cartridges in the other, and announced to everyone that he had come to kill all white men trying to take away his land. Fortunately, Young-Man-Afraid-of-His-Horses and a number of Indian soldiers from the agency restrained the emotional Little Big Man and then put themselves between the commission's cavalry escort and the enraged Sioux. Although a major disaster was apparently averted, it was obvious that the Lakotas, with their overwhelming numerical superiority, could have wiped out all the soldiers and federal negotiators if that is what Red Cloud and the other Sioux leaders had wanted to do.

Fortunately, much more substantive business was accomplished by the Sioux and the Allison commission three days later at a meeting that was limited to twenty chiefs and held in the much more insulated stockade at the Red Cloud Agency. The tribal representatives, having had almost seven days to mull over the government's proposals, were more relaxed and congenial, but the position they took seemed completely unreasonable to the surprised commission members. The Sioux would give up the Black Hills, but the price would be governmental care for seven generations.

Red Cloud probably gave the most details for this sweeping

new Lakota plan: "For seven generations to come I want our Great Father to give us Texan steers for our meat. I want the Government to issue for me hereafter, flour and coffee, and sugar and tea, and bacon, the very best kind, and cracked corn and beans, and rice and dried applies, and saleratus and tobacco, and soap and salt, and pepper, for the old people." The Sioux leader, determined to get the most for his people if they ceded the cherished Paha Sapa, also wanted a light wagon with horses and "six yoke of working cattle" for each of his Sioux followers, a proposal bound to appeal to those idealistic whites who yearned for the day when all Indians would be peaceful and industrious farmers.

Although Red Cloud and Spotted Tail were often at odds over major questions of policy, the two chiefs were in full accord on this demand for support for seven generations. Indeed, Spotted Tail put the case in even stronger terms than Red Cloud did when he asserted that the Sioux expected compensation for their loss of the Black Hills for as long as they lived on this earth. The Cheyenne and Arapaho representatives expressed very similar sentiments. Obviously, all these Plains tribes who had lived and hunted around the Black Hills for three generations or more wanted to be compensated if they were going to give up this favorite spot in their once vast hunting range. Because some wanted more in return for this sacrifice than others, rumors began to circulate that the Indians' total price for the hills could be anywhere from thirty to fifty million dollars.

The final two days of the conference were almost as difficult for the Allison commission as the disruptive meeting on September 23. Red Cloud not only repeated his demand for seven generations of support but also added a few more conditions to complicate the situation. He wanted to prohibit liquor from being brought onto his reservation, a practice he had long denounced; indeed, there were charges in the press that drunkenness was especially widespread at this conference. The resolute Oglala leader also demanded that Catholic missionaries be sent to his agency, an obvious slap at the Episcopal church, which had provided all the Indian agents thus far appointed for his people. Red Cloud was once again demonstrating his penchant for muddying the waters at big conferences such as this.

The Allison commission's final proposal, as a consequence, was not presented with much enthusiasm. The federal government offered the Indians four hundred thousand dollars a year for leasing the Black Hills for as long as that lease would last. If, on the other hand, the Indians were willing to sell Paha Sapa outright, the government would pay them six million dollars in fifteen annual installments. But for either alternative congressional ratification was required, and if the hills were sold outright, three-fourths of all adult males from each tribe would have to sign the agreement.

Neither of these two proposals had much appeal for the Lakotas and their allies. In fact, disenchantment was so great that Red Cloud missed the last day of the conference in order to attend an Arapaho sun dance, leaving Spotted Tail as the unenthusiastic spokesman for those conferees who remained. The outcome of the meetings seemed close to failure for several reasons. First, in the eyes of the commissioners, the Indians had asked too much for the Black Hills; curiously, though, Spotted Tail had suggested six million dollars as a fair price before the negotiations had ever begun, and there is some evidence that the more responsible Indian leaders at the conference, including Red Cloud, did not ask for more than seven million dollars. The opening of conference sessions to all tribal members was also looked upon as a mistake; the exceptionally restless and suspicious northern tribes, who had no part in the Fort Laramie Treaty proceedings in the first place, proved particularly disruptive at these more open meetings near the White River. The lack of presents was probably another unwise decision on the part of Allison's commission. Even though gift-giving may have been regarded as cynical and degrading by most commission members, it was part of a time-honored ritual in the more than two centuries of white-Indian relations.

The disheartened commission members were especially bitter about the allegedly baleful influence exercised at the conference by certain persuasive traders, contractors, and interpreters (many of whom were of mixed blood). There is no question that this particular group of men had exercised a decisive influence over Red Cloud's thinking for a long time. It was also generally believed by outside white observers, as well as by the commissioners themselves, that these convincing "hangers-on" were encouraging the Indians to accept nothing less than a high annual payment for the hills in their negotiations on the basis that they would get a significant portion of that money through their dealings with the tribes involved.

In the end, Senator Allison and his commissioners returned to Washington distressed and angry over their failure to settle the Black Hills question. To regain some of their lost prestige, they recommended that Congress adopt a "take-it-or-leave-it" approach with the Sioux and their allies. The government should offer a "fair equivalent" for the acquisition of the coveted hills, which should be "presented to the Indians as a finality." It further suggested that, in the future, Congress should take the initiative in all aspects of Indian relations, abolishing all existing agencies and reorganizing the entire Sioux service as part of the process. The Allison commission's new approach was tantamount to an ultimatum, a rather dangerous stance considering the surly attitude of an estimated four hundred northern tribesmen who were now drifting away from the White River conference site and heading into the still largely wilderness area that made up the unceded Indian territory defined in the treaty of 1868.

Although the commission's visit had created a dangerous situation, given the tensions generated by the illegal Black Hills gold rush, the federal government still did not realize how close it was to a major Sioux war. Many in the country blamed the new crisis on the ineptitude of the Allison commission. The *Omaha Weekly Herald*, in its October 1 edition, faulted the commission for not involving Red Cloud more in its negotiation proceedings. If more attention had been paid to Red Cloud, "who has more brains than the whole Commission put together," it argued, and less to the other chiefs, some substantial progress could have been made in this last-ditch effort to solve the Black Hills problem.

Although this western newspaper had the reputation of being an astute observer of Lakota life, its conclusions regarding Red Cloud's involvement in the negotiations is highly debatable. In fact, Red Cloud probably constituted the essence of the government's problem. In presenting the Sioux plan for seven generations of support, Red Cloud was certainly one of the Sioux's leading spokesmen. He had much better relations with the small but disruptive northern tribesmen than Spotted Tail had; indeed, in the tumultuous months that preceded the commission's visit, Red Cloud was accused by a number of treaty Indians of tolerating, if not cooperating with, Crazy Horse's Oglalas and the notoriously uncompromising Miniconjous. But the most striking fact about the *Herald*'s assessment was the continuing importance of Red Cloud in all Lakota affairs. This man had remained the dominant Sioux leader ever since he stalked out of the Fort Laramie conference in 1866; many apparently felt he could still be a crucial factor in the solution of the Black Hills dilemma.

But the events of the coming months would be largely out of Red Cloud's control. For one thing, an estimated fifteen thousand miners were illegally prospecting and digging in the once remote Black Hills. Although most southern Lakotas, including Red Cloud, were deeply distressed by these illegal violations, many of the northern group were becoming alarmingly hostile toward the miners. To Sitting Bull and his stubborn Hunkpapas, the beautiful dark hills, generously covered with lodgepole pine, provided abundant firewood and shelter for a wealth of small game; they were the source of much of the meat for the Lakotas and their allies, and, unlike their southern brethren, these Sioux hard-liners were not about to give up the hills under any circumstances. As a consequence, unmistakable tensions began to build during the fall of 1875 at the scattered Sioux agencies in both Nebraska and the Dakota Territory as well as throughout the unceded territory east of the Bighorns. Even though those Lakotas living by the treaty had reduced earlier tensions by surrendering their hunting lands south of the Platte and by showing some willingness to relocate the Red Cloud and Spotted Tail agencies somewhere outside the state of Nebraska, the attitude of leaders such as Sitting Bull, Crazy Horse, and Black Twin was becoming a matter of real concern for government officials.

As a result of these anxieties, Commissioner of Indian Affairs Smith, who had said in his annual report that not even as few as "five hundred Indian warriors will ever again be mustered at one point for a fight," started to express some serious reservations toward the end of the year. Particularly ominous was Agent Saville's report on October 1 that many Indians were leaving the Red Cloud Agency and heading north. Although he tried to reassure his superiors that their main purpose was to hunt in the unceded lands—a practice that had become commonplace during the past several years—military commanders on the Northern Plains had become noticeably nervous. To the War Department, these wandering bands of Lakotas, now being joined by young and increasingly restive treaty Indians from the agencies, constituted a real threat, particularly in light of the large number of vulnerable white miners in the Black Hills.

Bowing to military pressure, the Indian Bureau sent to this dangerous area U.S. Indian Inspector E. C. Watkins to study the situation. When Watkins, an unusually hawkish bureaucrat, returned from his extensive reconnoitering, he issued a report on November 9 which confirmed the War Department's worst fears. He insisted that the bands roaming the unceded Indian country of Wyoming and Montana, while small in number, were both independent and disdainful and posed a threat to the reservation system because they could attract enough of the younger treaty warriors to create an imposing fighting force. Watkins's recommendation was to employ force, a solution that many military commanders had long regarded as the most viable one.

Less than a week before Watkins had filed his disturbing report, a secret meeting was held at the Executive Mansion (now the White House) on November 3. At that conference

President Grant worked on a plan with his senior generals and his high Indian officials to deal with these troublesome Sioux and their allies. But the government faced some difficult dilemmas. The Black Hills belonged to the Indians by treaty, and the independent bands had a perfect right to wander and hunt in the unceded lands to the west of the hills. The Allison commission had failed to "extinguish Indian title" to the Paha Sapa, and there was no time to launch a new political effort. The choices faced by Grant and his confidants could be lumped into one question: How could the federal government crack down on these defiant bands without seeming to violate its obligations under the Treaty of Fort Laramie? Grant made two important decisions in response to this question. First, the government would continue its prohibition against mining in the Black Hills but would deliberately not enforce it. And second, it would compel the northern hunting bands to leave their unceded lands and take up settlement at one of the agencies.

In instituting these two new policies, the government played down the acquisition of the Black Hills as a motivation. Instead, it justified its actions on the basis of a series of depredations against Montanans on the Upper Yellowstone during the building of the Northern Pacific, depredations that were greatly overstated, according to historian Robert M. Utley. It would also stress the disruptions caused by new Sioux raids on such friendly tribes as the Crows and the Arikaras, a practice as natural for the Sioux as their nomadic wanderings. Both of these provocations were interpreted as violations of the 1868 Fort Laramie Treaty and were to be used to legitimize a war against a people who, in the case of the northern tribes, had never subscribed to this oft-ignored treaty in the first place. Despite the weak legal basis for Grant's new policy, however, it would probably solve the Black Hills problem by populating the coveted Paha Sapa with white miners, an act of possession that could severely hinder the power of northern bands to prevent the sale of the hills to the U.S. government.

Six days after these two presidential directives were secretly hammered out by Grant's inner circle, Inspector Watkins returned from his trip to the Upper Missouri with a report that would more than justify the provocative actions they had proposed. But the more cautious Indian Bureau was hesitant to launch Watkins's most extreme proposal: a winter attack on the Indians; the aggressive official had wanted to confront the northern tribes and "whip them into subjection." Indeed, on December 6, Commissioner Smith directed the Sioux Indian agents under him to send runners to the Indian camps scattered throughout the unceded country and order them to return to their respective agencies by January 31, 1876; if they refused, they would be considered hostile.

But the government's tough new ultimatum did not work as it was supposed to. One factor which could not be controlled was the weather; the winter of 1875–76 was an especially severe one, and when runners finally arrived at their destinations, they discovered that Sitting Bull and his Hunkpapas were huddled around campfires on the Yellowstone, while the Miniconjous and Sans Arcs (along with their Cheyenne allies) were encamped further west on the Tongue. The response of most of these nontreaty Indians was pretty much one of disbelief. Some interpreted it as an invitation, such as the one they had received four months before to confer with the Allison commission. Others understood the true gravity of the message but, because of a different concept of time, did not attach as much importance to the January 31 deadline as they should have. Few apparently understood the dire consequences of ignoring the federal government on this score; they apparently had little realization that troops would be sent to force them to return.

There was also a good deal of resentment over Washington's high-handed new policy, which extended to agency as well as nonagency Indians. James S. Hastings, Saville's successor as the new agent at Red Cloud, reported a decided lack of support among Red Cloud's people for this controversial ultimatum; he had to promise a reward to find anyone at the agency willing to go north with the message. Although the Indians at the Spotted Tail Agency viewed the ultimatum as an effort to intimidate the nontreaty Indians with whom they had serious differences, they resented it as an unwelcome interference in an essentially family quarrel. Because of a generally uncooperative attitude among Lakotas on and off the reservation, a serious impasse was reached. When January 31 came and none of the independent bands had arrived at their assigned agencies, the future of the Sioux was promptly turned over to the military.

This development gave General Sheridan an opportunity to launch a surprise winter campaign against the Lakotas before they could use the good fighting weather of late spring. This particular element of surprise was one of Sheridan's contributions to Indian warfare on the Great Plains; he had successfully employed it several years earlier against the Southern Plains tribes. His plan called for a three-pronged movement, with General Terry leading troops westward from Fort Abraham Lincoln in Dakota Territory, General Crook marching northward from Fort Fetterman, and Colonel John Gibbon marching eastward from Fort Ellis in Montana. But because of the exceptionally long and cold winter in 1875–76, Sheridan's winter campaign became a late spring one; Terry did not leave Fort Abraham Lincoln until May 17, and Crook was unable to start his major campaign against the defiant Lakotas until May 29.

General Crook's tardy start was probably caused by bad weather as much as anything else. Heeding Sheridan's wishes, Crook left Fort Fetterman in mid-March, in temperatures of forty to fifty degrees below zero, and headed north in search of the obstinate Lakota bands. On March 17, his subordinate, Colonel Joseph J. Reynolds, made a dawn attack on a village of about 735 people on the Powder River; the encampment was comprised of Oglalas, Northern Cheyennes, and a few Miniconjous. This unexpected assault through deep snow was an instant success; the surprised Indians, however, rallied their forces, and Reynolds was eventually forced to abandon the village. Colonel Reynolds, who later faced a court-martial for his performance at what would be called the Battle of the Powder River, could boast of little in the way of tangible success; a herd of ponies that he captured during the battle was retaken by the Indians that night. Even his claim that he had successfully attacked the camp of the redoubtable Crazy Horse on that cold March morning proved unfounded; Crazy Horse's own village was located downriver.

If Crook had hoped to break the back of the defiant Sioux by this early campaign, he had badly miscalculated. Indeed, the freezing, poorly clad refugees from this village sought shelter in Crazy Horse's camp first and in Sitting Bull's later; their graphic accounts of how the soldiers had burned their village, leaving them to freeze to death, resulted in a strong vow of unity on the part of Sitting Bull, Crazy Horse, and the other Sioux and Cheyenne leaders. In fact, they pledged to stay together for as long as necessary.

Throughout the late months of that difficult spring, an unusually large village of Indians was in the process of following the buffalo westward. They were traveling in six separate tribal circles, which included representatives from all seven of the Lakota tribes (actually there were not enough Blackfeet and Two Kettle Sioux for each of these tribes to have its own circle). The Cheyenne circle took the lead, selecting the campsites; because of its immense size, the village was limited to a stay of no more than five days before it began to affect the environment adversely. The Hunkpapa circle, which brought up the rear, was given the responsibility of protecting the huge encampment from behind. By early June the 360 lodges that comprised this unwieldy village had grown by the addition of 100 more lodges, giving it a population of about thirty-one hundred. Military commanders in the area, who tended to have higher estimates of Indian strength anyway, were convinced that a number of agency Indians were contributing to the growth of this threatening behemoth.

General Crook was a strong believer that there was significant collusion between nontreaty and agency Indians. He claimed that Colonel Reynolds had discovered "a perfect magazine of ammunition, war material, and general supplies" in that ill-fated Cheyenne-Lakota village he had surprised. To Crook these items were strong evidence of help from agency Indians. He also insisted that the independent bands and agency Indians were in an effective "co-partnership" and that the spoils of war of these nontreaty Indians had been taken to the agencies in return for needed supplies. The agents at both the Red Cloud and Spotted Tail agencies heatedly denied Crook's allegations. Hastings claimed that all Reynolds found in the way of ammunition at the unsuspecting village was "five pounds of powder, twenty of lead, and six boxes of percussion caps." He also warned that Crook's inept, if not disastrous, winter campaign had probably reawakened old feelings of superiority on the part of the Sioux. A new war of words between the army and the Indian Bureau had evidently started.

Crook felt so strongly about these charges that in early May he visited the Red Cloud Agency. The general, who had achieved his envied reputation as an Indian fighter in the Southwest because of his wise use of Indian scouts and sure-footed mules, was becoming increasingly well known among the Sioux. Sometimes called Gray Eagle, perhaps because his braided blond beard had a gray tint—Red Cloud called him Gray Fox—he was best known among the northern tribes as Three Stars. This latter nickname has been the source of some conjecture. Although as a brigadier general Crook could wear a star on his hat and one on each shoulder, he almost always dressed in a casual canvas suit, wearing a cork helmet. Ordinarily a reticent man, his remarks to Red Cloud elicited Red Cloud's most aggressive response to white provocations since 1868, when the stubborn Sioux leader finally put his mark on the Treaty of Fort Laramie. Red Cloud warned Crook that the Lakotas were ready for action; they had enough warriors, guns, and ponies to meet any challenge. "They are not afraid of the soldiers or of their chief." The unusually militant Red Cloud also told Crook that every lodge "will send its young men, and they all will say of the Great Father's dogs, 'Let them come!'"

Because of the prominence Red Cloud had achieved during the last decade, his remarks had strong repercussions throughout the country. The *New York Herald* claimed in early June that the "corruption" of agents, the "perfidy" of the government, and the "selfish and persistent encroachments" of its citizens on

Indian lands had driven Red Cloud, "the best of his race," to the point of desperation; if he felt alienated, think how his less disciplined, less patient tribesmen must feel. In truth, it had become increasingly evident that Red Cloud was giving at least moral support to those defiant tribesmen to the north. His son, Jack, for example, went off to join "the hostiles," presumably with his father's approval. This fact provides additional proof of Red Cloud's ambivalence regarding this crisis—an ambivalence that was not new. Although he was always the government's mainstay in helping Washington implement its policies toward the agency that bore his name, his cooperation had always been qualified by his own perception of what the Fort Laramie treaty really meant. Indeed, throughout the first six years of his reservation life he either questioned or challenged almost every major federal policy that affected his people. This new and very real threat to the Black Hills, however, may have cast some doubt in his mind about the merits of giving the government even reluctant cooperation.

A dissatisfied Crook returned to his command in the Powder River country still harboring suspicions of a conspiracy. On June 17, 1876, the general, while playing whist with his officers, became the victim of a surprise attack on his camp along the Rosebud. Only the alertness of Crook's Crow and Shoshone scouts prevented this engagement, the Battle of the Rosebud, from becoming a disastrous setback. The Sioux and Cheyenne warriors, although fewer in number, fought with a ferocity never seen before. Although Crook ultimately drove them off and declared victory, he found it necessary to return to his base camp in the south to replenish his supplies, and for six weeks his army was, in effect, out of commission. The Indians, convinced that they had won, returned to their base camp, that large village comprised of six tribal circles. But by late June this mammoth encampment had moved to the juncture of Reno Creek and the Greasy Grass, the river whites called the Little Bighorn. There for six days they celebrated their triumph over Crook.

It was during those summer days following the Battle of the Rosebud that agency Indians began arriving in large numbers.

As part of the army's conspiracy theory regarding collusion between treaty and nontreaty Indians, a number of officers, besides Crook, had been concerned about a major exodus of young warriors from the agencies. On May 28 one alert lieutenant, upon his return from the Powder River country scouting for Crook, reported seeing seven hundred to eight hundred agency warriors heading north to join Crazy Horse and Sitting Bull. On June 2, Colonel Wesley Merritt passed along even more disturbing news. As a result of his conversations with Captain Jordan from Camp Robinson and Indian Agent Hastings, he believed that fifteen hundred to two thousand Indians had left the Red Cloud Agency since May 10. Hastings, however, was unwilling to concede that they had left to join the northern bands, nor would he admit that Red Cloud was abetting this unusual migration; Red Cloud had given him the rather unlikely explanation that many of these Lakotas had left to recover stock that their northern brethren had stolen.

It seems that before early June, the anxieties of the army regarding this exodus to the north were not well founded. But after the bloody encounter on the Rosebud, the situation did change dramatically. During a period of only six days, the great village along the Little Bighorn had doubled in size, growing from 450 to 1,000 lodges. There were now seven thousand Indians in the six tribal circles; the village's fighting force had grown from eight hundred to eighteen hundred warriors in less than a week. This was the encampment that the daring Lieutenant Colonel Custer blundered into on June 25, 1876, resulting in the loss of his entire command and the disastrous mauling of the outnumbered companies of the Seventh Cavalry led by Major Marcus A. Reno and Captain Frederick W. Benteen. How prominent a role agency Indians played in this, the now famous Battle of the Little Bighorn, is still debatable, but one fact cannot be denied: the death of Custer, the one the Sioux called Long Hair, and the heavy losses incurred by his Seventh Cavalry derailed General Sheridan's three-pronged effort to surround and subdue the northern bands for weeks. Moreover, it led to almost a year of vicious fighting before the hostilities of the Great Sioux War of 1876–77 were brought to an end.

There is evidence that the Indians did not plan for such a startling victory. Sitting Bull and Crazy Horse apparently only wanted to fight a defensive war. They only struck at the overconfident forces under Crook and Custer after they realized that the army sought the kind of major conflict that would endanger not only their lives but also the lives of their women and children. But once the news of this disaster reached the East, where proud citizens were celebrating the nation's centennial, the collective might of the country, which Red Cloud had nervously observed during his Washington visits, was ready for the kind of campaign against the Sioux that Crazy Horse and Sitting Bull would have dreaded the most. Armed with more material and political support than ever before, the military, whose humiliation was shared all the way up the ranks to former General of the Army Ulysses S. Grant, was eager to avenge this astonishing Sioux triumph.

General Crook's response to this fiasco was to restart his heretofore sputtering campaign. On August 10 he rendezvoused with General Terry along the Rosebud, bringing to this renewed campaign a combined force of four thousand troops. The large village that had destroyed Long Hair's command, however, had already disbanded; it was a decision based more on the migration of buffalo and the Indians' indispensable need for more game than on military strategy.

Although Crook would later engage in some serious campaigning to the east, which on September 9 involved him in a largely inconclusive battle with Little Bighorn veterans at Slim Buttes in Dakota Territory, the officer who would make the most significant difference in the campaigns that comprised the Great Sioux War was Colonel Nelson A. Miles. Warmly clad in a long overcoat trimmed in bear fur, this talented but vain officer, whom the Sioux called Bear Coat, relentlessly pursued Crazy Horse's followers up the Tongue River during the freezing month of January 1877. He also successfully pressured Sitting Bull and his Hunkpapas to migrate northward, where they crossed into Canada in early May.

But the agency Indians would also secure their share of unwanted attention from the aroused military. Indeed, after Custer's death army officers were even more convinced that there was collusion between Red Cloud's treaty Indians and those now hunted victors who had brought such shame to the U.S. Army at the Battle of the Little Bighorn. One of the first policy changes proposed by the vengeful soldiers was to replace civilian Indian agents with nearby military commanders; thus, at the Red Cloud Agency the army wanted to replace Hastings with the officer in charge of Camp Robinson, and at the Spotted Tail Agency it wanted to replace Agent E. A. Howard with the commander at nearby Camp Sheridan. A law passed by Congress in 1870, however, required officers to surrender their military commissions if they assumed the duties of a civilian Indian agent. After some heated wrangling, the army settled for an arrangement whereby civilian agents would remain but would be under military control; at Red Cloud this new plan worked out well, as the new appointee, Dr. James Irwin, a onetime Shoshone agent, managed to mix well with almost all the agency's diverse factions.

Another policy the army aggressively pursued was General Sheridan's idea of arresting and disarming all those Indians returning to the Red Cloud Agency from the north. (Jack Red Cloud had already quietly slipped back to the agency during the summer of 1876.) But the scrappy little Sheridan decided to wait until Colonel Ranald S. Mackenzie could arrive from Fort Sill with six companies before enforcing this policy.

While the army was cracking down on all the Lakotas and Cheyennes, Congress, also eager to avenge Custer's defeat, organized another Sioux commission, which was to pursue the inevitable outcome of Senator Allison's proposed ultimatum: the surrender of all Indian claims to the Black Hills. George W. Manypenny, a former commissioner of Indian affairs, was elected to chair this group, which included Bishop Henry B. Whipple, who was sometimes compared favorably with Father De Smet as an honest and trusted peacemaker, and Newton

Edmunds, who drew up the meaningless treaties with the Sioux in 1865. In mid-September of 1876 at a conference with Manypenny at Red Cloud, the agency chiefs, including Red Cloud, agreed to give up the Black Hills and the unceded territories west of the hills. Although the agreement required the Lakotas at the agency to resettle along the Missouri River, Manypenny told the unhappy chiefs that Grant still wanted them to settle in Indian Territory, and if they would agree to the government's latest terms, they could stay at the Red Cloud Agency for the rest of the season. Red Cloud was openly sullen over the prospect of his people surrendering their historic lands, but he did agree to allow some of his young warriors to go to Oklahoma and assess the possibilities of a future home there. But in the end, the U.S. government, responding to pressure from the railroads to develop Indian Territory for white settlement, eliminated this distasteful option for the Lakotas.

The Manypenny commission, elated by its success at the Red Cloud Agency, went to the Spotted Tail, Standing Rock, Cheyenne River, Crow Creek, Lower Brulé, and Santee agencies and easily won agreements at all of them. His success in this endeavor was not necessarily because the commission's members were more knowledgeable about Sioux affairs than the members of the Allison commission had been, but because of a new set of factors that emerged during the negotiations. For example, Manypenny's commission completely ignored Article 12 of the Treaty of Fort Laramie, which required the approval of three-fourths of all the adult Indian males for any land cession of this kind; only the signatures of the chiefs, plus one head man from each tribe, were required by this latest Sioux commission. A second factor was the thinly disguised threat that if the Sioux were not cooperative, they would be denied the rations and annuities that they had come to depend upon. A third factor, probably the most important of all, was the army's unrelenting pressure to settle the Black Hills question once and for all.

General Crook remained one of the main figures in this get-tough policy with all Lakotas, whether they had participated in Custer's downfall or not. In this regard his views were in perfect harmony with those of Colonel Mackenzie when that veteran of highly successful campaigns against the Kiowas and Comanches arrived to take command of the garrison at Camp Robinson. Mackenzie proved uncompromisingly firm; he even opposed the Manypenny commission's plan to allow young Sioux warriors to visit Indian Territory until he was overruled by the president himself. Both Crook and MacKenzie were convinced that Red Cloud was in direct communication with the independent northern bands, which were still militarily resisting the will of the U.S. government. In October 1876, Crook went to Camp Robinson to direct the disarming and dismounting of all Sioux warriors at the Red Cloud Agency. In this action he was acting very much in tandem with General Terry, who was doing the same thing at the Standing Rock and Cheyenne River agencies.

Before implementing this strict new policy, the army ordered Red Cloud to move his band, which was encamped at Chadron Creek about thirty miles away from the agency stockade, back to the reservation. The stubborn Oglala leader refused, asking that all of his rations be sent to Chadron Creek in the future. As for the sturdy stockade that had served as the center of life for the Red Cloud Agency during the past four years, Red Cloud offered the army all of the buildings of that once busy compound.

Red Cloud's cavalier attitude prompted direct action on the part of Crook. On October 22, at nightfall, Colonel MacKenzie, acting under Crook's orders, led eight companies from Camp Robinson to Chadron Creek to deal with this defiance. Indicating the army's single-minded determination to prevail, MacKenzie's already sizeable force was joined en route by veteran Indian fighter Major Frank North and his brother Luther. These two men had the services of forty-two Pawnee scouts, who had little love for the Sioux, whether peaceful ones or not. About four miles from Chadron Creek, Colonel Mackenzie divided his force into two battalions; one went to Red Cloud's encampment, the other went to the nearby camp of the like-minded chief Red Leaf. At dawn the unsuspecting

Lakotas at both camps awoke surrounded by troopers who were itching for a fight. The fifty-five-year-old Red Cloud, many years past his prime as a warrior, had no alternative but to surrender without a shot.

Mackenzie, who was in charge of the force that surprised Red Cloud, did not prove gracious in victory. His soldiers disarmed all the warriors under both chiefs, while Pawnee scouts rounded up their horses. Although both bands were well mounted—Major North collected 722 animals from the two camps—their armaments were confined to a few old guns and pistols and a paltry supply of ammunition; the favorite army refrain that all treaty Indians were well armed and a sure source of weaponry for the "hostiles" proved invalid, at least in this case. The hard-working Lakota women were ordered to take down the tipis, after which these proud people were escorted back to the agency by unsympathetic blue-coated soldiers certain they were avenging Custer's death. All of the Lakotas, except for the old and feeble, were forced to walk. When darkness descended, the more able-bodied men were compelled to march all night until they reached Camp Robinson. Although these resentful Lakotas were jailed upon their arrival, they were released the following day and allowed to return to their agency homes. As for the horses so indispensable to the Sioux, Colonel Mackenzie gave each Pawnee scout a mount, while Major North took the rest of the herd to Cheyenne for sale.

Red Cloud's humiliation, however, would not end here. General Crook gathered the demoralized Sioux in the agency stockade and, without any of the characteristic courtesies that had accompanied his earlier meetings with Red Cloud, told the agency's leading Lakota, in front of his peers, that he was no longer chief of the Oglalas. Indeed, from then on Spotted Tail would be recognized as the leader for both the Red Cloud and Spotted Tail agencies.

The uproar caused by the precipitous actions of both Crook and Mackenzie should have been expected. Red Cloud was almost in disbelief; his deeds of unquestioned leadership had accustomed him to a deference that had not prepared him for this ignominious incident. He tended to blame the Great White Father. "What have I done that I should receive such treatment from him whom I thought a friend?" Curiously, though, he was not as alarmed by Spotted Tail's elevation to power as he was by the loss of his horses. He confidently knew that his old rival could never replace him in the affections and respect of his people; indeed, to Spotted Tail's credit, he never tried. But the loss of Sioux ponies, especially to the Pawnees, was a real affront to Red Cloud and his warriors. Even the members of the Manypenny commission, which had a much better understanding of the Indian value system, criticized the seizure of the horses. In fact, thirteen years later the U.S. Congress appropriated $28,200 to compensate the bands of Red Cloud and Red Leaf for the loss of their ponies.

As for Crook, he was convinced that he had done the right thing. The favorable views of his fellow officers certainly left him no doubt about the validity of his actions. An elated General Sheridan sent him a congratulatory telegram three days later. "Go right on disarming and dismounting every Indian connected with the Red Cloud Agency," Sheridan chortled. Crook was so confident of his course that he began recruiting for the army Indian scouts from the Red Cloud and Spotted Tail agencies. In fact, the opportunity to ride a horse and carry a gun proved very alluring to many of these once formidable warriors; four hundred of them enrolled at Red Cloud and a hundred at Spotted Tail.

The events of the following year would provide a most confusing picture of Red Cloud's life. The results of the Battle of the Little Bighorn had seriously threatened his heretofore illustrious career. His power base had eroded. He remained confused about the future; the cause of the independent bands under Crazy Horse and Sitting Bull had little chance for success, yet, like all Sioux, Red Cloud still cherished the way of life for which they fought. His personal agenda looked bleak, too; Red Cloud, of all the Lakota leaders, had the dubious distinction of being not only disarmed and dismounted, but displaced as well. It was under such discouraging circumstances that the

Oglala leader became involved in a number of very serious controversies. One of them dealt with the surrender of Crazy Horse. Having been relentlessly pursued throughout the harsh winter of 1876–77, Crazy Horse's loyal followers were hungry and tired; they had already reached the limits of their endurance. Crook, who had not enjoyed much success against the Sioux on the battlefield, finally decided to play the role of the peacemaker. Couriers were sent north to try to induce the charismatic Crazy Horse to surrender; one party headed by Few Tails and Hunts the Enemy (later called George Sword) departed in January 1877 and, after a successful parley with Crazy Horse, got him to agree to come to the Red Cloud Agency and join his relatives.

In mid-February, Spotted Tail, Crazy Horse's uncle, also became involved in the increasingly frenzied peace efforts. But his participation was met by a host of frustrations. Although he struggled for weeks to find Crazy Horse's camp, when he reached it the elusive war leader was not there. The best he could do was to receive assurances from Crazy Horse's father that Crazy Horse would bring in his exhausted camp of Oglalas and Cheyennes, comprising some four hundred lodges, as soon as the weather had improved. Yet when Crazy Horse finally arrived at the Red Cloud Agency on May 6, it was Red Cloud who rode with him at the head of the two-mile column of subdued but not broken Lakota and Cheyenne warriors.

The debate still rages over how Red Cloud managed to upstage his old rival in inducing Crazy Horse to surrender. Some have insisted that Red Cloud, seeing his power and authority slipping away, convinced General Crook, whom he was anxious to please, that if given the supplies to feed Crazy Horse's starving warriors, he could bring them in faster than Spotted Tail could. Others have insisted that Lieutenant William P. Clark, the officer at Camp Robinson who was assigned to deal with Crazy Horse, was anxious to have that now-famous Sioux holdout surrender to Red Cloud rather than to Spotted Tail, because this arrangement would bring distinction to his post at the Red Cloud Agency. William ("Billy") Garnett, an interpreter of mixed blood who was a familiar figure during these proceedings, testified that Clark told Red Cloud that if he would bring in Crazy Horse, Clark would use his influence to get General Crook to reinstate Red Cloud as a chief; he would also make Red Cloud a First Sergeant, a rank that would make him the "highest officer in the Indian Scout Service."

Whichever version is correct, Red Cloud, who was ultimately restored as leader of the Oglalas, was given a hundred men and adequate supplies to feed Crazy Horse's hungry followers. When he finally rendezvoused with that maverick leader on April 27, Crazy Horse was already on his way to the agency. The tired and discouraged war chief spread his own blanket on the ground for Red Cloud to sit on and gave this old comrade from the 1866 siege of Fort Phil Kearny his shirt as a sign that he was surrendering to him. Never close to Red Cloud, the supple, muscular Crazy Horse, twenty years younger than the veteran leader, still bore the facial scar inflicted by Red Cloud's ally No Water in that bitter dispute over Black Buffalo Woman. Yet they were apparently on cordial terms during their ten-day trip together to the Red Cloud Agency. When the disarming and dismounting of Crazy Horse's people began after reaching the agency, Red Cloud made the whole process run reasonably smoothly by carefully explaining to Crazy Horse all the steps involved in the procedure. In all, some 899 persons surrendered, giving up two thousand horses and mules and 117 guns and pistols; it was one of the last important acts of the Great Sioux War.

The debate over Red Cloud's role in Crazy Horse's death on September 5, 1877, is the most heated and acrimonious of them all. That he was jealous of the younger man's popularity is a given. But so were many of the Indian leaders who comprised the old guard at the Red Cloud and Spotted Tail agencies, including Spotted Tail himself. Also, Crazy Horse would undoubtedly be a difficult person to assimilate into the reservation system. He had only surrendered because his band and the Cheyenne warriors with whom he fought were starving and exhausted from the relentless pursuit by soldiers such as the tenacious Bear Coat. Crazy Horse had been given to understand by General Crook that if he did end all resistance to the U.S. government, he and his people would receive their own agency in the Powder River country. As it turned out, Crook and the other authorities (both military and civilian) were anxious to include Crazy Horse in a Sioux delegation to be sent to Washington to meet the new president, Rutherford B. Hayes. They wanted to show Hayes as well as the rest of Washington that the Great Sioux War was indeed over. More ominous for Crazy Horse's future was Crook's ultimate plan to put the troublesome warrior in a prison cell on the Dry Tortugas off the coast of Florida.

Crazy Horse's problems were a mix of potentially dangerous circumstances that stemmed not only from the jealousies of other Sioux leaders, such as Red Cloud, but also from the ambivalent attitude of many of the military men involved. Crazy Horse, carefully coached by Red Cloud, was more than gracious during his surrender. When his bedraggled party reached the Hat Creek stage station on the road to the cherished Black Hills that had provoked the conflict in the first place, Crazy Horse shook hands, perhaps for the first time with a white man, Lieutenant William Rosecrans of the Fourth Cavalry, who had been dispatched northward with ten wagonloads of rations and one hundred head of cattle. Crazy Horse gave Rosecrans a war bonnet, a pipe, a war shirt, and a beaded sack as tokens of his sincerity. Moreover, he showed no resentment that Crook was away in Washington and that the still sullen Colonel Mackenzie was not present, even though he was headquartered at Camp Robinson. To many army officers Crazy Horse was a worthy foe; he was as glamorous a figure to them as he was to most young Lakota warriors.

Civilian officials were not immune from Crazy Horse's charisma either. When Inspector Benjamin Shipp held an important council with the Sioux on July 27 to plan the Washington peace trip, he did not oppose Young-Man-Afraid's gracious proposal that Crazy Horse be given the honor of hosting a feast to mark this promising occasion. Although no one openly objected, Red Cloud and several like-minded Indians abruptly left the meeting; that evening two of the unhappy men warned Agent Irwin on behalf of Red Cloud that Crazy Horse was an unreconstructed warrior who could not be trusted. They were especially adamant in their opposition to a pledge made by General Crook to allow Crazy Horse to participate in the last great buffalo hunt on the Powder River.

As the summer of 1877 gave way to fall, the inevitable friction between Crazy Horse and his caretakers (as he regarded government authorities) began to surface. The fiercely independent Lakota leader, neither trained nor willing to play the game as Red Cloud and Spotted Tail had done, became uncooperative, even refusing to sign receipts for the necessary rations the government was obligated to give his people. According to Catherine Price, Crazy Horse's unwillingness to handle these rations, an important role for a tribal leader, forced some of his followers to seek another *itancan* fo fulfill their needs. Agent Irwin, no doubt influenced by older, more established Oglala leaders such as Red Cloud, Little Wound, American Horse, and No Flesh (and even the more conciliatory Young-Man-Afraid-of-His-Horses) grew critical of Crazy Horse. Irwin claimed that the intransigent Sioux warrior was "silent, sullen, lordly and dictatorial," even toward his own people. One incident that created exceptional divisiveness at the agency was General Crook's effort to recruit Lakota scouts to help round up Chief Joseph and his resolute Nez Percés. Crazy Horse was evidently convinced that Crook's real target was Sitting Bull, now living in exile in Canada, and on August 31, the day the scouts were ready for departure, he threatened to take his people and head north.

When Red Cloud and the other older compatriots told Agent Irwin that they could do nothing to calm Crazy Horse, they provided the increasingly disenchanted Irwin and General Crook, who arrived at Camp Crawford on September 2, the excuse they needed to arrest him; in fact, on the following day, Crook ordered Lieutenant Colonel L. P. Bradley, his new commandant at Camp Robinson, to take Crazy Horse into custody. On the morning of September 4, as a consequence of these grave developments, four companies of the Third Cavalry and four hundred Indians, including Red Cloud, Young-Man-

Afraid, Little Wound, and American Horse, started for Crazy
Horse's camp, six miles below Camp Robinson, but, when they
arrived, the camp had already been abandoned and Crazy Horse
and his wife Black Shawl had fled by horseback to Spotted
Tail's agency. Crazy Horse's brief stay with Spotted Tail was
even more tumultuous; the Brulés were stoutly opposed to this
arrangement, but the seven-foot-tall Touch-the-Clouds and his
Miniconjous, who were also at the agency, disagreed, and a tense
standoff ensued. Spotted Tail, who made it very clear that Crazy
Horse must recognize Spotted Tail's leadership if he stayed,
finally persuaded his potential young rival to return to the Red
Cloud Agency and explain to the authorities that the rumors of
his mischief, including the one that he intended to kill General
Crook, were untrue.

Accompanied by Touch-the-Clouds and Spotted Tail and a
party of Brulé warriors (along with Spotted Tail agent Jesse Lee),
Crazy Horse made the forty-five-mile trip from the Spotted Tail
Agency to Camp Crawford in relative calm and peace. However,
when the group arrived on the evening of September 5, things
deteriorated quickly. The large gathering confronting them was
highly agitated; some, including supporters of Red Cloud and
American Horse—who apparently both were there—exhibited
open hostility. One partisan follower of Red Cloud called
Crazy Horse a coward, almost causing instant violence. An
uncooperative Colonel Bradley refused to confer with Crazy
Horse, ordering that he be incarcerated in the guardhouse next
door to the adjutant's office. When Crazy Horse caught sight
of the dark, three-foot by six-foot cell inside the guardhouse,
he made a break for the door, allowing thousands of Lakota
onlookers to witness the shameful deed which was about to
occur.

After Crazy Horse drew a concealed knife to aid in his escape,
one of his once steadfast warriors, Little Big Man, grabbed
him by the arms so he could not use his weapon. Some of the
more hostile officers who observed this dangerous encounter
allegedly called for Crazy Horse's death. When the strong, agile
thirty-five-year-old war leader finally broke free, one or more
of the nervous soldiers surrounding him with drawn bayonets

(probably Private William Gentles of Company F, Fourteenth Infantry) delivered the fatal thrust. When Crazy Horse was brought into the adjutant's office to die, he was treated by the post physician, Major Valentine T. McGillycuddy, who, as a future Oglala agent, would one day play a major role in Red Cloud's life. Although most accounts refer to one fatal wound—some even speculating that it was accidentally inflicted by Crazy Horse's own knife—the most convincing version insists that there were two wounds: a bayonet cut on his side and one on his back, which even penetrated his kidney.

There seemed to be plenty of people around to share the blame for this sad episode in Sioux history. The controversial Little Big Man was apparently able to convince most of his people that he was simply a peacemaker struggling to prevent a potentially violent incident. Two army accounts, those of Lieutenant Clark, who remained on good terms with Crazy Horse longer than any other officer, and the less-than-friendly Colonel Bradley, both stressed the accidental nature of Crazy Horse's death, no doubt hoping to absolve the army of any blame. But Crazy Horse's own people, including Red Cloud, must bear their share of the responsibility. Stephen E. Ambrose, in his comparative study of Crazy Horse and Custer, is probably the most critical of Red Cloud on this score. He sees the "fine hand" of Red Cloud, the "master politician," behind the destructive rumors about Crazy Horse's alleged perfidy that inevitably led to the maverick warrior's death. To Ambrose, the rumors regarding Crazy Horse's proposed return to the warpath, the recommendations of many older chiefs that General Crook shoot Crazy Horse before Crazy Horse could shoot him, and the poisoning of Agent Irwin's mind against Crazy Horse were largely inspired by Red Cloud.

In the final analysis, though, while Red Cloud's role in Crazy Horse's demise is undeniably a serious blemish on his character and one that has discredited him in the eyes of many modern Lakotas, his opposition to Crazy Horse in 1877 was not nearly as controversial then as it is now. The Sioux were tired of war before this tragedy; the events of the past year had disrupted nearly everyone's life. Many felt that unity among the Sioux was

more important than ever before. With the U.S. government
threatening to move the Oglalas and the Brulés back to the
Missouri River, where they had not lived for three generations,
many of those who had believed in Crazy Horse's cause now
felt that they needed a more savvy, experienced leader like Red
Cloud to deal with their persistent white adversaries. Ironically,
because of this new attitude, Red Cloud's star was once again on
the rise, notwithstanding the difficult days that preceded Crazy
Horse's death.

CHAPTER 8

The Feud with McGillycuddy

THE Sioux were on the threshold of one of the most depressing decades in their history. Most of them were not nearly as aware of the dire consequences of the Great Sioux War as Red Cloud. Before the Battle of the Little Bighorn, they had been largely shielded from the hard realities of life. During the early years of reservation life, Indians from the Red Cloud Agency and the other Lakota agencies could come and go as they pleased; many would leave for their unceded lands in the spring to hunt for buffalo and live the Sioux's traditional way of life and return in the fall before the heavy snows and cold weather could bring hardship. Even for those who stayed at the agency by choice, life did not change much. They lived in tipis, often miles from the agency headquarters, where they picked up rations and annuities, usually about every other week. Although there was often a great deal of talk about learning to farm and to graze stock, few of them really felt compelled to do it, at least not before 1877.

Most Sioux were oblivious to those forces already in motion that could end this idyllic way of life. Only grudgingly did they acknowledge that their great commissary on the plains, the enormous buffalo herds, was being depleted at a frightening rate by organized parties of hide hunters; the discovery by an eastern tannery in 1871 that buffalo hides could be an excellent source of commercial leather accelerated the slaughter until by 1878 the southern herd was obliterated and five years later the northern herd shared the same fate.

The demise of the buffalo was, according to Robert M. Utley, a "cultural catastrophe." It left the Plains Indian no alternative to reservation life; moreover, the structure of Sioux life, based primarily upon warfare and the hunt, became largely outmoded. Without buffalo, the elaborate organization of tribal circles and the institution of police societies to oversee the hunt and guarantee its harmony with tribal custom were no longer necessary. Without buffalo, the vital tasks of Indian women in preparing meat and hides and crafting tipis and clothing no longer had much validity. Without buffalo, warfare, with its ritual, its emphasis on courage and decorative display, would have little relevance, for much of it was predicated on competition with rival tribes over control of the horses used to pursue the buffalo. Indeed, the existence of the buffalo herds, which in 1877 still roamed the unceded lands in dwindling numbers, was the key to those deeply held Lakota beliefs in the spiritual connection between the Sioux and these indispensable animals.

The gradual erosion of this compelling alternative to reservation life was not fully realized before Crazy Horse and Sitting Bull led their people northward in defiance of the U.S. government. Many government authorities and a large segment of public opinion were reluctant to force the Lakotas to accept the reality that they had become much too dependent on the federal government for their food and subsistence. There was still a real concern about alienating the treaty Indians for whom Red Cloud, who still had the support of many influential easterners, was a conspicuous symbol. But with the Great Sioux War, this public attitude changed significantly. The army took over many of the responsibilities once cherished by civilian authorities and spearheaded a campaign to avenge the nation for the "Custer Massacre." The results of this great offensive altered the lives of the Sioux and their Cheyenne and Arapaho allies in ways they could never have imagined. This last great Indian war was followed by a drastic curtailment in the freedom and mobility of these once dominant Plains tribes.

Red Cloud was more keenly aware of this change than were most Sioux leaders, although he was quite successful in concealing his thoughts. He also had many concerns of a personal nature. His status as a tribal leader was still not totally secure, despite his improved relations with General Crook. Challenges by rival chiefs, always a problem in Sioux leadership, seemed especially serious during this time of trial. And then there was the question of his role in the next great challenge to face his people: the dreaded move to the Missouri mandated by the U.S. government.

Although the Sioux had given their consent for a Missouri move during the troubled negotiations over the Black Hills in 1876, their agreement was contingent upon the promise that they could confer with the Great White Father. Fulfillment of this pledge was one reason for the importance of the proposed Sioux trip to Washington in 1877. Meeting the new president, Rutherford B. Hayes, was a particularly strong incentive for Red Cloud, a major leader of this Washington-bound delegation, which included Spotted Tail and his son, three Arapaho leaders, and four representatives of those Lakotas who had openly flouted the authority of the federal government during the Great Sioux War, including the highly controversial Little Big Man.

When this Indian delegation gathered in the East Room of the White House on September 27, shortly after their arrival in the capital, they were faced with a formidable array of national leaders. The distinguished looking Hayes was there with his wife, along with four cabinet officers, including Secretary of State William B. Evarts and Secretary of the Interior Carl Schurz, who was determined to achieve those Indian reforms long advocated by influential easterners. Edward P. Smith, the outgoing commissioner of Indian affairs, was present along with Ezra Hayt, the incoming one. General Crook and Bishop Whipple added extra allure to this illustrious gathering, as did William Welsh, former chairman of the Board of Indian Commissioners.

Red Cloud showed that he still enjoyed the recognition he once took for granted. He was, for example, the first member of the Indian delegation to speak. After shaking hands with the new Great Father, he declared, with all his old forcefulness, his opposition to the relocation of the Sioux along the Missouri River. He also gave shrewd reasons for this position, including his contention that the Oglala Sioux could not support themselves in this new location as well as they could along the Tongue River northwest of the Black Hills, where there was "good grass, [a] fine country for stock." He referred to the government's proposed location for the new agency at the juncture of the Missouri River and Yellow Medicine Creek as being on the roundly disapproved "whiskey road," no doubt an effective appeal to the president's wife, "Lemonade Lucy," who had banned alcoholic beverages at White House functions.

Red Cloud had much support for his stand on this issue. Spotted Tail, who spoke the following day, insisted that it was never his understanding that the signing of the Black Hills agreement committed his people to live on the Missouri; Washington authorities had planned to relocate Spotted Tail's Brulés at the old Whetstone Agency, which was across the Missouri from Fort Randall, where they had lived from 1868 to 1871. General Crook, who had shown his critics that he could keep his word by advocating that northern Lakotas should be allowed to live on the Tongue River, if not the Powder, argued for favorable presidential action in behalf of Red Cloud's Oglalas. He insisted that they had behaved very well since the bands of Red Cloud and Red Leaf were disarmed and dismounted eleven months before.

As a result of these appeals, the new president made a major concession: the Sioux could look for another reservation site in the spring. They would, however, have to spend the winter on the Missouri, because the government had already sent supplies there. Moreover, the Ponca Indians had been removed from that area to Indian Territory to make room for them. Although Red Cloud and the other delegates were so delighted with this concession that they wore white men's clothing at their final meeting, they still resisted the idea of wintering on the Missouri River. But the president remained firm: the Oglalas and the Brulés should at least move closer to their supplies on the Missouri, he insisted. He also pledged General Crook's assistance to ease the hardship of this journey.

On October 26, a month after these negotiations, the Lakotas from the Red Cloud Agency began their long and dreaded migration to the east. Although the government could offer them little in the way of food for their 250-mile trip, except for beef on the hoof, General Crook did provide them with much of their transportation, which included "teams of broken down cavalry horses." When eight thousand Sioux, including two thousand of the still restless northern tribesmen, assembled for the trip, they formed a column eight miles long. Their journey proved a difficult one; many members of the long cortege were sick and poorly clothed. The immense evening encampments, as a consequence, were always welcomed; the quickly assembled tipis sometimes extended for three miles from the head of the column to the exhausted stragglers in the rear.

The unpredictable attitude of the northern Indians was the greatest concern; it included the gloomy mood of Crazy Horse's mother and father, who brought Crazy Horse's body along for some future resting place along the trail. When the long and shivering column reached a point along the White River, about seventy-five to eighty miles west of its Missouri River winter destination, Red Cloud, now fully restored as the most competent of the Sioux chiefs, boldly announced that his people would go no further; they would spend the cold months of this always difficult season, already plagued by early snows, on the banks of the White River rather than at that designated point where Yellow Medicine Creek empties into the Missouri.

General Sherman, still very influential and continuing to grow in popularity as General of the Army, was outraged when he heard about Red Cloud's decision. "Don't allow them a pound of food anywhere except at their proper agency," he wired his friend and subordinate, General Sheridan. Sherman was equally outraged when he heard that Agent Irwin was supporting Red Cloud's latest stand. "No Indian agent has the right to change the destination of the Red Cloud party." But the Indian Bureau backed Irwin in his decision, and even General Sheridan was not certain he could legally stop the flow of supplies to a peaceful people. In the end, the Indian Bureau prevailed. Red Cloud's people were allowed to spend the winter on the White River. It was decreed that from that temporary home they could travel to the Missouri once a week to get supplies from the newly authorized Yellow Medicine Agency. The willful Red Cloud, just one year after his demotion by Crook, proved again how formidable a leader he could be.

Red Cloud may have won this tiff with the government, but deciding on a permanent location for his people could be a much more troublesome problem. General Crook had parted company with most officers when he urged that all parties involved should adhere to President Hayes's pledge to let the Lakotas select their own agency site, a decision that could give them considerable latitude, as the Sioux reservation encompassed the entire southwestern corner of Dakota Territory. Red Cloud, who had pushed for the Tongue River when he was in Washington, had, with Agent Irwin's advice, settled for a site on White Earth Creek (now White Clay Creek). It was a relatively isolated area located as far up the White River as the Sioux could get without being in Nebraska.

The stalemate that developed over the new location lasted for six months. To end it the federal government resorted to one of its favorite devices: it created another committee. On June 20, 1878, Congress authorized Secretary of the Interior Schurz to appoint a commission to find a permanent location for followers of Red Cloud and Spotted Tail. Schurz selected a group of three men for this difficult responsibility; it included Colonel David S. Stanley, an army officer who had gained favorable recognition during the Yellowstone campaign five years earlier. This commission, sometimes known as the Stanley commission, traveled west to ascertain the views of the unhappy Lakotas. In its talks with Spotted Tail and Red Cloud, the commission surprisingly found Spotted Tail more adamant than Red Cloud in resisting any location at or near the Missouri. Spotted Tail told Stanley and the other two commissioners that in ten days he and his people would break camp and move to a site on Rosebud Creek near the South Fork of the White River.

Red Cloud, for his part, insisted on White Clay Creek as the new home for his people. Once again dunning the government for something, he also asked for five hundred cows and a Catholic priest during his conference with the new commission. Red Cloud and Spotted Tail, incidentally, were both partial toward Catholic missionaries. In fact, Spotted Tail had asked President Hayes for Catholic clergymen during his Washington visit: "I would like to get Catholic priests. Those who wear black dresses." The reference to the popular black-gowned Jesuit priests was to a large extent a tribute to Father De Smet's fair and usually evenhanded relations with the Sioux. In addition, Red Cloud's clashes with many of the Episcopal agents who had been sent to his agency had probably influenced his like-minded views on the subject of Jesuit clergymen. But the attitude of the Catholic church at this time cannot be discounted; the Bureau of Catholic Indian Missions, organized in 1874, was one of the few missionary bodies willing to give the Indians some say in how they conducted their lives.

Although the Stanley commission may have listened to Red Cloud and Spotted Tail, it did not heed their advice. The commissioners recommended that Red Cloud's people settle on nearby Wounded Knee Creek rather than on the White Clay and that Spotted Tail's people settle on the South Fork of the White River rather than on the Rosebud. It was during this discouraging stage of the impasse that the Oglalas and Brulés decided to take the initiative. On September 19 the Oglala leaders asked Irwin to tell the Great Father that they were going to move to White Clay Creek in two days in order to avoid another cold winter at their present location. Commissioner of Indian Affairs Hayt, who had still hoped to persuade the Sioux to settle along the Missouri, happily capitulated; indeed, he appointed James R. O'Beirne, a clerk in his office, to help in this latest migration. Consequently, when Red Cloud and Little Wound arrived at White Clay Creek at the head of a small party on October 7, O'Beirne, who was given the functional title of special removal supervisor, was there to greet them. Using

Camp Sheridan as his major headquarters, O'Beirne had already arranged to have building materials brought from the old Red Cloud Agency near Camp Robinson or from the railhead at Sidney, Nebraska.

The warm reception given to O'Beirne's hard work by the Red Cloud party was a great relief to the U.S. government: Dull Knife and his desperate band of Cheyennes had escaped from their unhappy homes in Indian Territory the previous month, and there was real fear that they would join discontented Sioux in Montana and launch a new Indian war. No doubt feeling reassured, the Indian Bureau generously supplied the Oglalas with ninety-seven wagons to carry their supplies to the White Clay, allowing the Sioux themselves to do the freighting. When the main body of Red Cloud's wandering people reached their new site on November 11, there was a healthy feeling of relief, notwithstanding the fact that only one small building for the new agency had been constructed. Most of Red Cloud's people evidently felt that they had found a permanent place after ten years of frustration on three separate reservations. But they would not have the privilege of naming their new home after Red Cloud; the Indian Bureau, probably blaming him for much of the acrimony generated by this move, refused to give Red Cloud that honor. The bureau instead called the new place Pine Ridge, even though most of the pines on the lonely prairie landscape that comprised the Oglala's new home were concealed in the many ravines that crossed it.

But Red Cloud would not enjoy the tranquility he felt he deserved for long. On New Year's Day of 1879, the Pine Ridge Agency lost a good friend. Irwin, who had been well liked by most Oglalas, resigned in disgust as a result of his differences with Hayt and the stinging criticism he received over his support of the Pine Ridge move. His replacement was the notoriously strong-willed Valentine T. McGillycuddy. Only thirty years old at the time, this energetic contract surgeon for the army, sporting one of the most elaborate mustaches found on the frontier, arrived at Pine Ridge on March 10. Tireless and combative, he immediately set the stage for a seven-year struggle with Red Cloud that drew national attention and caused such acrimony that Pine Ridge became known to many Sioux as the "Place Where Everything is Disputed."

To those who wanted to tighten control over the Sioux, Dr. McGillycuddy seemed like the perfect choice. His previous experiences in dealing with Lakota issues had been rich and varied; he had served as a topographer on the Jenny expedition to the Black Hills in 1875, and he was the post surgeon who attended Crazy Horse after he was fatally wounded at Camp Robinson in 1877. As the man who treated Crazy Horse's wife, Black Shawl, for tuberculosis, the new agent, who felt his relationship with Crazy Horse had been a special one, may have already prejudged Red Cloud. McGillycuddy's hostility toward tribal government, in fact, was barely concealed; he ardently believed that the Indian agent should be the major source of authority on any reservation.

His sharp differences with Red Cloud surfaced at his first meeting with the major chiefs at Pine Ridge. Red Cloud, who presided over the gathering, was conciliatory at first, passing the proverbial peace pipe to McGillycuddy and asking his compatriots to listen carefully to what their new agent had to say. But McGillycuddy quickly shattered this early harmony by making it clear that the Sioux would have to change their traditional way of life. Presenting a new map of the agency, he pointed to the many fertile valleys that marked Pine Ridge's rolling landscapes and insisted that his Indian charges should go out and cultivate them as independent farmers instead of clustering idly around the new agency's headquarters.

A surprised Red Cloud quickly objected, asserting that the Great Spirit had created the Sioux for hunting and fishing, not farming. He bitterly complained that the government, which had already seized the bountiful lands of the Lakotas, now wanted to rob them of their identity. Such a policy was wrong, he insisted. The "white man owes us a living for the lands he has taken from us." After this clash the two men seemed to be at odds over almost everything. For example, when McGillycuddy proposed the creation of an Indian police force so that army troops could be removed from Pine Ridge, Red Cloud opposed him, insisting that his people could police the agency themselves.

But the struggle between Red Cloud and McGillycuddy was being duplicated throughout almost all the agencies that comprised the still immense Sioux reservation. The experiences of Canadian-born James McLaughlin provide another example of this familiar discord. In 1881 McLaughlin became the agent at Standing Rock after having served in that position at the Devil's Lake Indian Agency for five years. He, too, pushed increasingly popular government programs to reform the vanquished but still proud Sioux. Like McGillycuddy, this man, who had the added advantage of being married to a Sioux, pressured the Lakotas under his jurisdiction to take up farming or stock raising. He was also persistent in pushing for Indian education and Christian religious values; his success in the latter category was largely a result of the strong support he received from the Catholic Church.

In most of the six agencies that comprised the Great Sioux Reservation, an area which encompassed forty-three thousand square miles of arid plains, there were fundamental struggles going on among the residents that often involved the agents. On the Standing Rock and Cheyenne River agencies, for example, where Hunkpapa, Miniconjou, Sans Arc, Blackfeet, and Two Kettle Sioux drew their rations, there was a curious blend of conflict and cooperation. At Standing Rock, McLaughlin clashed bitterly with Sitting Bull when the great Hunkpapa medicine man finally surrendered and moved to the reservation in 1883. Sitting Bull became the leader of a group of traditional Sioux who were often called "nonprogressives"; these more intransigent Lakotas were located on every agency where those who believed in the old values were strong and organized. At Cheyenne River, these traditional Lakotas were led by Big Foot and Hump. At the Brulé agency on the Rosebud, Crow Dog and Two Strike were the leading nonprogressives. At Red Cloud's Pine Ridge Agency, Big Road and Little Wound were best known for their leadership in this resistance.

But there were also some rather strident government support-ers at these agencies; they were usually called "progressives." McLaughlin, for example, enjoyed the support of John Grass and Crow King in his battle with Sitting Bull; even the great Gall, who had led the charge against Custer at Medicine Tail Coulee ford on the Little Bighorn, often backed McLaughlin in his disputes with Sitting Bull.

McGillycuddy could also rely on tribal progressives to support him in some of his most violent disagreements with Red Cloud. Young-Man-Afraid-of-His-Horses, who no doubt was resentful because Red Cloud had displaced his father as leader of the Oglalas, often sided with McGillycuddy on divisive tribal issues. American Horse, who claimed to have killed the luckless Captain Fetterman in 1866, was usually cooperative; in the two major motivations for cooperation, opportunism and an awareness that Indians could no longer change things, American Horse was often put in the first category by his critics.

Interestingly enough, both Red Cloud and Spotted Tail tried to avoid identification with either camp. Although most participants in this cultural struggle between the Sioux and the government, which marked the early 1880s, probably regarded these two men as nonprogressives, they were both careful to avoid the kind of irreconcilable impasse that characterized relations between Sitting Bull and McLaughlin throughout much of the decade. They would sometimes challenge an Indian agent or some other government official with whom they disagreed, but if forcefully rebuffed, they could either compromise or turn to another cause.

Their participation in educational matters is one example of the limited cooperation they were willing to give. In 1879, Captain Richard Henry Pratt visited the Pine Ridge and Rosebud agencies in search of promising young Lakotas for his off-reservation boarding school in Pennsylvania. Pratt, who had served as a jailer for imprisoned Plains Indians in Florida after the Red River War, was the founder and superintendent of the soon-to-be-famous Carlisle Indian Training School. This institution, which had recently used some unoccupied military barracks to house Indian pupils, was supposed to transform young Indians from a "savage state" to a civilized one. Although Pratt had no experience in his new endeavor, his dogmatic nature gave him an aura of confidence and authority. Also, his belief in the total immersion of Indian children in the dominant white culture won him the support of many self-styled reformers. As a result, he was able to recruit for his noble experiment sixty boys and twenty-four girls from both agencies.

Because of the deep anxiety of most parents over Pratt's new project, a delegation from the Pine Ridge and Rosebud agencies, including Red Cloud and Spotted Tail, visited Carlisle a few months later, in June 1880. Both chiefs were shocked by what they found: when Spotted Tail saw that his own children were dressed in military blue uniforms, their hair closely trimmed, he abruptly removed them from the school, vowing to oppose any further cooperation with Carlisle. The self-righteous Pratt, his angry eyes staring over his prominent Roman nose in characteristic fashion, was furious with both Spotted Tail and Red Cloud during their disruptive visit. Pratt attacked the hostile speeches made by both men as being "offensive and prejudicial to the discipline of the school."

Not surprisingly, Red Cloud and Spotted Tail became wary of almost all the new educational systems being foisted on their people. Although they would eventually prefer on-reservation day schools and boarding schools to off-reservation institutions such as Carlisle, they would remain suspicious of all government-sponsored schools. While this position would categorize Red Cloud as a nonprogressive for many years, it would have only a short-lived effect on Spotted Tail, who was shot and killed by a rival named Crow Dog in 1883, an event that triggered bitter factionalism at the Rosebud Agency for years.

Red Cloud and Spotted Tail also clashed with the government on the nature of the religious institutions that their new overseers insisted they embrace. Both men, as mentioned before, wanted Jesuits or other Catholic orders to manage their spiritual and educational affairs. But in a predominantly Protestant country during a predominantly Protestant century, there was great opposition to too much Catholic participation in Indian affairs.

The religious issue was one of the first to divide Red Cloud and Agent McGillycuddy. On April 30, 1879, for example, a Benedictine priest, Father Meinrad McCarthy, arrived at Pine Ridge to establish a mission among the Oglalas. Red Cloud was ecstatic over McCarthy's project, urging the priest to stay at his home until he could get settled. But as McGillycuddy and other reservation employees knew, Pine Ridge, like the previous Oglala agencies, was the spiritual monopoly of the Episcopal Church; McGillycuddy, therefore, informed the priest that he would have to leave. When the disappointed clergyman pitched a tent two miles south of the agency, near Camp Sheridan, to wait for a final decision, Red Cloud begged him to return. McGillycuddy, however, remained stubborn, forcing Red Cloud to try a new tack: he told the tribal council that he did not care if the Episcopal missionary at Pine Ridge stayed as long as his people could also have Catholic missionaries to teach their children. After a four-month stalemate, Father McCarthy's superiors recalled him.

The uncomfortable seven-year relationship between Red Cloud and McGillycuddy would provide few respites from the bitterness that marked their initial encounter. A few weeks after McGillycuddy located on the Pine Ridge map those valleys where he felt Oglalas could farm, Red Cloud, buttressed by twenty-one other chiefs, including the ordinarily more progressive Young-Man-Afraid, sent a letter to President Hayes asking that McGillycuddy be replaced by his predecessor, Dr Irwin. The uneasy relationship between the two became all but impossible after that incident.

Despite McGillycuddy's determination to stay at Pine Ridge, ouster efforts against him never ceased. On September 4, 1880, fifteen months after Hayes received that controversial letter in behalf of Irwin's reinstatement, another letter, this one signed by American Horse, reached the president. Acting as spokesman for the tribal council, American Horse, who was often the reservation gadfly, reiterated the call for McGillycuddy's removal:

"We ask and beg of you to take our present Agent from us and give us another in his place so our people can be at peace once more which will never be as long as he remains with us."

American Horse's provocative communication was in response to McGillycuddy's effort to usurp most of Red Cloud's powers. The intense, balding Indian agent had called a tribal meeting to depose his rival. He had even sent the head of the Indian Police, an organization he had created over Red Cloud's objections, to bring the reluctant Red Cloud to the meeting. But the results of this maneuver were a big disappointment to McGillycuddy. The Council of Chiefs, made up of more than one hundred men, placed all but five sticks in Red Cloud's pile as each participant was given the chance to cast a stick for his choice for tribal leader. American Horse spoke for a substantial majority of the Oglala people when he informed Hayes that Red Cloud was their selection: "He has been our head chief, he is now and always will be, because the Nation love, respect and believe in him."

But McGillycuddy would not accept the council's verdict as final; indeed, from that point on he always referred to Red Cloud as "the former chief" of the Oglalas. The embattled agent was also convinced that there was a conspiracy behind the council's action; he insisted that American Horse's pro–Red Cloud letter to Hayes was inspired by H. C. Dear, a trader close to Red Cloud whom McGillycuddy banished from Pine Ridge for "disorderly conduct." McGillycuddy's attitude toward Red Cloud, who was about thirty years his senior, was nothing short of contemptuous. "Red Cloud is now an old man in his dotage," McGillycuddy wrote the commissioner of Indian affairs, "childish and not responsible for what he does."

Red Cloud's next attempt to eliminate his hostile rival occurred after President James A. Garfield was inaugurated on March 4, 1881. The persistent chief, although sixty years of age, showed few signs of being in his dotage. He wrote the new president in late April that McGillycuddy ran Pine Ridge more like a military post than a reservation. Also, reverting to that self-serving role noted by many of his critics, the enduring Oglala leader chided McGillycuddy for not supplying him with the ox teams and wagons he had promised.

On May 12, two months later, Red Cloud and ninety-six chiefs petitioned Garfield for McGillycuddy's removal. Although this petition did not represent any new strategy on Red Cloud's part, the charges contained in it were much more serious. The chiefs accused McGillycuddy of stealing and lying at their expense. The enraged agent was so incensed at Red Cloud for these attacks on his character that he openly challenged the leader at a conference called in connection with the Sioux's annual sun dance on June 22. He demanded that Red Cloud either affirm or deny the charges in the Garfield letter that McGillycuddy had stolen and lied. As he had responded to Saville in the scandal at the Red Cloud Agency over inferior food in 1875, Red Cloud backed down when personally confronted. In fact, he told McGillycuddy that he never accused him of lying and stealing; that was not what he wanted the letter to Garfield to say. What he really wanted from the president was a trip to Washington so he could straighten out the problems that divided the two.

Ironically, Red Cloud got his chance for another Washington trip two months later. But the main purpose of his visit this time was to help solve the Ponca Indian controversy rather than to settle differences with McGillycuddy. The Ponca Indians had been moved from their ancestral lands along the Missouri River to Indian Territory in 1877 to make room for the Sioux. The displaced and courageous Poncas captured the sympathy of the American people when a number of them, led by Standing Bear, tried to return to their homeland. Their arrest and the controversial trial that ensued ignited so much public emotion that President Hayes appointed a special commission to look into the matter. When this body recommended that the Poncas be allowed to return to their ancestral lands, the government was in a difficult bind. Red Cloud's willingness to have the Sioux make room for the Poncas as well as for those unhappy

Cheyennes who wanted to leave Indian Territory took the president off the hook and won for Red Cloud and his people many new friends.

Even McGillycuddy was grateful to Red Cloud for his flexibility on the Ponca question. But this more benign mood toward Red Cloud soon changed when he heard that Red Cloud had secured Secretary of the Interior S. J. Kirkwood's permission for white men married to Lakota women to stay on the reservation as long as they behaved themselves. McGillycuddy was a longtime critic of Red Cloud's white friends, whom he felt were behind most of the chief's troublemaking activities. The agent also believed that much of the drunkenness at Pine Ridge was caused by these unprincipled "squaw men," who were also the tribe's major suppliers. Indeed, in an obvious appeal to puritanical America, he not only implied that Red Cloud was unduly influenced by John Barleycorn, but also that those white friends were responsible for "several broods" of illegitimate children of mixed blood who were now corrupting life at the Pine Ridge Agency.

Despite these interesting differences, tensions between the two men eased following Red Cloud's visit to Washington. In a January 1882 report to the commissioner of Indian affairs, Red Cloud even complimented McGillycuddy: "The Agent with us is a good Agent." But two months later, McGillycuddy was again making new charges against Red Cloud, accusing him of using the traditional spring councils to lobby for the agent's removal.

The Sioux sun dance in June was of particular concern to Dr. McGillycuddy because Red Cloud could communicate with a large number of Lakota Sioux at that ceremony. This ritual, found among many of the Plains tribes (although sometimes under different names), was the ultimate expression of Lakota gratitude to Wakan Tanka, the Great Spirit, whom the Sioux believed was manifested in everything from the rays of the sun to the most minute aspect of nature. The most dramatic feature of the sun dance, a twelve-day ceremony, was the suspension of brave young warriors from the sun dance lodge pole. These young men, as part of their tribal sacrifice, were tied to the sturdiest pole the Sioux could find by rawhide lines attached to skewers implanted in their skin. By hanging there in great pain, eyes fixed upon the sun, these intense young Lakotas were helping to ensure the blessings of the Great Spirit for the coming year. It was a ceremony that involved all tribal members in one way or another. The young men, who were usually involved in their own quest for a personal vision, were the most obvious participants, but the more virtuous of the tribal women were also included. They were given the honor of locating the sacred cottonwood tree that would be used as the ceremonial lodge pole.

McGillycuddy had been opposed to the sun dance from the beginning. He wrote to South Dakota state historian Doane Robinson many years later, on December 28, 1923, that the "dance was interfering with the propress [sic] of civilization among my charges." In fact, in 1882 he warned the Oglala leaders, including Red Cloud, that the dance must cease after the June ceremony. Confirming that this stand seemed unnecessarily reckless to many in government was his admission that the Indian Bureau only gave him lukewarm support. Even General Sheridan feared that McGillycuddy had overestimated his influence with the more progressive Oglalas: there was widespread apprehension that McGillycuddy could trigger a "general outbreak" at Pine Ridge. The fact that the sun dance, minus those rites that cause physical suffering, remains an important Lakota ritual today is convincing proof of how serious McGillycuddy's misconceptions were about the beliefs and values of his Indian charges.

Red Cloud himself must have sensed McGillycuddy's vulnerability on this issue. Indeed, the aging warrior was a major participant in the sun dance that year. Dressed in breechcloth, Red Cloud, painted and wearing feathers for the occasion, helped his people bring back their great visions of the past. He also worked to undercut McGillycuddy's influence during a number of conferences with Indian delegations at the ceremony. Indeed, the entire atmosphere at this gathering was made more dangerous by the presence of a large number of Sitting Bull's

Sioux and Northern Cheyenne followers; the once-powerful medicine man had just returned from his Canadian exile during the past year. McGillycuddy credited the leading progressive at Pine Ridge, Young-Man-Afraid-of-His-Horses, for preventing the potential violence that Red Cloud's provocations could have produced; Young-Man-Afraid, who had become Red Cloud's chief rival for tribal control, strived, along with McGillycuddy's reliable Indian Police, to keep order at these intense sun dance festivities.

Two months later, however, an even more serious eruption occurred when Red Cloud and fifty of his followers left Pine Ridge in mid-August without permission to attend a feast at Louis Shangrau's Nebraska ranch; Shangrau, of mixed blood, was a former scout for General Crook whom McGillycuddy had evicted for bad conduct. A number of McGillycuddy's detractors attended this feast, including William J. Godfrey of Colorado, a good friend of Secretary of the Interior Henry M. Teller, whom President Chester A. Arthur had appointed after Garfield's assassination. Godfrey had a letter, calling for McGillycuddy's removal, for Red Cloud and his followers to sign; this communication also included a provocative ultimatum that if McGillycuddy was not gone "within sixty days," or if there was not an investigation of his "gross misconduct" during this same period, he would be escorted off the reservation by the letter's signatories. To compound this new problem, Red Cloud, usually a very cautious and politic leader, unwisely threatened to kill some freighters who were preparing to leave for Thatcher, Nebraska, to pick up a load of freight. McGillycuddy used these uncharacteristic indiscretions on Red Cloud's part to win the support of Commissioner of Indian Affairs Hiram Price; in fact, the agent tried to persuade the bewildered commissioner to send Red Cloud to the old prison in Leavenworth to avoid further chaos.

The climax of this particularly bitter dispute occurred in the summer of 1882 when Red Cloud appeared at Pine Ridge's agency headquarters, a mile from his village, to hear McGilly-cuddy read Commissioner Price's telegram authorizing Red

Cloud's arrest and incarceration if such a move were necessary to maintain the peace. During this visit a fight broke out which resulted in Red Cloud's being unceremoniously locked up in the guardhouse. Although there were accusations on both sides, Red Cloud was the main participant threatened with violence during this incident, according to his friend Charles P. Jordan, the chief clerk of the body chosen to investigate the controversy. In fact, at the same time Red Cloud was summoned to McGillycuddy's headquarters to hear the Price telegram, he was warned by his nephew, a member of McGillycuddy's Indian Police, that McGillycuddy planned to make good on previous threats to kill him. Red Cloud, in Jordan's own words penned twenty years later, responded to this threat by ordering his followers to disarm. He also sent his son, Jack, back to the village to raise the American flag over his house as a gesture of peace and goodwill.

McGillycuddy's apparent victory over Red Cloud in this incident made him overconfident. When he left Pine Ridge the following day for a business trip, his enemies quickly regrouped. On August 21, some of his most important subordinates, including his clerk, the reservation trader, the chief of police, and the agency physician, wrote Commissioner Price, warning him that McGillycuddy's treatment of Red Cloud could provoke a bloody outbreak at the agency. This telling complaint, plus others coming from people on both sides of the question, led to the appointment of a special inspector, W. J. Pollack. This new troubleshooter was sent to Pine Ridge in September to determine who was at fault in the dispute. Pollack, in a two-part report to Secretary Teller, sided with Red Cloud in the confrontations, which had already drawn a great deal of national attention to the unhappy state of affairs at the Oglala agency.

In the second part of Pollack's report, filed on October 14, the special inspector cited a number of serious irregularities at Pine Ridge. One charged that McGillycuddy was living high at the expense of his Indian charges, unfairly depriving Red Cloud of his rations while giving his Indian policemen and other favorites more than they actually needed. But the account of another inspector, filed the same day, exonerated McGillycuddy of Pollack's more serious charges. The net effect of this exchange was a decision by the Indian Bureau against further investigation of these accusations. McGillycuddy's survival in this latest fray should not be all that surprising. Although his contentious nature tended to keep things in an uproar, his record shows that he was probably more honest and efficient than most Indian agents at that time.

During these stormy summer months in 1882, Red Cloud's rivalry with McGillycuddy shifted from struggles over jurisdiction and authority to those over governmental land policies. The shift was triggered on August 7 when Dakota's territorial delegate to Congress, Richard F. Pettigrew, successfully offered an amendment to a congressional act calling for the appropriation of five thousand dollars to enable the secretary of the interior to negotiate for modifications of existing treaties with the Sioux. The delegate was acting in behalf of impatient constituents who wanted a land corridor through the Great Sioux Reservation, which at that time extended from the Missouri River to the gold fields of the Black Hills. To implement this new legislation, Secretary Teller appointed a commission headed by Newton Edmunds, the former governor of Dakota Territory whose interest in Indian affairs had remained strong. Joining Edmunds on this new commission was Peter Shannon, former chief justice of the Dakota territorial supreme court, and James H. Teller of Cleveland, Secretary Teller's brother.

Before the new commissioners started west to negotiate with the Lakotas on the proposed land corridor, the government decided to ignore the provision in the Fort Laramie Treaty that required the concurrence of three-fourths of all adult males for any major treaty modification. As a result of this decision, only the signatures of the major chiefs and headmen were required in a procedure similar to the one used when the government acquired the Black Hills in 1876. Although somewhat reluctant at first, Teller gave in to Edmunds on this new requirement, accepting Edmunds's arguments that it would be impossible to get the necessary three-quarters of the adult males to vote because of the distance and other logistical problems. He did refuse, however, to provide the commission with the funds necessary to feast the Indians as a way of winning their agreement to this proposed land cessation.

The new and revised accord that the Edmunds commission took west with them had indeed proposed some major changes. It not only called for the Sioux to cede the land between the White and Cheyenne rivers for a corridor to the Black Hills, but it also called upon the Sioux to cede the land above the Cheyenne River west of the 102nd meridian (the northwest corner of present-day South Dakota). Approval of this proposition would mean an end to one large, contiguous Sioux reservation; the entire reservation, as a matter of fact, would be divided among the existing Sioux agencies, some of the land going to Pine Ridge, some of it going to Standing Rock, and so forth.

The land loss for the Lakota tribes would be enormous; estimates of the acreage involved range from 9,000,000 to 11,000,000 acres. In return for this sacrifice, each head of family would receive 320 acres of land and each minor child would receive 80, in accordance with the Treaty of Fort Laramie. Moreover, the Lakota Sioux as a people would be given twenty-five thousand cows and one thousand bulls as a foundation herd. So that this herd could grow, none of these animals could be sold or slaughtered without the permission of an agent. The Edmunds commission presumably felt that it had the support of most Indian reformers in these provisions to make the Sioux people farmers and stockmen; appropriately enough, each participating family would receive a cow and a pair of oxen for its own use.

When the hopeful commissioners reached Pine Ridge on October 22, 1882, they found themselves uncomfortably in the middle of the Red Cloud–McGillycuddy rivalry. Red Cloud's first reaction to their presence was an unequivocal refusal to discuss their new plan. At that point Edmunds sought McGillycuddy's help. The agent, in a test of strength with Red Cloud, won over a number of the younger Lakotas, who, in defiance of Red Cloud, consented to the new agreement. The commissioners also collected the required signatures from the rest of the agencies, except for the Lower Brulé and the one at Crow Creek. Republican President Arthur, at Teller's behest, submitted the agreement to the Forty-seventh Congress, and it looked as though Dakota homesteaders could now move into the thousands of newly opened acres that once had belonged to the Sioux.

But before such action could be taken, information got out that the Edmunds commission had not legally complied with that treaty provision requiring the signatures of three-fourths of the adult males for any major change. One of the chief opponents of the Edmunds commission was Republican Senator Henry L. Dawes of Massachusetts, who was becoming the chief spokesperson for the nation's Indian reformers. Although Senator Dawes did not object to those provisions that encouraged the Lakotas to become farmers and stock grazers, he opposed any land cession that did not have the approval of three-fourths of all Sioux men. Dawes proceeded to block ratification of the Edmunds agreement, forcing the commission to return to the agencies in order to get additional signatures.

Not surprisingly, Pine Ridge proved to be one of the most difficult places to get new names. McGillycuddy did assemble enough chiefs to hear the commission's position presented by the Reverend Samuel D. Hinman, a man whose earlier participation on the Allison commission of 1875 was largely negated by the fact that Red Cloud did not like him. Predictably, Red Cloud proved unyielding, insisting that he would not permit the acquisition of additional signatures. The inflexible old warrior, however, under pressure from the other chiefs, did permit Hinman to visit the villages at Pine Ridge one by one with the understanding that, if he could secure the requisite number of adult males, the council would be called to ratify his results.

Hinman, accompanied by one of Pine Ridge's leading progressives, George Sword, traveled throughout the far-flung agency in their quest for more signatures. Although he was able to win support in some of the villages, most notably Little Wound's, he soon became aware of a host of new problems.

Sioux males were often known by several names. Moreover, the job of determining who was a minor and who was not made Hinman's task almost impossible. Also, Hinman was certain that Red Cloud had sent runners ahead of him, threatening to banish all those Lakotas who agreed to the land cession. Ultimately Reverend Hinman and George Sword gave up on getting the required number of signatures and settled instead for a list of adult males willing to sign the new agreement. Hinman's insistence that the 633 names he did gather constituted three-fourths of this adult male group did not seem too convincing; McGillycuddy was already feeding 1,226 adult males as part of Pine Ridge's program of rations and annuities.

When Hinman returned from his exhaustive mission, he learned that Red Cloud had left the agency, with a pass from President Arthur himself, to visit his old Shoshone rival Washakie in Wyoming. This latest setback was minor, however, compared to the arrival of the Dawes committee in late August 1883. The Dawes committee was created at the same time that Congress required the Edmunds commission to get its additional signatures. The committee's untimely presence at Pine Ridge was almost embarrassing; although Senator Dawes could accept the division of tribal lands among individuals as a step toward civilization, he could never condone a blatant land grab. In fact, Dawes's appearance spelled an end to the fumbling efforts of the Edmunds commission.

The Dawes committee proved more than willing to allow the Sioux adequate opportunity to express their true views regarding severalty; not unexpectedly, Red Cloud led the way, accusing Hinman and the Edmunds commission of deceiving his Oglalas and demanding that the controversial land agreement be torn up. To the surprise of many, all the leaders at Pine Ridge, including most of the agency's progressives, lined up behind their old leader, leaving McGillycuddy in the embarrassing position of explaining why he supported such a questionable agreement. McGillycuddy, when he testified before the Dawes committee at Rosebud, tried to rehabilitate his image by resurrecting two of his favorite targets, the reservation's "half-breeds and squawmen," the longtime supporters of Red Cloud. These men opposed severalty, he insisted, because, if the Sioux's reservation land were divided among individuals, they would have to face the dreary prospect of becoming self-supporting for the first time.

Dawes's intervention greatly strengthened Red Cloud's standing in his struggle with McGillycuddy. Before this event, Red Cloud's position was beginning to slip; in fact, during this crucial year of 1883, Young-Man-Afraid-of-His-Horses had been elected by a three-to-one vote over Red Cloud to head the Indian council. Now the power of the resilient Red Cloud was again in the ascendancy; most Oglalas were apparently returning to his brand of skeptical, but cautious, leadership. But the Dawes committee still thought that the Great Sioux Reservation was too large for the needs of the Lakota people. And like the Edmunds commission, it, too, wanted to divide the reservation among the existing agencies and open up the surplus lands to white settlement. Under its plan, however, the remaining acreage would be paid for with money rather than with cows and bulls.

During this stage of the struggle, Red Cloud acquired a new friend among those eastern humanitarians who were challenging land-hungry westerners and eastern capitalists recklessly eager to develop the West, regardless of the consequences. This new ally was Dr. Thomas A. Bland, one of those leaders, along with former Oregon Indian superintendent Alfred B. Meacham, who organized the National Indian Defense Association. This unusual organization, founded in 1885, believed in Indian self-determination at a time when most Indian reform groups were calling for the prompt assimilation of all Indians into the dominant white society. Through its journal, *The Council Fire*, edited by Bland, the association constantly criticized the way the government was handling Indian policy. To the perceptive Bland, McGillycuddy, whose feud with Red Cloud continued to draw national attention, was a perfect foil for those involved in his struggle.

In June 1884, Red Cloud, with Secretary of the Interior

Teller's permission, invited Dr. Bland to visit Pine Ridge. When the noisy reformer arrived at the agency, however, McGillycuddy had him brought to his office by a sullen escort of Indian Police and told him to leave immediately, notwithstanding Secretary Teller's consent. Bland was ordered into a carriage and spirited off the agency, ending up on Jacob Ganow's ranch in nearby Nebraska. Red Cloud, who had offered a hundred men to escort him back to Pine Ridge, visited Bland at the ranch with some 150 followers. But he could not persuade Bland to return to the agency. When Bland finally left for Washington in mid-July, however, he created a national furor in *The Council Fire* with his account of his abrupt and legally questionable expulsion. But the feisty McGillycuddy struck back, insisting that Bland had only come to Pine Ridge to cause trouble; indeed, in the agent's opinion this outspoken reformer had created more chaos "than a Sun Dance and two or three barrels of whisky."

Bland's intrusion into Pine Ridge affairs caused a real uproar in Dakota Territory. John R. Brennan, superintendent at Pine Ridge during the early 1900s, remarked in 1904 that Dr. Bland and his "white fool friends" had sneaked onto the reservation after giving Red Cloud "some very bad and malicious advice." Bland might well have succeeded in his provocative intentions if it had not been for Young-Man-Afraid, Little Wound, and the Indian Police, who again gave crucial support to McGillycuddy. Perhaps even more damaging to Red Cloud's cause was the attitude of Senator Dawes toward Bland. Dawes believed him to be an unreliable person, one whom McGillycuddy had every right to order off the reservation. This attitude was bad news for the tenacious old chief because Dawes represented the new mainstream of the Indian reform movement, while Bland was regarded as nothing but a radical out on the fringe.

Senator Dawes was associated with a relatively new and vital Indian reform movement that received its impetus in 1883 at a meeting at Lake Mohonk, a rather posh resort in upper New York State near the Catskills. There had been important efforts to improve the Indians' lot as early as the late 1860s, including the initiatives of the Quakers who had prompted Grant to enunciate his Peace Policy. By the time of the divisive Bland incident these efforts had been refined into some persuasive and carefully justified precepts. Assimilation was probably the key word for this new approach. The new reformers wanted to assimilate the Sioux and other western tribes into the nation's social structure as soon as possible. They wanted to Americanize the Indians as they had Americanized (or tried to Americanize) the multitude of immigrants who had arrived during the late nineteenth century. They wanted to educate the Indians in Christian values, which in the 1880s meant Protestant values. They also wanted to instill in them the work ethic, or Protestant ethic, so that they could become industrious farmers or stock grazers willing to become responsible for themselves.

Even more controversial, these new reformers of the Dawes stripe wanted Indian assimilation to occur so swiftly and efficiently that the reservation, as a training ground for Indian acculturation, would become outmoded and eventually disappear without notice. As Senator Dawes phrased it at the 1887 Lake Mohonk Conference, the reservations "will pass like snow in the springtime, and we will never know when they go: we will only know they are gone." The major problem with his vision, as far as Red Cloud was concerned, was its hostility toward tribalism; to achieve the kind of individualism to make total assimilation complete, tribal leadership and the communal values embodied by Indian chiefs would have to disappear along with the reservation system.

Dr. Bland's belief that change should come through Indian rather than white initiative was also out of step with the new Indian movement. Outmoded, too, because of its emphasis on Indian initiative and self-reliance was the Bureau of Catholic Indian Missions, which was increasingly regarded as a threat to Protestant dominance because of the work of its tireless missionaries among the western tribes. But the voices of these reformers were weak when compared to those who advocated reform at the four-day conferences held yearly on the shores of Lake Mohonk; an example of how illustrious these Mohonk gatherings were was the presence of former president Hayes at the 1889 conference.

Indeed, the personalities of this new movement largely set the pace for Indian reform throughout the rest of the Gilded Age. Two of its major spokespersons were Albert K. Smiley and his twin brother, Alfred, owners of the Lake Mohonk resort. Another was Thomas Jefferson Morgan, a Baptist educator who would become commissioner of Indian affairs; he may have embodied the "spirit of Mohonk" better than anyone else. Patrician Senator Dawes of Massachusetts was also among their number. But the most successful of these Indian reformers was Herbert Welsh, founder of the Indian Rights Association. This slender young man from one of Philadelphia's most aristocratic families toured the Great Sioux Reservation in 1882 with a friend. As a result of that trip he launched the association, in his own home, with thirty like-minded people. This group, which dedicated itself to the improvement and civilization of all tribes, became the premier fact-finding and lobbying organization among the largely upper-crust Eastern reform groups.

Although Red Cloud may not have been truly cognizant of the intent of this new movement, he remained, notwithstanding Bland's unsuccessful intervention, determined to replace McGillycuddy at Pine Ridge. The election of President Grover Cleveland in 1884 gave him new hope, as Cleveland was from another political party. Armed with optimism, the chief, now sixty-three years old, agitated for a Washington visit in the hope that Cleveland, the first Democrat elected to the presidency since James Buchanan, would be more sympathetic than his predecessors. Characteristically, McGillycuddy refused to fund Red Cloud's Washington trip from agency revenues. But friends from Valentine, Nebraska, a Democratic stronghold, raised enough money so that the old chief could go to Washington and personally lobby this newest Great Father. Red Cloud, who took Todd Randall (one of McGillycuddy's despised "squaw men") with him as his interpreter, also received financial help from Dr. Bland for his Washington trip. Bland, who was much more comfortable on his own Washington turf, was doing battle with Senator Dawes for criticizing him and with former secretary of the interior Teller for giving Indian agent McGillycuddy another four-year term.

On March 18, 1885, Bland took Red Cloud to see Cleveland. The portly new executive, in office for only two weeks, listened intently to Red Cloud's criticisms of McGillycuddy: "Our agent is a bad man. He steals from us, and abuses us, and he has sent all the good white men out of our country and put bad men in their places." But Cleveland and his secretary of the interior, L. Q. C. Lamar, were deliberately cautious about committing themselves to McGillycuddy's removal. Cleveland had campaigned on the issue of civil service reform in the 1884 election and was reluctant to replace a Republican, such as McGillycuddy, with a Democrat unless there was just cause. Lamar, a former Confederate with considerable sympathy for the Indians, had issued Red Cloud white men's clothing, which the patient Oglala leader seemed more than willing to wear in exchange for presidential support. He also invited the aging but still vibrant Red Cloud to attend the swearing-in ceremony of John Atkins, the new commissioner of Indian affairs. In the meantime, while Red Cloud awaited the president's decision on McGillycuddy's tenure, he delighted Bland and his friends with personal appearances which showed that none of his charisma had been lost since his 1870 Washington visit.

Red Cloud's patience was finally rewarded. On April 3, Commissioner Atkins ordered McGillycuddy to come to Washington to respond to Red Cloud's charges. Although the embattled Indian agent brought such loyal progressives as Young-Man-Afraid-of-His-Horses and George Sword with him for support, McGillycuddy encountered an impressive array of talent during a tense hearing held specifically to review Red Cloud's complaints. One of McGillycuddy's adversaries was Judge A. J. Willard, a noted lawyer and political leader from South Carolina. The judge believed, along with Bland, that the Indians could work out their own destiny if left alone. Another opponent of the agent was former commissioner of Indian affairs George W. Manypenny, who had dealt with the

Sioux firmly but honestly during the painful negotiations over the Black Hills nine years before. Although Atkins reprimanded McGillycuddy for calling the proceedings a farce, this high-level hearing could not produce sufficient evidence to allow Cleveland to replace McGillycuddy without appearing to be a partisan spoilsman. Indeed, as the hearing dragged on it became clear that the essence of the dispute was a bitter personal rivalry.

The Cleveland administration, unwilling to take a decisive position on the McGillycuddy affair, decided to gain time by implementing a March 3 congressional appropriation authorizing the Speaker of the House to appoint a committee of five "to investigate the expenditure of appropriations for the Indians." Because the Democrats now controlled the House, this committee, composed of three Democrats and two Republicans, was chaired by Democratic Congressman William S. Holman of Indiana. Although the fledgling committee was perceived throughout the country as an instrument to investigate the Red Cloud–McGillycuddy feud (such was the importance of the Sioux to the reservation system at that time), the Holman committee ended up taking testimony at almost all the Indian reservations in the West.

When the Holman committee started its hearings at Pine Ridge on July 22, McGillycuddy and Red Cloud were both present to give their side of the story. McGillycuddy, insisting that Red Cloud had the allegiance of only a fourth of Pine Ridge's total population, argued fervently that his perennial adversary had always been a hostile obstructionist. Red Cloud, in addition to calling for McGillycuddy's removal, took an especially shrewd tack in his testimony, asking the government for all those things that the increasingly intrusive white assimilationists expected them to have, such as plows, oxen, mowing machines, and all other things that successful agriculturists need.

When the committee submitted its report to Congress on March 16, 1886, after its travels throughout the West, the results, not unexpectedly, reflected deep party divisions, thus depriving the Cleveland administration of the type of mandate it needed to oust McGillycuddy without appearing too partisan. To Red

Cloud's great satisfaction, though, the Democratic majority did urge caution in any plan to break up the Great Sioux Reservation. But the Republicans wanted a quick partition of all reservation lands and then ultimate allotment on an individual basis. Also, the Democrats, in a partisan swipe at McGillycuddy, insisted that a good Indian agent secures the "respect and confidence" of his charges. Republicans, equally partisan, insisted that good Indian agents had to be tough because there were "insubordinate and turbulent" elements found among many tribes. In only one portion of the Holman report was Red Cloud critically dealt with, and this was in the area of educational reform. The willful old warrior was especially vulnerable on this question; he had long opposed the church and government Indian schools springing up throughout the country. Indeed, he generally resisted efforts to have his own children and grandchildren attend these schools.

The Cleveland administration stalled for six weeks after the Holman report before it did anything decisive. Clearly, both sides in this widely publicized feud had their own arguments and their own viewpoints. The sturdy Democratic president with his walrus mustache, however, would in the end be persuaded more by politics than by logic. His party having been out of power for a quarter of a century, Grover Cleveland was grudgingly but assuredly giving way to persistent Democratic office seekers who cast covetous eyes at all available governmental positions, including those in the Indian service. McGillycuddy's job was certainly one of the more alluring prizes of the western spoils system, and western Democrats, along with Bland and his aggressive friends, were demanding McGillycuddy's political scalp. There was also a fear, still prevalent on the shrinking northern frontier, that McGillycuddy could goad Red Cloud into some kind of bloody outbreak. Although Democrats tended to stress this dreaded possibility more than Republicans did, Republican Senator Charles F. Manderson of Nebraska admitted that Red Cloud had the power to "rally every discontented element in the Sioux nation to his standard."

Given the difficulties inherent in McGillycuddy's removal,

President Cleveland, still nurturing his reputation as a civil service reformer, decided against any frontal attack on the temperamental McGillycuddy. Instead he decided to bait the Indian agent and let him hang himself. The effort, which showed a keen understanding of McGillycuddy's prickly nature, began inauspiciously. The Indian Bureau in May 1886 sent Inspector E. D. Bannister to Pine Ridge with instructions, already approved by both Cleveland and Secretary Lamar, that McGillycuddy replace his clerk, Donald Brown. When McGillycuddy indignantly refused, as his superiors anticipated he would, the stubborn agent was replaced by Captain James M. Bell of the Seventh Cavalry. The move was only temporary, however; five months later Indiana Democrat H. D. Gallagher became Cleveland's permanent choice for this top governmental post at Pine Ridge.

Red Cloud could not have been more delighted with this unceremonious end to McGillycuddy's controversial tenure. In a letter to his friend Dr. Bland, reprinted in Bland's *Council Fire*, he insisted that he would not "prove ungrateful to the authorities in Washington" for rescuing him and his people from these "long-continuing acts of persecution and injustice." He even started to sound like an assimilationist, or progressive, telling the people of Chadron, Nebraska, at a Fourth of July parade a month or so after McGillycuddy's removal that while whites and Indians were "traveling two different roads," they should now "become as one nation with but one heart and mind."

Just how sincere Red Cloud's intentions were is difficult to ascertain. The feud had been highly personal; both men had unquestionably contributed to its bitterness. Although McGillycuddy's actions were open and above-board, his disrespectful attitude toward Red Cloud, a man many years his senior, was barely concealed after their initial confrontations. Red Cloud's tactics, on the other hand, were more devious; his approach characteristically consisted of petitions or behind-the-scenes pleadings to the government for McGillycuddy's removal. Indeed, McGillycuddy often raged against his rival for going behind his back in the unceasing campaign to oust him. Historian George E. Hyde saw this approach as so typical of Red Cloud that he described the low-key and circuitous strategy of the Cleveland administration to replace McGillycuddy as "vintage Red Cloud." But McGillycuddy was probably the most uncompromisingly provocative of the two. W. R. Jones, who recalled the feud during a frank interview with Judge Ricker in 1907, characterized McGillycuddy as a man of ability and courage, but one who was "out of his element in those things requiring tact and kindness." In truth, once McGillycuddy got down on a person, he rarely relented.

But the feud was more than just a clash of personalities. Although Red Cloud in his crusade to eliminate McGillycuddy almost lost sight of the overall picture, as he had against Agent Saville a decade earlier, his alarm over McGillycuddy's reforms were not without merit. The hot-headed Indian agent was as anxious to change the Lakota way of life as Senator Dawes and his Mohonk colleagues were. The main difference between McGillycuddy and these other detractors was that McGillycuddy had neither the patience nor temperament to seek an acceptable consensus with the Sioux; he seemed reluctant even to persuade his Sioux charges that things like assimilation and severalty were best for them. Instead, he curried the favor of such Indian allies as Young-Man-Afraid-of-His-Horses and George Sword, who, with the help of his loyal Indian Police, acted as an effective counterpoise to Red Cloud and the older chiefs. McGillycuddy failed in his grand design to dominate affairs at Pine Ridge largely because of Red Cloud's unyielding spirit and the fickle political currents of the time. But now the victorious old chief would have to face a new and very determined Indian reform movement that would not accept token changes among his people. Whether the veteran Lakota leader was really as much of an assimilationist as he sounded in his Fourth of July speech in Chadron remained to be seen.

CHAPTER 9

The Ghost Dance Troubles

THE final months of 1886 were especially satisfying to Red Cloud. He had not enjoyed such power and prestige for years. Not only was the erosion of his authority under McGillycuddy reversed, but there was also a new and much desired unity among the Lakotas at Pine Ridge. Red Cloud even worked out his differences with the agency's progressive leader, Young-Man-Afraid-of-His-Horses. Progress in this reconciliation, however, was slow; McGillycuddy had built a power base for Young-Man-Afraid that Red Cloud's younger rival was reluctant to yield. Nevertheless, on July 26, 1887, after a year of careful negotiations, the two men were able to sit in council together, smoke a peace pipe, and agree to cooperate in their people's difficult transition from the old life to the one now being mandated by the U.S. government. Red Cloud appeared sincere in his efforts to achieve this reconciliation; he told a representative of the commissioner of Indian affairs who was visiting the reservation that he and Young-Man-Afraid-of-His-Horses had agreed to "pull together and hereafter sit side by side in council as brothers."

Federal authorities, too, learned an important lesson from the Red Cloud–McGillycuddy feud: namely, that order could best be maintained at Pine Ridge by working with, rather than against, Red Cloud. This new realization was reflected in the tenures of McGillycuddy's two successors, Captain James M. Bell, the temporary appointee who replaced McGillycuddy, and Hugh D. Gallagher, the man who replaced Bell. Captain Bell, for his part, not only treated all Pine Ridge Lakotas alike, irrespective of their "former cliques and clans" (to quote Red

Cloud), but even successfully catered to their aging chief, who could still be temperamental at times. The tactful army officer, for example, restored all the ration tickets to Red Cloud that the Oglala chief insisted McGillycuddy had stolen from him. Moreover, when Red Cloud wanted to take approximately three hundred of his followers to Wyoming for a visit with the Shoshones, Bell consented with an almost good-natured amiability.

When Gallagher took over as Indian agent on October 1, he, too, showed an admirable sensitivity toward Red Cloud. He also brought to his new position a kind of calm, even-tempered disposition rarely displayed by McGillycuddy. Robert O. Pugh, an issue clerk at Pine Ridge during Gallagher's tenure, called him "one of the best Indian agents in the service," praising Gallagher's honesty in a governmental post that did not always attract the best men. Gallagher really delighted Red Cloud most, however, by permitting the Holy Rosary Mission to be established at Pine Ridge. McGillycuddy, representing governmental policy at the time, had opposed Catholic missionary activity among the Oglalas; his resistance to Father McCarthy in 1879 provided an especially telling statement. Gallagher, on the other hand, was Roman Catholic and felt differently about this issue. Moreover, as a Democrat and a Cleveland appointee, he was not as closely tied to the Protestant establishment as was his Republican predecessor, McGillycuddy. At any rate, when Father Florentine Digmann arrived in August 1888 to head the new mission, Red Cloud, who at some point in his life had been baptized a Catholic, was elated to have the black-clad Jesuits attending to the spiritual and educational needs of his people.

Ironically, many of the policies pursued by Bell and Gallagher were very much like those pursued by McGillycuddy. For example, in 1886 Captain Bell, unquestionably aware of Red Cloud's long-standing opposition to a tribal census, conducted a count of Pine Ridge inhabitants that trimmed the agency's total population from 7,649, the number for McGillycuddy's 1885 census, to only 4,873. Yet, knowing that a reduction of population figures at Pine Ridge could result in a reduction in food rations, Bell took great pains to placate Red Cloud, treating him and his tribesmen with the kind of respect not always accorded them by McGillycuddy.

Gallagher, too, pursued many of McGillycuddy's controversial policies. For example, he cut the beef ration at Pine Ridge to match the reservation's reduced population. But, like Bell's, his approach was tactful enough to avoid any unpleasant disruptions. He was even successful in persuading a group of Red Cloud's people to abandon their village on White Clay Creek, near the agency headquarters, and take up farming in another, less accessible, village; when McGillycuddy had first recommended a move of this nature in 1879, he had one of his first important disagreements with Red Cloud.

Red Cloud responded to this new respect with optimism and good cheer. He wrote George Manypenny on October 7, a week after Bell's tenure ended, that things had improved to such a degree on the reservation that Manypenny would "hear of no more strife and dissatisfaction from Pine Ridge Agency in [the] future."

But nine months after McGillycuddy's removal, a series of setbacks affected Red Cloud's people with results about as fatal as those that followed the Great Sioux War. On February 8, 1887, President Cleveland signed into law the Dawes General Allotment Act. This congressional law, one of the great landmarks in Indian legislation, mandated the allotment of tribal lands. By this measure, each family head would receive 160 acres of reservation land to cultivate, each single male adult 80 acres, and each minor 40 acres. In the case of tribal grazing lands, these amounts could be doubled. Also, title to the allotted lands would be withheld for twenty-five years in order to protect the inexperienced new landowners from covetous whites. Anticipating some Indian resistance, the government could select individual plots of land after four years for those tribal members who failed to make a selection. Such a stipulation was very shrewd, given the continuing opposition of leaders such as Red Cloud to the allotment concept. On a more positive side, U.S. citizenship would be granted to those Indians who took their allotments.

The most potentially divisive provision of the new law was the one authorizing the government to purchase surplus reservation lands and open them for white homesteaders. The execution of this section of the Dawes Act, which could be implemented by the secretary of the interior before or after the allotments were made, would eventually have a devastating effect on Indian landownership; from 1887 to 1934, government-purchased reservation lands not needed for allotment, plus individual land plots sold by Indian owners after the twenty-five-year trust period, reduced the total acreage of Indian holdings from 138 million to 55 million.

The concept of allotment on reservation lands had many supporters throughout the country. Eager western homesteaders and business interests anxious to develop the West, of course, would find any law of this kind appealing. Circumstances in Dakota Territory during the late 1800s provide a prime example of this attitude; any congressional law that would unlock those lands on the Great Sioux Reservation between the Missouri and the Black Hills would be enthusiastically embraced by enterprising Dakotans. Even though severalty bills had been debated in Congress during the 1870s, it was not until the 1880s, when Indian reformers of the Mohonk stripe began their intense lobbying, that conditions were ripe for the passage of a law as sweeping as the Dawes Act. In truth, it was no surprise that Senator Dawes pushed his bill through a more-than-friendly Senate while his allies in the lower house pushed it through that less committed body.

Among the reformers most delighted over this new law were those who believed that the Indian could be made over into the white man's image. Charles C. Painter, Washington lobbyist for Herbert Welsh's Indian Rights Association, for example, likened the Dawes Act to the Magna Charta, the Declaration of Independence, and the Emancipation Proclamation as far as its future impact on the American Indian.

The arduous process of applying this new law to the Great

Sioux Reservation started on April 30, 1888, when Congress passed the controversial Sioux bill. This measure, fundamentally the same one under which the Edmunds commission had operated, called for the division of the Sioux reservation into six smaller ones and allowed all surplus lands to revert to the public domain. There were, however, two important differences between this new bill and that under which the Edmunds commission discharged its business. First, the Sioux bill, instead of having the surplus lands homesteaded outright, specified that they would first be sold for fifty cents an acre, the proceeds going to an Indian trust fund. Second, a provision put in the Sioux bill by Senator Dawes required the president to negotiate for surplus lands according to the procedures of Article 12 of the Fort Laramie Treaty, which required the approval of three-fourths of all adult Lakota males before any land cession could take effect. Senator Dawes's main opposition to the Edmunds commission, it should be recalled, was its disregard for Article 12.

Opponents of the Sioux bill saw the introduction of Article 12 in the ratification fight as their best hope for success. Members of Dr. Thomas A. Bland's National Indian Defence Association, in particular, encouraged the Lakota Sioux to withhold their approval of this measure, which would alienate thousands of acres of Sioux land. Judge Willard, for example, angered Agent Gallagher when he sent Red Cloud a letter urging him to withstand the mounting pressure to partition the Great Sioux Reservation. But Willard really had no need for concern. Red Cloud and most of his Lakotas on the far-flung Sioux reserve clearly saw the dire implications of the Sioux bill.

Cleveland's new secretary of the interior, William F. Vilas, who replaced Lamar in 1888, started the ratification campaign for the Sioux bill by appointing Captain Richard H. Pratt to head the commission that would visit the reservation for that purpose. Pratt was a poor choice. The dogmatic bureaucrat, still acting as superintendent of the well-known Carlisle Indian School, was as determined an Indian assimilationist as Senator Dawes. Unfortunately, he lacked the political skills of the respected Massachusetts legislator. In fact, Pratt's gruff and self-righteous manner was a major liability; he had already alienated Red Cloud when Red Cloud and Spotted Tail visited the Carlisle school in 1880. Consequently, it was probably a wise decision that the first stop on the Pratt commission's travel agenda was Standing Rock, not Pine Ridge. Yet, discouragingly enough for the government, Pratt and his colleagues encountered surprisingly strong resistance at Standing Rock; indeed, after a month of strenuous persuasion, they were only able to acquire twenty-two signatures out of an adult male population of more than a thousand. Equally disappointing results were obtained at Crow Creek and the Lower Brulé Agency. In a state of utter discouragement, Pratt abandoned plans to visit the Pine Ridge, Rosebud, and Cheyenne River agencies and instead sought a desperate conference with Secretary Vilas.

The unhappy Pratt, with Vilas's support, finally decided to put the Sioux bill into effect without the signatures required by the 1868 treaty. His first step in this radical new strategy was taken at the Lower Brulé in a conference for Indian agents and selected chiefs and spokesmen from all six agencies. Significantly, Red Cloud was not there; he was not invited. This omission was a sure sign of the government's great frustration; according to Robert M. Utley, the Sioux had completely stymied the government by unequivocally saying no to all of Pratt's pleas and recommendations. But at this fateful Lower Brulé conference, their united front began to crumble; they began to argue over certain provisions of the new measure, implying to federal authorities that a more liberal law would be acceptable. The biggest mistake the Indian conference made, however, was to suggest that another trip to Washington might yet yield a satisfactory compromise.

Correctly perceiving the Washington trip as a chance to erode Sioux resistance, the government invited sixty-seven Lakotas and Cheyennes and their agents and interpreters to the capital in October. Once again, Red Cloud was excluded. Nor was his new ally Young-Man-Afraid-of-His-Horses invited to come along. Although the omission of these two at the Washington conference was part of Pratt's strategy of going over the heads of major chiefs to reach the rank and file, it was becoming clear that the federal government was rethinking its twenty-year policy of recognizing Red Cloud as his people's chief spokesman. Although this newest Washington delegation did have a few leaders of consequence, such as Little Wound, George Sword, American Horse, and Little Chief of the Cheyennes, most of these new delegates were simply not in the same leadership category as Red Cloud and Young-Man-Afraid.

Even so, if federal authorities and Mohonk reformers thought they could monopolize the time of these less experienced Lakota and Cheyenne delegates, they were in for a disappointment. Eastern opponents of the Sioux bill, including people such as Bland and his supporters, maintained a constant stream of criticism, much to Pratt's frustration. But the Lakotas themselves were also dubious about a bill that could result in the loss of half their reservation land. They complained about the price the government set for their surplus lands. Why should the Sioux receive $0.50 an acre when the government asked $1.25 an acre for its lands? To the embarrassment of their white counterparts they recited the broken promises made in regards to the 1868 treaty and the Black Hills cession. They were especially vocal about the government's lack of action on the much heralded inducements for farming and education. They scolded federal authorities for not surveying reservation lands, a compelling point, given that the Sioux were uncertain which lands would be taken from them as surplus acreage.

Secretary of the Interior Vilas, convinced that the Dawes Act offered "a brighter promise for the adult Indian race" than anything else Washington ever offered, soon lost patience with this barrage of criticism. To salvage the conference, however, he was willing to make some changes, including a hike in the price of surplus Indian lands to a dollar an acre. But ultimately the discouraged interior secretary sent the delegation home to think about the government's newest recommendations to improve the Sioux bill. The mood of the Sioux, however, changed little after their return home. At Pine Ridge, for example, a letter drafted in December by Red Cloud, Young-Man-Afraid, and Little Sword repeated many of the criticisms made at the Washington conference. This defiant message also bemoaned the fact that, while Lakotas now dressed like white people and sent their children to white schools, they were still treated with disdain.

But the authorities in Washington were determined to settle this matter as soon as possible. Dakotans anxious to achieve statehood believed that the Great Sioux Reservation denied them a contiguous state and served as a barrier against their access to the Black Hills. As for the Mohonk reformers, many of them were convinced that if the Sioux did not agree to severalty now, they would be compelled to take something far less agreeable later. Responding to attitudes such as these, the lame duck session of the Fiftieth Congress enacted a new Sioux bill, which President Cleveland signed two days before his term expired on March 2, 1889.

The basic provisions of the new Sioux bill were the same as those of the spurned 1888 one. But some sweeteners were added to make the new law more acceptable. Those who purchased ceded Sioux land would now have to pay $1.25 an acre for the first three years, $0.75 for the next two, and $0.50 thereafter. Moreover, land would be surveyed at government expense, and a $3,000,000 Sioux trust fund would be established. Curiously, even though it was obvious that Washington had become disenchanted with Red Cloud, a special provision was included in the new bill to compensate Red Cloud and Red Leaf and their followers for the horses taken from them in 1876 by Colonel Mackenzie after the Battle of the Little Bighorn.

While this second Sioux bill was being debated by Congress, the highly frustrated Red Cloud wrote the commissioner of Indian affairs for permission to come to Washington to discuss the new piece of legislation. But with the change of administrations in Washington, conditions were even less favorable for Red Cloud. The new Great White Father, Benjamin Harrison, was much more susceptible to the wishes of the Mohonk reformers, including Senator Dawes, who, after all, was one of the strongest leaders from Harrison's own party. Yet nothing could have been more symbolic of the new Washington order than Harrison's choice for commissioner of Indian affairs. Baptist-educated and a Mohonk regular himself, Thomas Jefferson Morgan, the new appointee, was, like Dawes, an assimilationist whose belief in the transformation of the Indian into a yeoman farmer was so strong that he was willing to disassemble tribal government and the whole reservation system to accomplish that purpose. As a consequence, the president's newly installed secretary of the interior, John W. Noble, rejected Red Cloud's request to visit the capital. Although the anxious old warrior left for the East before receiving this negative response, his trip to Washington on this occasion proved of little consequence.

On May 19, eleven weeks after his inauguration, President Harrison announced the names for yet another commission to win Lakota approval for the Sioux bill. Unlike Captain Pratt's commission, this body was comprised of some exceptionally high-powered men. Former Ohio governor Charles Foster headed the three-man board. Missouri Senator William Warner, a former Union general and national commander of the Grand Army of the Republic, was another member. The most important person on the new commission, however, was the recently promoted Major General George Crook. The inclusion of Three Stars Crook, as the Lakotas still called him, created a combination of fear and anxiety on the part of Sioux leaders, who were most anxious to present a united front against this latest version of the disruptive Sioux bill. Although many Lakotas felt that this familiar figure could be trusted, others believed him to be a man who could bring a regiment of cavalry into the picture by a mere nod of the head.

The new commission was well equipped for its tough assignment. It had its own special railroad car, which left Chicago on May 29 for the Great Sioux Reservation. A sum of twenty-five thousand dollars had been appropriated for its mission; in 1889 this was a substantial amount of money, certainly large enough to fund those grand feasts which in the past had made the Sioux amenable to compromise. And, of course, it had the full support of Lake Mohonk's self-designated Friends of the Indian, whose influence had largely overwhelmed the desperate lobbying of Dr. Bland and his associates.

Crook's return to Sioux country after his military campaigns in the Great Sioux War revealed the significant changes that had taken place at Pine Ridge. Even though the government had encouraged its Sioux charges to build the log cabins that dotted the landscape, most families preferred to spend much of their time in tipis erected nearby. Indeed, if the government had hoped to set an example by the two-story frame house it built for Red Cloud in 1879, it had not been very successful with most Oglalas at Pine Ridge. Although Lakotas were more apt to dress like white homesteaders or stock grazers, on special days it was obvious that they preferred their own traditional regalia. Also, the substantial wood or brick missions, schools, and government offices on the reservation were in sharp contrast with most of the Indian dwellings. But one thing had not changed: the often fractious clans or bands, which were divided even more by the clash of progressive and nonprogressive viewpoints, were still present. And Crook understood better than his fellow commission members how to exploit these divisions.

The commission's first stop was at the Rosebud Agency. There Crook implemented Pratt's failed strategy of going over the heads of the leading chiefs to reach a tribal consensus. The savvy general worked on all the diverse Rosebud factions, who sorely missed Spotted Tail's forceful leadership. One particularly susceptible group was made up of mixed-bloods and white men married to Indian women. As late as 1882, full-blooded Sioux still had not accepted these people as social equals. Yet this group, which overwhelmingly favored the Sioux bill, proved more than willing to add its numbers to meet the ratification requirement of three-fourths of the adult males. Eventually Crook and his associates won the support of most full-bloods by implying, in the friendly, low-keyed manner used by all three commissioners, that those who resisted would miss out on all the advantages of those who did not.

The commission employed a similar strategy at the other agencies, enjoying unusual success at all of them but Pine Ridge. In fact, although 4,482 signatures were acquired out of a total of 5,678 adult males on all the agencies collectively (225 signatures more than the required three-fourths), the commissioners could win only the approval of 684 of the 1,306 eligible adult males at Pine Ridge. What made the Pine Ridge results so different was the resistance of Red Cloud, Young-Man-Afraid, and Little Wound to the blandishments of Crook and the other commissioners. The aging Red Cloud, nearly blind by this time, even turned his tribe's presentation against the Sioux bill over to the younger, more energetic American Horse. This remarkably articulate chief spoke almost continuously on the Sioux bill and on related and unrelated topics for more than two days. Although the opportunistic American Horse was one of the few prominent Oglalas eventually to agree to the controversial land provisions of the Sioux bill, discipline was maintained among almost half of the Pine Ridge Sioux because of the steely determination of Red Cloud and his allies.

The commission ultimately accomplished its purpose through the use of questionable but timeworn strategies. On the day the commission arrived at Rosebud, for example, it dipped into its substantial war chest to pay for fifteen beeves to feast the suspicious Sioux, who had never lost their taste for meat. To some, the commission's methods were out of character for General Crook, whom Red Cloud had grown to trust. "He, at least, had never lied to us," the old chief observed when Crook died less than a year later. Yet the general admitted in his autobiography that he had unsuccessfully offered two hundred dollars each to Red Cloud, Young-Man-Afraid-of-His-Horses, and Little Wound so they could feast their bands as a reward for supporting the Sioux bill.

Unfortunately, the government proved most ungracious toward Red Cloud, despite its widely heralded triumph. The sixty-eight-year-old veteran, who stood up to Crook and orchestrated the campaign that stalled the commissioners at Pine

Ridge much longer than anticipated, was not to be forgiven. Secretary of the Interior Noble wrote Acting Commissioner of Indian Affairs R. V. Belt on July 1, after the Crook party had left Pine Ridge, that he wanted American Horse rather than Red Cloud to be the "Chief of the Sioux, or the one favored by the government." He asked Belt if any written authority existed whereby the "obstructionist" Red Cloud should continue to be recognized as the voice of the Sioux people. Belt replied that no such paper existed in his office file, although Red Cloud's name was included among those chiefs and headmen who signed the 1868 Fort Laramie Treaty and the 1876 Black Hills agreement. Belt also prepared three drafts of a letter to Agent Gallagher, directing him to recognize American Horse as the true chief of the Oglalas, but Inspector W. J. Pollack of the Indian Bureau, a longtime supporter of Red Cloud, dissuaded him from this project. Nevertheless, when the Lakotas were called to Washington in December 1889 for a final conference on the Sioux land agreement, American Horse, rather than Red Cloud, headed Pine Ridge's delegation.

The banishment of Red Cloud from decision-making circles at this time was a serious mistake. If ever a man of his talents and experience was needed, it was now. Even though the Lakotas had reluctantly agreed to the Sioux bill, an overwhelming majority of them opposed the controversial allotment section, which, after all, entailed the loss of about half their reservation land. But at Pine Ridge, Red Cloud, Young-Man-Afraid, and Little Wound had largely thwarted the Sioux commission, or the Crook commission, as it was sometimes called. Consequently, many frustrated Lakotas turned approvingly to leaders such as Red Cloud, who had earned their trust, rather than to leaders such as American Horse, who had betrayed it. But now the amazingly resilient Red Cloud was being ostracized at a time his presence was most required.

In many ways, circumstances in 1889 seemed to be conspiring against improved relations between the Sioux and the U.S. government. One concern that dogged the Crook commission during its negotiations was the fear of many Sioux that land losses would be accompanied by ration reductions. For years Lakotas on the reservation had inflated their population figures to avoid ration cuts. They had justified this deception on the basis that weight shrinkage for their beeves was 30 percent between the government's delivery and the animals' slaughter, a development that was decidedly to their disadvantage. As this disparity had long been a sore point, nonprogressives on the Great Sioux Reservation, who honestly believed that any land loss could justify a governmental cut in the beef ration, took special note of a federal census that had been initiated at Rosebud even before the arrival of the Crook commission.

Predictably, the dire consequences forecast as a result of that census count were not long in coming. In fact, two weeks after the Crook commission left Rosebud, a government order reduced the beef issue at Rosebud by two million pounds and at Pine Ridge by one million; proportional beef reductions were also made at the other agencies. Also, about the same time, Congress, in an economizing mood, used the same Indian Appropriations Act that had created the Crook commission to cut the Sioux's subsistence appropriation for fiscal year 1890 to nine hundred thousand dollars. This reduced appropriation, one hundred thousand dollars less than that of the two previous years, was widely interpreted as a serious threat by the Sioux, who had seen government rations steadily decline since 1886. Commissioner of Indian Affairs Morgan, in response to these disturbing developments, felt he had no alternative but to cut the food rations of an already unhappy people.

Crook and the other commissioners were as chagrined by this cut as those tribal progressives who had supported the Sioux bill; Foster, the commission's chairman, sent a sharply worded note of protest to Morgan. Ironically, the commissioners had not lied to the Indians. The land agreement in the Sioux bill had nothing to do with their beef rations. Tragically, the timing of the cuts could not have been worse; the Sioux, who already felt they had been tricked into signing a dubious agreement, now felt worse than ever. American Horse, who along with No Flesh ultimately broke with Red Cloud over the Sioux bill, was especially embarrassed: "The Commission made us believe that we could get full sacks if we signed the bill, but instead our sacks are empty."

The Crook commission vainly tried to remedy this embarrassing situation during the Sioux's December visit to Washington. There, the Indian delegates, who always enjoyed the bustle and excitement of Washington, were treated to a brief visit with Benjamin Harrison, the remote little president who had been their Great Father for ten months. What really cheered the delegates the most, however, was the commission's report to Secretary of the Interior Noble. In it were some minor recommendations that Secretary Noble could act upon at his own discretion, such as Indian employment on the reservation, equality of mixed-bloods with full-bloods, and an end to the ban against those traditional dances the government considered "innocent." More important were the commission's recommendations to Congress, which called for the restoration of one hundred thousand dollars for the beef ration, increased educational appropriations, and prompt availability of interest on the newly created three-million-dollar Sioux trust fund. Although Congress looked with favor on the set of recommendations for the interior secretary, it balked at those directed toward itself; the more friendly Senate approved this second set of reforms in April of the following year only to have the House eventually reject them.

But the most disruptive development occurred two months after the Sioux's Washington visit, when President Harrison announced that, because three-fourths of their adult males had approved of the land agreement, he would now open the reservation's surplus lands to white homesteaders. Under his February 10 proclamation, these ceded lands would be available to outside settlement immediately, even though the survey that had been promised to ascertain the boundaries of the six now separate reservations had not been made. Moreover, no provision had been included for those Indians living on surplus lands to take an allotment elsewhere. It was a no-win situation for the Sioux. Either their newly ceded lands would be flooded by eager white settlers (as occurred when aggressive town boosters promptly staked out claims on freshly opened Lower Brulé lands) or they would lose substantial revenue if settlement on these surplus lands was sluggish, the $1.25 per acre price only remaining in effect for three years. Ironically, because of drought conditions developing in the Dakotas at the time, the disposition of these newly ceded lands was lethargic.

The unhappy Lakotas did not even benefit from Harrison's submission of the Crook commission's report to Congress, along with a proposed bill incorporating its recommendations, because of the unfortunate indifference of the House. This body not only obstructed the president's wish to placate the Sioux but also further complicated Indian relations by delaying the regular Indian Appropriations Act until mid-August of 1890, thus slowing the arrival of clothing and other needed annuity goods until well into the winter. Also, this same appropriation measure only earmarked $950,000 for the subsistence of the Sioux, including some widely publicized efforts to civilize them. Indeed, the amount was still $50,000 short of the figure necessary to restore their old allowance.

Many Sioux were outraged. One disgruntled Indian told Reverend William J. Cleveland, a member of the old Pratt commission who was most familiar with reservation conditions, that the government's word was worth very little: "They made us many promises, more than I can remember, but they never kept but one; they promised to take our land and they took it."

But conditions other than Washington's controversial policies were also creating despair among the Sioux. In the late 1880s and early 1890s the weather itself seemed to be conspiring against the Lakotas. A series of devastating droughts that scorched the Great Plains plagued not only the Sioux but white settlers as well, driving many of them into angry agrarian protest movements. But the serious crop damage caused by the weather was complicated by other problems. Many of the Sioux, who reluctantly returned to their wretched little farms after time-consuming meetings with the Crook commission, claimed that during their absence cattle had been killed, chickens stolen, and crops damaged or eaten. Commissioner of Indian Affairs Morgan tended to blame mismanagement for the state of Indian agriculture in 1889, although he admitted that some of the neglect might have been a result of the time spent with the Crook commission. The virulent cattle disease blackleg, which tended to kill young animals, had also appeared. The real coup de grace to the welfare of the Sioux, however, was the searing summer drought of 1890. Add these adversities to the cuts in government rations going back to the mid-1880s, and the result is a truly desperate situation, one compounded by reduced appropriations, which were significantly less than what they had been.

The upshot of all these depressing circumstances was hunger, perhaps even starvation, at Pine Ridge and the other reservations partitioned from the Great Sioux Reservation. Even Morgan, still comfortable with his Mohonk certitudes, admitted that the government's ration reductions came at a bad time; nevertheless, he insisted that the cuts had not reduced the Lakotas to starvation. Bishop Hare, on the other hand, forcefully asserted that the Sioux died when taken ill "not so much from disease as from want of food." Whether lack of food or disease was the chief culprit for this high fatality rate, the epidemics of influenza, measles, and whooping cough sweeping the forlorn collection of new Sioux reservations were taking their toll; at Pine Ridge alone, according to George Sword, the death rate for the 5,550 residents ranged from 25 to 45 a month; tragically, most of these victims were children.

It was during this low point in Sioux life that an unusual piece of news, which gave them their first real feelings of hope in many years, reached the stricken Lakotas. The source of the new optimism was a Paiute shaman from western Nevada, named Wovoka, who claimed to be a new Indian messiah. His revelations of a better future soon spread across the western plains like an insatiable wildfire. Wovoka, whom some Indian faithful declared bore nail prints on his hands and a spear wound on his side, claimed that, while stricken with fever during an eclipse of the sun in 1881, he was taken to the afterworld to visit the Supreme Being. There he saw all those who had died years ago, enjoying their traditional way of life. And there he was told to return to earth and tell all Indians to love one another, live at peace with whites, and work unstintingly for a rebirth of their once glorious world.

A slow, shuffling dance, which involved both men and women, constituted the essence of the hard work necessary for this rebirth. Because this dance, and the mournful songs that accompanied it, would reunite all Indians with their dead ancestors, it was called the Ghost Dance by suspicious whites. Even more alarming to the nervous settlers living near the six new Lakota reservations was the belief that this dance, continually performed in Wovoka's fashion, would result in the disappearance of all whites and the restoration of the buffalo herds; in short, the Ghost Dance would bring back Red Cloud's free and cherished life of the past.

Reports regarding this new faith came from a variety of sources. As Wovoka's revelations spread eastward from Nevada, they probably reached other Plains and mountain tribes before the Sioux were exposed. In September 1889, for example, Father Aemilius Perrig, a missionary from Rosebud, heard that Jesus had appeared, crowned with thorns, to an Arapaho hunting party located west of the Sioux. A month later, one of Father Perrig's students claimed that God had appeared to the Utes in the Rocky Mountains, warning them to beware of the corrupting influence of whites or risk extinction. Historian James C. Olson has speculated that the Sioux heard about the new Indian messiah from the Shoshones in Wyoming, who were once mortal enemies until Red Cloud reconciled with them during the 1880s.

There is almost as much confusion over when the Sioux heard about Wovoka as how. Elaine Goodale, the supervisor of education in the Dakotas, inserted in her diary, as early as July 1889, the testimony of an Indian who claimed that Christ had appeared to the Crows, announcing himself as the same Savior who came to earth before only to be killed by whites.

It was only a matter of time before the Sioux, desperate and miserable, would want to investigate these rumors. In the fall of 1889, Good Thunder, Brave Bear, and approximately four other inquisitive Lakotas left Pine Ridge for the Far West to see if the tales of an Indian messiah were true. Although they did not see Wovoka himself, they did confirm all the rumors about his existence. Indeed, it was obvious to them that Wovoka was the Son of God, whose return this time was for the benefit of Indians. In the spring, a larger Sioux delegation, representing the Pine Ridge, Rosebud, and Cheyenne River reservations, was organized. Sanctioned by important Lakota leaders, this delegation included Good Thunder, Kicking Bear, and Short Bull, all of whom became ardent disciples of Wovoka after visiting him in Nevada. Upon their return, Good Thunder preached the new religion at Pine Ridge, and Short Bull preached it at Rosebud. Kicking Bear enjoyed only limited success in his efforts to win converts at Cheyenne River but later went to Standing Rock at Sitting Bull's invitation and did very well until Agent McLaughlin expelled him.

The most conspicuous mark of the new religion, which ultimately resulted in the conversion of about a third of the Lakotas, was the somber Ghost Dance. Although under Wovoka's Paiutes it was a circle dance in which men and women moved slowly to the left, the Sioux changed it to harmonize with their own culture. Remembering their beloved sun dance, they put a sacred tree or pole in the center and danced around it with such persistence that many of them dropped from exhaustion. Being a more militaristic people, the Lakota Sioux also gave the Ghost Dance a certain twist never endorsed by the pacifistic Wovoka. They claimed that the shirts designated for the Ghost Dancers were bulletproof, making those who believed in the new faith invincible to white attacks. Thus, by the late summer of 1890, during the worst of the widespread drought, many Lakotas, dressed in special costumes featuring representations of animals and heavenly bodies, could be heard by apprehensive settlers feverishly dancing and singing. Although some Sioux leaders such as Red Cloud were skeptical, most Ghost Dance participants were deeply touched by Wovoka's revelations. They had visions of dead ancestors back on earth once again in pursuit of the buffalo. Moreover, their hopes were mounting that the whites, who had radically changed their lives, would disappear forever, as Wovoka had promised.

In the Dakotas, many whites who lived near the now downscaled Sioux reservations were alarmed over the Ghost Dance's growing popularity. The Christian elements of this new faith were particularly confusing to them. Although they should have known that with women participants the new dance could not have been a war dance, many actually feared it could lead to war. The Sioux themselves were divided over the significance of their new religion. The Ghost Dance was much more popular in the southern part of what was once the Great Sioux Reservation than in the northern part. The largest number of Ghost Dancers ever to have gathered, as a matter of fact, was at Red Cloud's Pine Ridge, where a great ceremony occurred at the Stronghold, a triangular plateau in the Badlands of the agency's northwest corner, a surprisingly secure natural fortress. Perhaps thirty-five hundred believers gathered there during the climax of the religious fervor. Curiously, most of them were Brulés from Rosebud, although a respectable number of Oglalas from Pine Ridge were also present.

Lakota leaders were as divided as their people over this new faith. Although many were skeptical, a number were hesitant to distance themselves too much from the movement in case Wovoka's revelations were true. Nonprogressives tended to believe in the new faith, while progressives tended to doubt it and even oppose it. At Pine Ridge, American Horse and Young-Man-Afraid-of-His-Horses remained unconvinced, but Little Wound, whose views had recently become more progressive, was unwilling to take a chance. "My friends," he told his followers, "if this is a good thing we shall have it; if it is not it will fall to the earth itself. So you better learn this dance, so if the Messiah does come he will not pass us by but will help us get back our hunting grounds and buffalo."

The Ghost Dance created a special dilemma for Red Cloud. Although schooled in the old beliefs, an active sun dance participant as late as the 1880s, notwithstanding his age, he had, more than anyone else, been responsible for the presence of Catholic clergymen at Pine Ridge. He had always been close to the church, according to Father Placidus Sialm, who served at the Holy Rosary Mission during the early years of this century. The priest was convinced that Red Cloud was never involved in the Ghost Dance movement; indeed, the old chief pitied those Lakotas who had fallen "into such depths of savagery and deviltry." Yet there is strong evidence that Red Cloud never really abandoned the old ways. Dr. James R. Walker, agency physician at Pine Ridge and a critic of Red Cloud, recorded a speech Red Cloud made several years after the Ghost Dance troubles in which he admitted that those who believed in traditional ways "lived happy and . . . died satisfied." Despite his genuine devotion to Catholicism, he yearned to be with his forefathers when he left this earth: "If this is not in the heaven of the white man, I shall be satisfied."

Moreover, the Ghost Dance was not inconsistent with many Sioux beliefs. Anthropologist Raymond J. DeMallie has refused to regard the Ghost Dance as a wholly alien faith. In fact, there were definite points of harmony between the new faith of Wovoka and that of the Sioux. A group of holy men at Pine Ridge once revealed to Dr. Walker that the Sioux had long believed that both mankind and the buffalo originated inside the earth before emerging on the surface. Consequently, whenever bison became scarce, it was because they had retreated back inside the earth, probably in response to some serious provocation by whites or Indians. The Sioux prophet Black Elk told of a holy man living during the mid-nineteenth century who prophesied years before that the "four-leggeds were going back into the earth." The power of this belief, of course, is that the buffalo really could return, making Wovoka's promise of a new abundance of game "completely consistent with the old Lakota system of cause and effect by which they comprehended ecology."

It would be difficult to argue that Red Cloud was unaffected by these new influences generated by Wovoka. In truth, for years his psyche had been a battleground for both the old and new beliefs vying for supremacy among the Sioux. Also, as the Sioux's most important spokesman until the late 1880s, he was painfully aware of the suffering of his people from crop failure, drought, disease, federal duplicity, and the humiliation that accompanied the loss of half their reservation. He believed that it was the abject despair of the Sioux that made the Ghost Dance so irresistible. In his opinion, many Lakotas did not know nor did they care whether Wovoka was the Son of God: "They snatched at the hope. They screamed like crazy men to Him for mercy."

Red Cloud reconciled his dilemma over how the Sioux should respond to this new messiah in much the same way that he dealt with the ramifications of the Great Sioux War. Secretly hoping for its success, he permitted his son, Jack, to be a leader in the Ghost Dance movement just as he permitted Jack to fight in the Battle of the Little Bighorn. The often paranoid Daniel F. Royer, who replaced Gallagher as the agent at Pine Ridge on October 1, 1890, reluctantly admitted in late November that Red Cloud had given him "no trouble of any character." Yet his earlier assessment of Red Cloud is probably more accurate: "While Red Cloud is not a prominent man in the dance, he is quietly encouraging his people to keep it going."

Indeed the Lakotas (especially those from Pine Ridge and Rosebud) kept the dance going and going until white settlers living on the fringes of the six new Sioux reservations became truly alarmed. As early as May 29, 1890, the citizens of Pierre, South Dakota, wrote perhaps the first letter of concern to the Department of the Interior. In truth, this community, capital of the new state of South Dakota, probably had good reasons to fear the disenchanted Lakota dancers, with their allegedly impenetrable Ghost Shirts, who wanted to hasten, through somber steps and mournful chants, the transformation to Wovoka's world without whites.

But Pine Ridge's self-confident agent, Hugh Gallagher, was not concerned, at least at first. He told Commissioner of Indian Affairs Morgan on June 10 that the excitement caused by the messiah craze would soon die down, "possibly to be supplanted by something equally as silly." By mid-July, however, he finally began to show concern. And by late August, while breaking up a ceremony with some two thousand dancers on White Clay Creek near Red Cloud's home, he and twenty reservation policemen were faced by a group of armed young Lakotas ready for a fight. The catastrophe was only avoided by the timely arrival of the still influential Young-Man-Afraid.

Unfortunately, Gallagher's replacement was not as calm and deliberate. Agent Royer, the new man, was a druggist and local politician from Alpena, a small town in recently admitted South Dakota. He was one of the beneficiaries of the country's indestructible spoils system, revitalized during the early months of the Harrison administration. The Mohonk movement was able to put one of its own in the Indian commissioner's office in the person of Thomas J. Morgan, but most of the lesser offices in government were again subject to the time-honored practice of political patronage. Under President Harrison's "Home Rule," Pine Ridge soon became known as "Pettigrew's Place," a recognition that the former delegate from Dakota Territory, now senator from South Dakota, Richard F. Pettigrew, would have the final say on who occupied such offices as Indian agent at Pine Ridge.

Royer, a nervous middle-aged man who was easily rattled, had only one qualification: he had worked in the South Dakota legislature to get Pettigrew elected as one of the new state's two U.S. senators. Pettigrew's choice was catastrophic. Former Pine Ridge agent Dr. Valentine McGillycuddy, himself a Republican and no friend of Gallagher, claimed that Royer's selection was "solely as a reward for political services." Robert Pugh, another Pine Ridge employee, referred to Royer and his chief clerk, Bishop J. Gleason, another product of Pettigrew's patronage, as two "broken-down politicians" and "political adventurers in search of a fortune," an assessment not far removed from McGillycuddy's.

The weeks following Royer's arrival at Pine Ridge saw conditions go from bad to worse. Throughout the reservation, Indians left their humble little cabins to set up tipis in the agency's scattered cottonwood groves, where they could dance and chant for days. Serious agricultural activity was curtailed even though many Lakotas were sick and hungry. The excitable Royer's efforts to deal with this worsening situation were totally ineffective. Repeatedly he warned the dancers to stop and return to their cabins, but he was not only ignored but also defied in the most provocative ways. Some of the Sioux called him Young-Man-Afraid-of-Indians, a nickname that admittedly took a few years off his age but one that again demonstrated how apt the Sioux were in coining appropriate names.

All of Royer's efforts seemed to encounter opposition. On November 8 he called a council of prominent chiefs to persuade them to give up the Ghost Dance. Their response brought yet another humiliation for the shaken agent, who was almost in a state of panic; the chiefs only laughed at him and refused to cooperate. Although Royer, in reporting this incident, did not name the defiant Oglala leaders except for Little Wound, "the most stubborn, head-strong, self-willed, unruly Indian on the Reservation," his omission of Red Cloud's name was very significant. For years almost all government reports on conferences with the Sioux, particularly with the Oglalas, had Red Cloud's name at the top. Now this well-known name was gone from much of the official correspondence; obviously Secretary of the Interior Noble's policy to ostracize this perennial Sioux leader was being implemented, notwithstanding the self-defeating nature of its effect.

Sometimes Royer's opponents skated perilously close to violence. On November 12, four days after Royer's unsuccessful meeting with the council, an Indian resisted arrest by brandishing a butcher knife, an incident made especially dangerous by the presence and support of two hundred armed Ghost Dancers. Royer told the government on this occasion, as he had on previous ones, that conditions at the agency were dangerous and that he and his employees needed immediate protection. The "Indians are dancing in the snow and are wild and crazy. . . . Why delay by further investigation, we need protection."

The entire country was soon aware of the unrest at Pine

Ridge, Rosebud, and the other Sioux reservations. In fact, nowhere else in the West was the Ghost Dance performed in such an aggressive manner and interpreted with such dire consequences for the future. Army observers were finally sent to see if Royer's troubled assessments were as serious as he claimed. Newspaper reporters and photographers eventually arrived, sensing the potential for a great news story. On November 13, 1890, President Harrison was convinced that army troops were needed, and a week later, to the dismay of Red Cloud and other Sioux leaders, Brigadier General John R. Brooke, commander of the Department of the Platte, arrived at Pine Ridge with five companies of infantry and three troops of cavalry. To augment this formidable presence, Brooke brought along one Hotchkiss gun and one Gatling gun. Troops were also sent to Rosebud, there to be scattered throughout that troubled reservation. And soldiers from the Nebraska National Guard were sent to guard the state's border with the Pine Ridge Agency.

The man eventually given overall command of these new forces was Major General Nelson A. Miles, whose high rank indicated the importance Harrison had placed on the crisis. In some ways the fearsome Bear Coat, as he was still called, was the best choice for this command, Crook having died of a heart attack eight months earlier. Miles showed some real understanding of the Sioux plight, expressing it in a December 19 telegram to the commander of the army, Major General John A. Schofield, and to the nation's most prominent Indian reformer, Senator Dawes:

> The difficult Indian problem cannot be solved permanently at this end of the line. It requires the fulfillment by Congress of the treaty obligations which the Indians were entreated and coerced into signing. They signed away a valuable portion of their reservation. . . . They understood that ample provision would be made for their support; instead their supplies have been reduced and much of the time they have been living on half or two-thirds rations.

On the other hand, this sometimes imperious general, who had a passion for self-advancement, could be a poor team player: his contempt for most civilian employees at the six scattered Lakota reservations was barely concealed. Moreover, he was hampered by a serious misconception: he was convinced that Red Cloud was one of "the principal incendiaries."

The arrival of federal troops at the Pine Ridge and Rosebud reservations tended to unite the Ghost Dancers instead of cow them. Soon even those Lakotas who were dubious about the new messianic movement, those often characterized as "friendlies," began to gather in confusion at the Pine Ridge Reservation near Red Cloud's home, while Wovoka's staunch believers retreated into the Badlands of Pine Ridge's northwestern corner with Kicking Bear and Short Bull, two of the most prominent Sioux emissaries who had visited Wovoka in his grass hut in distant Nevada. There, significantly bolstered by some unusually militant Brulés from Rosebud, they continued their persistent dances in the so-called Stronghold.

Toward the end of this increasingly turbulent year, Red Cloud had a change of heart regarding the Ghost Dance. Perhaps the Sioux's greatest realist, especially when it came to the welfare of his people, Red Cloud was becoming truly alarmed at the prospect of a bloody conflict resulting from this divisive religious craze. He wrote a poignant letter to the editor of the *Chadron Democrat* in nearby Nebraska on November 20, 1890. His concern seemed genuine: "I hear that the soldiers at Fort Robinson are coming here tomorrow. I tell you because I do not want to have trouble with the soldiers and other good white people that are near me." Deprived of the comfortable contacts he once enjoyed with federal authorities, he urged the editor not only to publish his letter for the people of Chadron but to write Washington as well: "If you can I want you to write the great father at Washington."

Because Red Cloud had been for years an unusually sensitive barometer in Indian-white relations, his depth of concern should have been important to both sides. Unfortunately, the people of Chadron had become exceptionally hostile and suspicious. Five days after Red Cloud's letter was published in the

Chadron Democrat, the citizens of the town, including Judge
Eli S. Ricker, who many years later interviewed both Lakotas
and whites involved in this conflict, passed an angry resolution
directed at Secretary of War Redfield Proctor. In it they condemned those Lakotas, "armed to the teeth," who were allowed
to remain undisturbed in the center of the "sparsely settled"
and vulnerable region around Chadron. They demanded that
these "savages" be subject to the same punishment reserved for
"traitors, anarchists and assassins." All Ghost Dancers should
be disarmed, they insisted, and their horses should be replaced
with oxen so they could once again plow instead of make trouble. Their call to disarm and dismount the restless Lakotas was
reminiscent of the outcry following the Battle of the Little
Bighorn. In fact, the policy of disarming alleged Sioux troublemakers would eventually result in the tragic battle on Pine
Ridge's Wounded Knee Creek.

Red Cloud, keenly aware of the nasty turn in the attitude of
his white neighbors, began actively to discourage participation
in the Ghost Dance. In early December, he persuaded Jack to
end his association with this controversial messianic movement,
but by that time the religious fervor had reached its high-
water mark. Brigadier General L. W. Colby of the Nebraska
National Guard described the excitement at Pine Ridge with
these alarming words: "Great lights and signal fires shone from
the bluffs and hilltops a few miles distant from Pine Ridge,
and the Bad Lands were ablaze with lights that could be seen
for miles." A kind of madness gripped the reservation. On
December 22, for example, a white man garbed in Indian clothes
came to Red Cloud's people, claiming to be the true messiah.
He asked for permission to visit the Badlands in order to spread
the word, but Red Cloud, whose patience with messiahs had
reached the saturation point, would have nothing to do with
this new one, a rural Iowan with millennial delusions. The old
chief contemptuously spat in his face: "You go home. You are
no Son of God."

Although Red Cloud had been persona non grata with civilian
government officials for eighteen months, some military officers

were aware of the prestige that this aging *itancan* for the Bad Faces still enjoyed among many Lakotas. General Brooke, who was one of them, did not want to waste the old chief's persuasive talents in his quest for peace. He asked Red Cloud to join him in a peace mission to the northern part of the reservation to deal with the die-hard followers of Short Bull, Kicking Bear, and Two Strike. The general was deadly serious; he was even prepared to give the Ghost Dancers food and safety in return for an end to their tumult. Red Cloud refused to go, although he did offer the services of his son. While some interpreted this rebuff as just another sign of Red Cloud's duplicity, it was probably the result of his diminishing physical vigor. The old chief, nearly seventy, bore little resemblance to the great warrior he once was. To many, little of the majesty was left in this now shrunken little man who was often seen wearing sunglasses to protect his failing eyes. The general, who nevertheless undertook his mission, almost succeeded in its accomplishment; Two Strike and forty followers agreed to come in, and according to General Colby, the Ghost Dancers who followed Short Bull and Kicking Bear actually returned to the old agency headquarters before a bitter quarrel ensued which drove them even further into the Badlands.

Curiously, when the conflict finally erupted, it occurred among northern Lakotas, where Ghost Dance activity had been far less popular. Moreover, the much anticipated violence was triggered by two botched arrests, not by any bloody repercussion from the controversial Ghost Dance. The first incident involved Sitting Bull, who, for political or religious reasons, was edging toward the new faith; his ominous vow to visit Pine Ridge and learn more about the Ghost Dance caused great consternation at Standing Rock Reservation. The ultimate decision to arrest this proud and stubborn Hunkpapa medicine man attracted widespread attention in the East, where Sitting Bull had displaced Red Cloud in fame and name recognition because of his role in the Battle of the Little Bighorn. James McLaughlin, the agent at Standing Rock since 1881, probably felt more hostility toward Sitting Bull than McGillycuddy felt toward Red Cloud. General Miles also wanted to arrest and remove Sitting Bull from the scene until the trouble had subsided. The vengeful McLaughlin, however, in collusion with the commander of Fort Yates, the military outpost near Standing Rock Agency, was able to undercut Miles's plan to use Sitting Bull's friend from the Wild West shows, "Buffalo Bill" Cody, to make a friendly arrest. Instead, McLaughlin at dawn on December 15 sent forty-three Indian policemen to arrest Sitting Bull at his cabin on the Grand River some thirty miles from the Standing Rock Agency. This preemptive move resulted in the kind of violence that could only worsen the situation with the restless Sioux: Sitting Bull and seven of his followers were tragically killed, while four policemen were left dead and three were seriously wounded.

The second of the two disastrous arrests involved a Miniconjou chief named Big Foot who lived on the Cheyenne River ten miles below its forks near the Cheyenne River Reservation in upper South Dakota. Big Foot was one of those unfortunate Sioux who was left outside Lakota territory when the Great Sioux Reservation was partitioned. Curiously, though, it was not this uncomfortable fact that put his name near the top of General Miles's list of troublemakers. It was Big Foot's warm identification with Wovoka's religion, a circumstance that took on new meaning when Hunkpapa refugees, fleeing Standing Rock after Sitting Bull's death, joined Big Foot and his Miniconjous in the slow and mournful chants of the Ghost Dance.

Although Big Foot was a nonprogressive like Sitting Bull, he was never a noted warrior or hardliner; in fact, about the same time Sitting Bull's Hunkpapas started arriving at Big Foot's camp on the Cheyenne River, the Indian leader was disassociating himself from the Ghost Dance. Lieutenant Colonel Edwin V. Sumner, an experienced campaigner now stationed in the Dakotas, was keenly aware that General Miles wanted Big Foot arrested, although the general had not yet issued direct orders for that purpose. But Sumner also knew of Big Foot's change of heart. Indeed, because of his trust in Big Foot's sincerity, Sumner allowed the Miniconjou leader to give him the slip and head southward.

Red Cloud and such peacemakers at Pine Ridge as Young-Man-Afraid, Big Road, No Water, and Calico were also aware of Big Foot's new attitude. In fact, they had urged Big Foot to come to Pine Ridge and help them end the trouble there, promising him and his followers one hundred horses in return for their assistance. Consequently, when Big Foot left his home on the south bank of the Cheyenne River at Red Cloud's behest, it was not to join "troublemakers" at the Stronghold but to join "friendlies" at the Pine Ridge Agency. Ironically, despite Red Cloud's exclusion by civilian authorities from any activity in behalf of peace, the invitation extended to Big Foot by Red Cloud and the other Pine Ridge chiefs would affect the entire Ghost Dance crisis. In fact, it would be a major factor in the events leading up to the tragedy at Wounded Knee.

Word of Big Foot's disappearance triggered a massive search on the frozen Dakota plains by troops prodded into action by an angry General Miles. Their frustrating lack of results, however, was not necessarily because of military ineptitude but because the army, convinced that Big Foot and his people were heading for the Stronghold and not for the agency, was conducting its search too far to the west. As a consequence, it was not until December 28 that a squadron of the Seventh Cavalry finally located Big Foot's bedraggled band near Porcupine Butte, north of Pine Ridge.

Shortly after this fateful encounter, a tired Big Foot, ill with pneumonia and carrying a white flag, met with the squadron's commander, Major Samuel M. Whiteside. At that meeting Big Foot readily agreed to move his people to a camp the army had prepared for him at Wounded Knee Creek, about twenty miles east of the agency. As a result, when dawn rose the next day, Big Foot's people, numbering approximately 350, were peacefully huddled in some one hundred tipis arranged as a crescent near Wounded Knee Creek. They were surrounded by troopers whose numbers were swelled to five hundred by the arrival the previous night of Colonel James W. Forsyth and the remainder of the Seventh Cavalry.

To an outside observer this forlorn encampment should have been guarantee enough that Big Foot and his people were not on the warpath. But Forsyth had orders to disarm them, always a risky enterprise. In fact, the slow progress of Forsyth's search for guns fueled the kind of tensions that often overcome logical behavior. Moreover, there were other dangerous irritants present that day. An obsessed medicine man named Yellow Bird pranced around, urging the most disgruntled warriors in camp to resist. Tense soldiers, nervously fingering their triggers, looked on with concern. One member of Big Foot's party, a deaf and unbalanced young man named Black Coyote, refused to surrender his rifle without being compensated for it. When two soldiers tried to wrestle the weapon from him, it went off accidentally. Simultaneous with this discharge, Yellow Bird tossed dirt into the air, which some soldiers interpreted as a signal. About a half dozen young Lakotas immediately dropped their blankets, revealing concealed Winchesters ready for action. Almost instantaneously, both sides fired point-blank at each other. It was an unnecessary tragedy that neither side had intended. Forsyth's troops were deployed in such a way that gunfire from one of his units could endanger the lives of another. The helpless dependents of the desperate Indian warriors were in such a vulnerable position that the Sioux bullets that missed Forsyth's men could accidentally hit the women and children fleeing the besieged village in terror.

During the murderous cross-fire that marked the first minutes of this unexpected conflict, the ailing Big Foot rose from his pallet only to be cut down, with most of his headmen, by a deadly volley of fire. At the same time, soldiers and Indians all around were engaged in bitter hand-to-hand combat. When the two sides finally separated, the Seventh Cavalry's four small-caliber Hotchkiss cannons, situated on a nearby hilltop, opened fire, flattening the Miniconjou tipis and filling the air with lethal shrapnel. When the smoke cleared after an hour of blood and carnage, 150 of Big Foot's followers, including the chief himself, were dead and 50 were wounded. But the army also paid its price, albeit a smaller one: twenty-five of its soldiers were dead and thirty-nine were wounded.

News of the bloody encounter spread rapidly; newspapers throughout the country were soon filled with its gory details. Understandably, the tenor of most editorial comment did not recognize any middle ground; some journals, most notably western ones, heralded the battle as a long-delayed vengeance on the part of the Seventh Cavalry for the Little Bighorn fiasco, while others condemned the Seventh Cavalry's attack as a wanton assault in behalf of greedy white land grabbers. The long-term result of this catastrophe is a bitterness that lingers today among many Lakota Sioux. The short-term result, however, was to prolong this last great Sioux uprising of the nineteenth century until at least mid-January.

One outcome of the conflict was an almost immediate investigation of the battle scene by 150 Brulé warriors; originally from Rosebud, they were followers of the aged and uncompromising Brulé chief, Two Strike. As soon as they heard the distant gunfire from Wounded Knee, the Brulés, painted for warfare, hastened toward the sound of battle ready for a fight. When they dejectedly returned to Pine Ridge, their news of the slaughter provoked many heretofore peaceful Lakotas to open fire on the unsuspecting buildings at the agency. General Brooke, however, refused to be panicked and denied his troopers permission to use their Hotchkiss gun against the restless Sioux, many of whom had gathered near Red Cloud's house.

In the midst of this chaos, Two Strike decided to take the "145 family lodges" that comprised his Brulé band and flee northward along White Clay Creek; a number of prominent Oglalas joined his hasty migration. Notwithstanding Brooke's admirable forbearance, this party, which was part of a great exodus involving four thousand Lakotas, rendezvoused with those two high priests of the Ghost Dance, Short Bull and Kicking Bear, who, after much soul-searching, were returning to make peace. When that troubled duo heard what had happened at Wounded Knee, however, they and their followers united with Two Strike and his band to travel to an abandoned camp some seventeen miles downriver. There they were joined by many survivors of Wounded Knee, some of whom were wounded but all of whom were bitter. The mood at the camp was ominously hostile.

Among the disenchanted Oglalas to join Two Strike willingly were Little Wound, No Water, and Big Road. Young-Man-Afraid-of-His Horses, probably the most steadfast progressive among the Oglalas, was in Wyoming at the time on a hunting trip. But the most surprising new members of Two Strike's band were Red Cloud and his family. Two Strike, who apparently resented Red Cloud's peace efforts, decided to abduct the old chief against his will. As the once great Sioux warrior described this humiliating episode in a letter to Dr. Thomas Bland, "the Brules forced me to go with them. I being in danger of my life between two fires I had to go with them and follow my family. Some would shoot their guns around me and make me go faster."

This episode was probably the lowest point in Red Cloud's life. The thought of the Oglalas' renowned chief being taunted in this fashion would have been impossible to envision a quarter of a century earlier, when Red Cloud forced the federal government to close the Powder River Road. Notwithstanding his mortification, there were still those who questioned his motivation, implying that he willingly conspired with his abductors. Ethnologist James Mooney from the Smithsonian Institution, whose history of the Ghost Dance period was the standard for many years, wrote historian Doane Robinson on February 20, 1904, that Red Cloud was probably not held against his will. How could such a respected leader, he asked, be denied freedom by his "own followers"? Of course the best rebuttal to this argument was that these kidnappers were not Red Cloud's "followers." Instead, they were exceptionally hard-line Brulés who had left Rosebud for Pine Ridge because most of the Ghost Dance activity was centered on the latter reservation. Other accounts of Red Cloud's surprise seizure have added to his ignominy. One of them, almost impossible to believe, alleges that when Red Cloud balked at Two Strike's entreaties to join him, Red Cloud's loyal wife of many years, Pretty Owl, threw his belongings in a wagon and declared that she was going on the warpath even if he was not.

The dangerous stalemate caused by these Sioux defectors, whose numbers had stabilized at about four thousand, was only broken when General Miles took personal command. The able commander knew the Sioux well enough to exploit the divisions among the camp's progressives and nonprogressives. At the same time, he skillfully used his troops to surround the defiant adherents of the Ghost Dance. He addressed a letter to the still formidable holdouts, telling them that if they would make peace, there would be no trouble. Significantly, the captive holdout, Red Cloud, found his name at the top of Miles's list of chiefs, which included Little Wound, Two Strike, Short Bull, Kicking Bear, Crow Dog, Big Road, and "all Indians away from their Agencies." Even though Red Cloud was being ostracized by civilian authorities and was in disgrace, Miles sent him another note, acknowledging his abduction by Two Strike's band and assuring him that it was the Indian Police, not the army, who fired on his house before those embittered Ghost Dancers had left Pine Ridge. This latter reference was to a widely held belief that Red Cloud had left because his home was shelled. Apparently still feeling that the old chief's support was necessary to end the impasse, Miles promised to return any personal belongings taken from Red Cloud or to compensate him for any possessions irretrievably lost. When all the Ghost Dance troubles finally ended, as a matter of fact, Red Cloud, along with many other Lakotas, successfully filed claims with the government for alleged property losses.

For two weeks the intense standoff persisted. Yet participants on both sides did exchange some surprising communications. For example, the obstinate Lakota holdouts, the majority of whom continued to intimidate the minority with threats of injury or death, insisted on a personal dialogue with Secretary of the Interior Noble and Commissioner of Indian Affairs Morgan. The strong-willed Miles responded to these insurgents in yet another letter, telling them that they had to deal with him first. Red Cloud's reply revealed the general confusion that prevailed; he claimed that Miles's letter was seized by a "crazy boy," who tore it up so that the rest of the camp could not read it. The old chief also implored General Miles to remove those troops who were aggressively circling the large and desperate Sioux encampment. Miles refused, telling Red Cloud that his men were only protecting the reservation and safeguarding the welfare of those Sioux who had remained friendly. He also promised those still intransigent Sioux leaders that if they would come to terms promptly, he would arrange a conference with President Harrison as well as Secretary of the Interior Noble. As a result of these strong assurances, a meeting was held with Miles the next day, January 5, 1891, which involved such important Lakota leaders as He Dog, Big Road, Little Hawk, and Red Cloud's son, Jack.

General Miles's optimism soon began to wane, however, when he realized how divided his adversaries were. But this stalemate could not continue forever. On January 9 an important break occurred. Red Cloud, He Dog, White Hawk, and their families made a dramatic late-night escape from the sleeping Sioux camp, where they had been virtually captives. According to one version of this episode, one of Red Cloud's daughters courageously led her almost blind and helpless father through a severe blizzard in order to reach the agency. Red Cloud's explanation for the flight was fairly simple: "I tried my best for them to let me go back, but they would not let me go, and said if I went they would kill me." Red Cloud's motives may have been more complicated than that, however; on January 7 one of Miles's officers, Lieutenant Edward W. Casey, was killed, and Red Cloud may have felt that he, too, would be held responsible for the death.

Despite Red Cloud's disturbing loss of prestige, his surrender undoubtedly had an important effect on those Sioux who still resisted Miles and his forces. How strong could their cause be if such a prominent leader as Red Cloud felt compelled to seek the protection of the U.S. Army?

The growing menace from Miles's troopers also threatened the resolve of such leaders as Big Strike, Short Bull, and Kicking

Bear, who had vowed to "die together" rather than surrender. But Miles was also able to undermine the confidence of these insurgents in two ways. He kept his promise to all those Lakotas who had surrendered earlier by giving them food and warm clothing, and he had used his influence to remove the inept Agent Royer, temporarily replacing him with the popular army officer Captain F. E. Pierce. Indeed, a general house-cleaning at all the Lakota reservations by the spoils-oriented Harrison administration was one result of this Ghost Dance fiasco.

When the defiant Sioux encampment finally surrendered on January 16, the once feared general mixed his characteristic sternness with a willingness to accommodate, an approach probably necessary to get the Lakota hard-liners to capitulate. He insisted that Short Bull, Kicking Bear, and twenty of their more fanatical adherents be arrested and sent to Fort Sheridan, Illinois, until all the Ghost Dance troubles had subsided; interestingly enough, many of them were eventually sent to Europe as part of Buffalo Bill's Wild West show. But Miles avoided Colonel Forsyth's tragic mistake; although he disarmed the zealous Ghost Dancers, he did not thoroughly search them for guns, even knowing that many had not complied with his order.

General Miles also kept his promise to allow a Sioux delegation to visit Washington for a conference with the president and his secretary of the interior. The delegation, which actually did represent several shades of opinion, was headed by the reliable Young-Man-Afraid-of-His-Horses, who was joined by such ordinarily friendly Lakota Sioux as American Horse, High Hawk, Big Road, and He Dog. Yet chiefs like Little Wound and Two Strike, despite their strong identification with the Ghost Dance movement, were also represented.

Significantly omitted from the delegation was Red Cloud; the old chief, who had been the voice of the Lakota Sioux for twenty-five years, had not been forgiven by Secretary Noble and the other civilian officials, despite the deference shown him by some members of the military. Red Cloud was obviously disheartened, rationalizing his omission on the basis of his failing eyesight: "Owing to the condition of my eyes, I was unable to accompany them." Yet he begged the moralistic and self-satisfied commissioner of Indian affairs, Thomas J. Morgan, to permit him to come to Washington when his eyes were better so he could give his side of what had actually transpired at Pine Ridge.

But Commissioner Morgan, who was socially and geographically from the same eastern establishment that had welcomed Red Cloud to Washington in 1870, apparently felt that the old chief was no longer useful. Morgan's cynical rejection was recorded on Red Cloud's January 26 request for a visit to Washington. It was a simple one-word response: "File." This terse dismissal of a once indispensable leader prompted historian James C. Olson to remark that while the careers of Crazy Horse, Sitting Bull, and Spotted Tail ended in violence, if not martyrdom, Red Cloud's was lost in a government file. The end of the bloody Ghost Dance troubles had truly marked the end of Red Cloud's great career as far as the U.S. government was concerned.

CHAPTER 10

The End of the Trail

THE years after the Battle of Wounded Knee Creek were dreary ones at Pine Ridge. The major lesson of the intense Ghost Dance movement was that not even an appeal for divine intervention could restore the old Sioux way of life. During the two decades before 1890 many Lakotas had harbored some hope that one day they could resume their old life, following the buffalo in the spring and fall and living in harmony with the ever-changing seasons. Not even their abandonment of hunting lands along the North Platte by treaty nor their loss of the Powder River country following the Great Sioux War of 1876–77 could totally discourage them from this hope. Even though being dispossessed of the Black Hills probably hurt them the most, it did not prepare them for the loss of half their reservation lands in the 1889 Sioux bill. But with the harsh suppression of the Ghost Dance in 1890, the Sioux could no longer ignore the fact that their cherished life-style was gone forever. After 1890, although some Lakotas at Pine Ridge and the other five reservations remained sullen and uncooperative, most of them grudgingly accepted the sedentary, agricultural life being imposed upon them by the U.S. government.

Probably no Lakota leader felt the continuing erosion of his people's lands and values more than Red Cloud. A quarter of a century before the bloody encounter at Wounded Knee, Red Cloud attracted national attention by closing the government-backed Bozeman Trail through the Sioux's treasured Powder River country. Although reluctantly agreeing to the Treaty of Fort Laramie in 1868, he disputed every point or interpretation that he felt worked against his people. Even though he refused to join Crazy Horse and Sitting Bull during the Great Sioux War, he used all his diplomatic talents to resist the painful cession of the Black Hills.

As the man the federal government recognized for years as the Lakota Sioux's chief spokesman, Red Cloud strove to preserve as many facets of his people's once free and nomadic life as he could. He was a reluctant farmer and balked at sending his children and grandchildren to white schools both on and off the reservation. He risked his leadership status in the late 1880s by resisting the government's last great land grab, the ominous Sioux bill. Although Red Cloud at first supported the Ghost Dance secretly, he had no illusions about the government's response when that religious frenzy began to show a dangerous side. In fact, he worked to stem the excesses of this spiritual revival even though federal civilian authorities no longer accepted him as the Lakota's chief representative.

When Red Cloud returned from his captivity at the hands of Two Strike's band, the state of his life as well as that of his people was at its lowest point. The comfortable house near the agency that the government had built for him had been looted. He was, along with many others at Pine Ridge, a claimant, seeking governmental compensation for all his losses. When Red Cloud signed his damage claim on July 29, 1891, he swore that he had not been "hostile, either by word or action," during the crisis marked by Wounded Knee. He set his losses as a result of the Ghost Dance troubles at $682.50. Although this figure was fairly substantial, his son's claim was $1,198.65.

The items for which Red Cloud made claims clearly indicate that while he may have resisted many of the white man's values, he accepted much of that race's material culture. Among the possessions for which he asked compensation were twenty-five loads of hay and eight loads of wood, two horses, one buggy, furniture (including two beds and two rocking chairs), dishes and utensils, a coffee pot, nonperishable foods such as beans and flour, and a washtub and basin. The government ultimately accepted Red Cloud's claims, although it lowered their value to $398.60.

Red Cloud must have felt lonely and unappreciated during those wintry days following his return from captivity. The home that he and Pretty Owl shared, stark by today's standards but the only two-story frame house at Pine Ridge, had been ransacked. His exclusion from the Washington delegation, which left for the capital in late January, hurt him deeply. The growing helplessness caused by his blindness and advanced age frustrated him, especially because his mind was still keen and his interest in Sioux affairs had not waned. Yet this tenacious man, still revered by many of his people as a symbol of their glorious past, would live for nineteen more years, largely ignored by the U.S. government.

Red Cloud not only maintained the respect of most Lakotas during those difficult years, but he also enjoyed the respect of many of the whites at Pine Ridge. In fact, his relationship with the former outsiders was a long one. Red Cloud's Bad Faces were among the last of the lingering Oglalas to move from their familiar encampments near Fort Laramie in the 1850s to the game-rich Powder River country in the north and the Republican River country to the south. Although Red Cloud was never as close to the white traders and soldiers at the fort as was the leader of his youthful days, Old Smoke, who chose to stay at Fort Laramie until his death in 1864, the aging chief was on friendly terms with a number of whites, both traders and soldiers, during the early nineteenth century. His warm relationship with Sam Deon, one of his favorite traders, to whom he told his life story in 1893, is one example of Red Cloud's closeness to those whites he trusted.

During Red Cloud's two decades as a negotiator for his people, many agents bargaining for the federal government became angry at Red Cloud for requesting governmental bequests to reward the services of one or more of his white translators or advisors. The exasperation of these federal officials, however, was not so much at Red Cloud's partiality toward these white favorites as it was toward the pro-Sioux advice he was getting from them; the livelihoods of these men were largely based upon successful trade relations with the Sioux. Indeed, Red

Cloud's inflexibility was often attributed to these white advisors, who, because of their mutual bond with the Lakotas, tended to identify with the Sioux's position against the government's.

The Oglalas generally had much closer relations with the whites than did the five northern Lakota tribes. The Oglalas' more intimate contact with the white strangers probably accounts for the major difference between Red Cloud's attitude toward the pushy newcomers and the attitude of such northern Lakota leaders as Crazy Horse and Sitting Bull. Crazy Horse was the major exception to this rule; he and most of his band of Oglalas, for example, deliberately maintained as much spiritual or psychological distance as they could between themselves and the increasingly numerous white traders and soldiers pushing into Sioux lands. Sitting Bull and his people, on the other hand, were insulated by a much greater geographical distance than was Crazy Horse. Indeed, the Hunkpapas and the other northern Lakotas were very remote in terms of miles from the encroaching white settlements. Thus, both Crazy Horse and Sitting Bull exhibited an intransigence often felt toward a rival with whom one has had few contacts and whom one can therefore demonize more easily. Red Cloud, for his part, knew many whites, both friends and enemies, and lived in harmony with the former while confronting the latter in battle or at the peace table.

To agency employees and other whites living in Pine Ridge, Red Cloud became a familiar figure during the last two decades of his life. He was remembered in the minds of many as that once fierce warrior who was now at peace with the U.S. government. Charles P. Jordan, a friend of Red Cloud who served in several important capacities at both Pine Ridge and Rosebud, recalled in a June 26, 1902, letter to historian Doane Robinson a remark that Red Cloud made at a Washington church reception in 1889: "When I fought the whites, I fought with all my might[.] When I made a treaty of peace in 1869–I meant it, and risked my life in keeping my covenant."

It was probably Red Cloud's pride as a peacemaker that ultimately made him controversial to many Native Americans of today. A number of Lakotas have criticized him for his lack of action in the face of continual government violations of the Treaty of Fort Laramie. His failure to join Crazy Horse and Sitting Bull in the massive resistance that led to the Battle of the Little Bighorn in 1876 has also been the subject of censure. Allegations that he was too comfortable as the Sioux chief the federal government most preferred have been leveled against him. It is true that at times he was a self-serving man. He demanded with unusual persistence compensation for the horses taken from his band and Red Leaf's band in 1876, and he enjoyed his wood-frame, two-story house at Pine Ridge, insisting upon compensation when it was looted as a result of the Ghost Dance violence. Yet Red Cloud risked all the power and influence he still had at his disposal to oppose the grossly unfair Sioux bill of 1889. And although he failed to recover his once cherished governmental prerogatives by unsuccessfully trying to defuse the Ghost Dance movement, it was an effort much more significant than historians have generally recognized.

It should also be remembered that whenever Red Cloud felt warfare was a feasible alternative, he did not hesitate to wage it. His dominant leadership role in the Fetterman and Wagon Box fights should not be forgotten, nor should his reputation as the most feared Oglala warrior before Crazy Horse. It was only after his visits to Washington that he realized that the overwhelming power of his white adversaries made further resistance untenable. It was at that point that he decided he could accomplish more for his people through negotiations than through the ambushes and sieges that characterized his war to prevent the government from federalizing the Bozeman Trail.

Red Cloud's successes as a diplomat and keen political leader did not leave him much better off than the people at Pine Ridge after the tragic outcome of the Ghost Dance movement. Because of his long service to them, many Oglalas still regarded him as their leader, and he remained the *itancan* of his own band, the Bad Faces. Yet most of the Sioux living on that hilly, largely treeless reservation were very poor; indeed, in 1994, a century later, Shannon County, South Dakota, which covers more than half of Pine Ridge's expansive acreage, ranked as the third poorest county in the United States. The federal government during the 1880s and 1890s had been aware of the deplorable conditions at Pine Ridge and the other Lakota reservations. On March 22, 1891, after the discouraged Sioux delegation returned from Washington, Commissioner of Indian Affairs Morgan urged all Sioux agents to clarify the rations, annuities, educational possibilities, and agricultural aid that their charges were entitled to under the Fort Laramie Treaty of 1868, the Black Hills cession agreement of 1877, and the Sioux bill of 1889. The agents were to assure the Lakotas that there was money to fund all these benefits. Moreover, additional funds had been appropriated to deal with the ration shortages that had made 1890 such a difficult year.

Even though Red Cloud had been effectively excluded from those tribal affairs that involved the federal government, Commissioner Morgan, in this letter, declared that Red Cloud's and Red Leaf's bands, from whom Colonel Mackenzie had seized ponies in that still-disputed controversy of 1876, should at least be compensated. More germane to conditions at Pine Ridge, he also announced that there would be compensation for friendly Indians, such as Red Cloud, who had suffered losses during the recent uprising. Morgan's letter provided a new carrot-and-stick approach toward the still unhappy Sioux. Although Morgan's mood sounded conciliatory, many of his superiors felt a hostility difficult to suppress. For example, Secretary of the Interior Noble, whose views against Red Cloud remained intransigent, wrote Morgan a week later that while he would try to be as "humane" as possible, any further trouble on the part of the Sioux would be met with "great severity" and the punishment necessary to "compel obedience."

Despite these well-intentioned governmental efforts to improve the lot of the Sioux, little progress was made on the Pine Ridge Reservation during the next two decades. The transformation of the Lakotas to a "state of civilization," the main creed for people like Commissioner Morgan and the other citizens representing the Mohonk movement, seemed stalled, to the surprise of many. But the fact that most Lakotas moved only grudgingly toward a sedentary agricultural life was not totally the fault of the government's policies. The nonprogressives among the Oglalas remained staunchly traditional, notwithstanding the efforts of such progressive leaders as Young-Man-Afraid-of-His-Horses, American Horse, and George Sword to adjust to the new ways.

Red Cloud, who had straddled both camps for years, became increasingly identified with the nonprogressive element the older he grew and the more isolated he became from the affairs of the federal government. He remained adamant against having his children and grandchildren attend white schools, believing that one of them died as a result of being at a government boarding school. His conviction that a farmer's life was degrading for a true Lakota warrior did not diminish significantly. Ironically, when the old chief finally took his land allotment under the Sioux bill in 1904, there was a noticeable break in the resistance at Pine Ridge against the allotment principle. Incidentally, Red Cloud's resistance to severalty was not based solely on ideological grounds; many Sioux at Pine Ridge believed their lands were ill suited for farming and should be held in common as grazing land.

Nor did Red Cloud ever become a cultural broker, to use historian William T. Hagan's term in his biography of Comanche Chief Quanah Parker. During the last quarter-century of Quanah Parker's life, that able Comanche mediator successfully dealt with Indian agents, Texas cattlemen, and the federal government for his tribe's benefit as well as his own. Although Red Cloud did make peace between his people and the federal government when he agreed to the Treaty of Fort Laramie in 1868 (and strove to maintain that peace under the most trying conditions), he was unwilling to be the kind of intermediary who could successfully broker relations between his people and the outside world. His strong devotion to traditional values was one problem; he often had to conceal his true attitude to protect himself and his people from federal retribution. The necessity of resisting treaty violations and audacious land grabs often made it difficult, if not impossible, to play the honest broker. Not only did Red Cloud's ambivalence make him a complex character during his lifetime, but also the strong inner conflict that waged within him might well have been mirrored at Pine Ridge eight decades later when angry Oglalas, under the leadership of the American Indian Movement, occupied the site of the Battle of Wounded Knee Creek during their highly publicized seventy-one-day siege in 1973.

Although Red Cloud's views were undoubtedly troubled during his declining years, he continued to maintain steadfast friendships with certain whites. One of them was Charles Jordan, who remained supportive of Red Cloud even after the old chief became irrelevant in the eyes of official Washington. Jordan regarded Red Cloud as a "grand old man," a natural-born gentleman always polite around the ladies. He also admired him as a leader who kept his word. Thomas Duran, a runner who carried an important dispatch to Red Cloud's camp near the end of the Sioux leader's war to close the Bozeman Trail, related a story to Jordan that illustrated the kind of integrity Red Cloud could display. Duran was captured by some of Red Cloud's allies and was being threatened with death when Red Cloud arrived with two hundred loyal followers. The Oglala leader, whose status as a chief still had not yet been fully established, immediately led his men into action, clubbing and dispersing the brash warriors who defied him. Red Cloud was particularly distressed over this incident, because Duran was under a flag of truce. To make up for this dishonor, Red Cloud gave Duran one of his favorite horses, about the most significant possession a Sioux warrior could bestow.

But Red Cloud had his detractors, too; even some of his own Oglalas were among them. Many of Little Wound's followers, for example, who traced their lineage back to Bull Bear, whom Red Cloud and his Bad Face comrades had killed in a drunken brawl, remained bitter against the old chief. This fateful episode, which ultimately divided the Oglalas into two groups, Old Smoke's followers and Bull Bear's followers, accounts for the fact that some Oglalas were in the Powder River country while others were in the Republican River valley at the time of Red Cloud's first encounters with large white migrations. Historical memories among these Oglalas were characteristically long; many of Bull Bear's people never forgot Red Cloud's role in Bull Bear's death. Man-Afraid-of-His-Horses, one of the Oglalas' great peace chiefs, was also a rival of Red Cloud, albeit a friendlier one. But his son, Young-Man-Afraid-of-His Horses, who became a leader of Pine Ridge's progressive element, was not always so friendly in his long rivalry with Red Cloud. Crazy Horse and many younger Oglalas were also critical of Red Cloud in the years before the Great Sioux War because he insisted on maintaining peace, even in the face of alleged governmental violations of the Treaty of Fort Laramie. In fact, Crazy Horse's biographer, Mari Sandoz, was as much responsible for Red Cloud's bad image as Crazy Horse's chief nemesis as anyone else; she tended to contrast every heroic trait of Crazy Horse with an ignoble one for Red Cloud.

There were formidable white critics, too. One was the Pine Ridge physician Dr. James R. Walker, who insisted in a November 21, 1906, interview with Judge Ricker that Red Cloud was exceptionally cruel in battle when he was young. Perhaps even more damaging is Walker's assertion, allegedly based upon Sam Deon's testimony, that Red Cloud could not command the respect of many Lakotas, some of whom even struck him in the face as if he were nothing more than a "cowardly woman." Again, this is another piece of testimony that seems to defy everything upon which Red Cloud's reputation was based. Sam Deon, for many years a close friend of Red Cloud, enjoyed the old chief's protection during the Sioux's prereservation years and helped him to assemble his autobiography in 1893. Moreover, to assault anyone as strong and aggressive as Red Cloud could only have been done after he was too old to defend himself.

As for the charge of cruelty against Red Cloud, it is true he gave no quarter in battle. American Horse, who allegedly killed Captain Fetterman in the famous ambush of 1866, never hesitated to boast about Red Cloud's great feats in battle. In one of American's Horse's interviews with Judge Ricker, for example, he claimed that Red Cloud had singlehandedly killed four Pawnee warriors in one conflict. Indeed, eighty coups were attributed to Red Cloud, making him the Lakotas' greatest warrior until Crazy Horse gained that distinction in his wars against the U.S. Army. Red Cloud's reputation as an illustrious warrior was probably the major catalyst for his elevation as the Sioux's most powerful leader of the post–Civil War period. It also guaranteed him much respect even after he became old and was discarded by federal authorities as a leader. In fact, many Sioux at Pine Ridge were to continue to revere him as a symbol of their glorious past until his death.

Although Red Cloud could bask in his past glory, he did have to share much of his people's destitution during the dreary decades that bridged the nineteenth and twentieth centuries. In 1902, Jordan poignantly described a visit from the old chief and his wife of almost sixty years, Pretty Owl. The two had driven 110 miles in an old lumber wagon from Pine Ridge to Rosebud, where Jordan was then employed. Jordan sympathetically depicted them as looking "dirty and destitute." The once renowned warrior, over eighty years of age, was "nearly totally blind." It was "a pathetic sight to see him led about by his 4 year old great grandson." Jordan, as a measure of his respect toward the aged chief, put Red Cloud and his little party up for three weeks, after which he "sent them on their way rejoicing."

Probably Red Cloud's happiest experiences during his latter days were the trips he took to get away from his frustrations at Pine Ridge. Usually he could endure his discouragements at Pine Ridge in silence. Yet there were times when he could no longer suppress his anger and frustration. He once told Warren Moorehead, a visiting anthropologist, that the government, after it had taken land away from the Sioux, had failed to "support and feed" them. "Now I, who used to control 5,000 warriors, must tell Washington when I am hungry. I must beg for that which I own. If I beg hard, they put me in the guardhouse." Although Red Cloud's complaints were sometimes admittedly self-serving, he did seem to feel responsible for the plight of his people. "We have great trouble here at Pine Ridge," he told Moorehead. "Our girls are getting bad. Coughing sickness every winter carries away our best people. My heart is heavy and I am old, yet there is not much more that I can do for my people."

Leaving the reservation from time to time, as a consequence, was good therapy for Red Cloud. Seeing the contrast between Pine Ridge and the once great hunting lands of the Lakotas to the west and south of it, however, could also be painful. After all, many parts of Nebraska and Wyoming were still remembered by both whites and Indians as Red Cloud country. This recollection was probably in Red Cloud's mind when he demeaned Pine Ridge in a conversation with Moorehead. "You see this barren waste," he complained. "Think of it! I who used to own rich soil in a well-watered country so extensive that I could not ride through it in a week on my fastest pony, am put down here." Trips to the ranch of his good friend Captain Cook in northwestern Nebraska were a bittersweet experience for him, because to get there he usually had to travel through the much prettier wooded and rolling country around Fort Robinson, which, until 1877, comprised the Red Cloud Agency, second of the Oglalas' four reservation homes.

Once Red Cloud reached Cook's Agate Springs Ranch, however, he was a happy man. In fact, he and his family probably felt more contentment camping along the wooded banks of the Niobrara River as Cook's guests than they did anywhere else. On his last trip in 1908, about the time he reminisced so nostalgically in that letter to Cook about the "old trails" followed by the Sioux for "hundreds of years," he spent ten peaceful days in that friendly environment. But not all of Red Cloud's trips away from the reservation were that successful. On a visit to the Shoshones and their healthful warm springs in Wyoming during the summer of 1894, for example, he was arrested for killing game out of season. Although he maintained his innocence, Red Cloud, who once held sway over that entire area, was briefly incarcerated in the Casper jail and fined sixty-six dollars, which he reluctantly paid by forfeiting two of his horses.

Although Red Cloud was largely neutralized because he had opposed the 1889 Sioux bill, he still made occasional forays into politics. Unfortunately, he achieved little success in these endeavors. For example, in 1891 he wrote a futile letter to Commissioner Morgan, on behalf of himself and Pine Ridge leaders such as Little Wound, American Horse, his son, Jack, and Young-Man-Afraid-of-His-Horses, in which he urged Captain Cook's appointment as the Oglala Sioux's new Indian agent. We are tired of eastern agents, Red Cloud wrote in this hopeful request, insisting that Cook, whom he had known for seventeen years, could be trusted. During the following year, Red Cloud tried, again unsuccessfully, to persuade James Cooper, a special agent of the Indian Service, to work for the abolition of the Indian Courts. He earnestly argued that everyone who appeared before these courts was fined, and nobody knew where the money went.

In 1897, Red Cloud made his last trip to Washington, still a cherished experience for the old warrior, who had been the center of attention during most of the fourteen earlier delegations of which he was a part. But the contrast between this trip and his first trip in 1870 could not have been more convincing. In 1870 he was greeted as the great Native American celebrity who had made the federal government back down in the Powder River country and had forced the entire nation to wait until he agreed to the terms of the Treaty of Fort Laramie. He was not only feted by official Washington but also welcomed with great enthusiasm along Fifth Avenue in New York City by thousands of New Yorkers, representing both the humble and the influential. In 1897, on the other hand, his testimony before the Senate Committee on Indian Affairs, along with Clarence Three Star's and American Horse's, was largely ignored, along with their lengthy memorial of grievances.

Most of Red Cloud's political activities, however, occurred at Pine Ridge. In 1898, for example, he unsuccessfully opposed the construction of fences on the reservation, a prime example of his continuing to cling to the traditional ways that most Sioux still held dear. In 1903, in another effort to reassert himself, Red Cloud, as the aging and frail *itancan* of the Bad Faces, celebrated the Fourth of July by abdicating his chieftaincy in favor of Jack, his only offspring to achieve influence and power in the tribe. The venerable leader, now in his eighty-second year, remembered how his maternal uncle White Hawk had stepped aside so he could become a chief. But what Red Cloud forgot was that he had achieved his status only because he was an incomparable warrior and a natural leader able to excel over competitors with better family connections. Indeed, even though the federal government, for its own reasons, often elevated certain Lakota leaders to positions of authority beyond that condoned by tribal practice, the concept of a hereditary chief was never recognized by the Sioux in any legal or binding way. For that reason, Jack was unable to achieve his father's high standing, although when he died in 1918, he was buried with honors.

In September 1903, Red Cloud addressed the Pine Ridge tribal council for the last time; it was probably his final political act of consequence. The occasion was a visit by South Dakota Congressman E. W. Martin. Martin wanted only a few hours of dialogue with those Lakota leaders who lived in his state. What he got was two days dominated by unhappy complaints, many of them dealing with the Black Hills cession and other infractions of the Treaty of Fort Laramie.

Aging leaders such as Little Wound, American Horse, and Blue Horse also spoke, but Red Cloud, still regarded by many as a living historical record, made the most telling remarks. Recalling the Allison commission's visit to the old Red Cloud Agency in 1875 to acquire the Black Hills, Red Cloud rekindled the lingering bitterness over the loss of Paha Sapa, those Sioux hills having become even more sacred during the past generation. He reiterated those comments of opposition he had made in the months before the Battle of the Little Bighorn, when the government offered to pay a mere six million dollars for the mineral-rich mountains. "The Black Hills is worth to me seven generations," he told Senator Allison and the other commissioners at that time, "but you give me this word of six million dollars. It is just a little spit in my mouth."

The old chief, who in 1875 had specified what seven generations of support for the Sioux would entail in terms of food
and supplies, still acted in 1903 as if he and his people owned
the hills. In fact, he said he would be willing to lend the "top
of hills" to the Great Father for mining. "That is just the rock
above the pines." His agreeableness on that score was based
upon the Sioux's dire need for money. "They should give us
the money for the Black Hills treaty because we need it now."
Eight decades later most Lakotas felt even more strongly about
the Black Hills, a position buttressed by the Supreme Court in
1980 when it ruled in the case of the *United States* v. *Sioux Nation of Indians* that the Lakotas were entitled to compensation
for the loss of the hills. The federal government, in fact, offered
the Sioux 105 million dollars; the figure included the 7 million
dollars that Red Cloud and some of the Sioux seemed willing
to take from the Allison commission in 1875, plus the 98 million dollars in interest that had accumulated since the cession of
the Black Hills in 1877. But the Lakota Sioux of the 1980s were
much more intransigent than Red Cloud; they refused the offer,
insisting that the Black Hills were theirs and citing the Treaty
of Fort Laramie to support that position.

Red Cloud died on December 10, 1909. Although he had
straddled two cultures and two sets of values for years, he was
buried with the full rites of the Catholic church in a small
cemetery above the Holy Rosary Mission, which he had loyally
supported since its establishment in 1888. Even though he
became largely lost in obscurity during the final decades of his
eighty-eight-year life, his death attracted widespread attention in
the national press; to many nostalgic Americans who lamented
the loss of the Old West, Red Cloud was one of the last of the
legendary figures to pass from the scene.

But Red Cloud's image was not always so secure; his importance as a dominant warrior and leader fluctuated significantly,
especially during the last four decades of his life. In 1870, when
he made his first visit to Washington as the Sioux chief who
had forced the federal government to abandon its road through

the Powder River country, he was probably the most famous Indian in the country. He thrived on that reputation until he was displaced by Crazy Horse and Sitting Bull, who captured the nation's attention by crushing the forces under Custer at the Battle of the Little Bighorn.

Yet even after this partial eclipse of his influence and power, Red Cloud remained a decisive force in Sioux affairs. He reemerged with surprising swiftness as the most prominent spokesman for the seven Lakota Sioux tribes because of the death of Crazy Horse in 1877 and because of the uncompromising attitude of Sitting Bull, which never wavered until that chief's death in 1890. As a consequence, Red Cloud, who had vowed never to fight again, was soon gaining attention for his stands on those issues that still separated his people from the policies of the federal government. Just as he opposed the surrender of hunting rights along the Republican River and the cession of the Black Hills before the Battle of the Little Bighorn, he opposed the removal of his people to the Missouri River and the loss of half of the Great Sioux Reservation in the 1889 Sioux bill in the years after Custer's defeat. Moreover, his feud with Agent McGillycuddy in the 1880s attracted about as much national attention as had his feud with Agent Saville in the 1870s.

During these struggles on behalf of his people after the Little Bighorn, Red Cloud showed an uncanny ability to stall a project he felt harmful to the Sioux, a position greatly bolstered by widespread support from many influential humanitarian groups in the East. With the advent of the Mohonk movement, whose members believed that individual land allotments were the only way to integrate Native Americans into the nation's white society, this crucial support for Red Cloud began to erode. By the late 1880s the venerable chief's white supporters had dwindled down to the members of groups such as Dr. Thomas A. Bland's National Indian Defense Association, which still believed that the Indians should set the pace of their assimilation into white society. After the tragedies that marked the Ghost Dance and the Battle of Wounded Knee Creek, Red Cloud's once surprising clout was almost gone. The reason for this demise was obvious; the federal government simply discontinued its policy of dealing with him as the Lakota Sioux's major spokesman. Nevertheless, he remained a revered figure at Pine Ridge until his death in 1909.

Red Cloud's enduring reputation was based upon his prowess as a warrior and his skill as a political leader. In fact, he was a warrior without peer who could not only command the respect of his own people but of his enemies as well. Indeed, the Crows, Pawnees, Utes, and Shoshones, and even the Arikaras to the east, witnessed with awe his boldness and give-no-quarter conduct in battle. It was a reputation that made him a popular leader for the Sioux to follow whether on a horse stealing expedition or a buffalo hunt. His success in warfare and his intimidating physical presence, which Captain Cook once likened to that of a tiger, almost guaranteed his eventual selection as a tribal shirtwearer, notwithstanding the humble circumstances of his birth.

Red Cloud's swift ascent as the most dominant of the Oglala chiefs, however, relied more on his abilities as a military leader and an exceptional political strategist. In both of these endeavors human intelligence was his most important asset. In fact, his exceptional mind helped him to comprehend the many mental vagaries that motivated his white adversaries, an understanding enriched by many early contacts with white traders and soldiers before the early 1860s. His resoluteness was another factor; it made him particularly effective in rallying his people against white encroachments during the first years following the Civil War. The most impressive display of this resolve was demonstrated at the peace conference at Fort Laramie in June 1866 just before Red Cloud's War. When Colonel Carrington's forces arrived at the conference on their way to occupy the Powder River country, which ironically enough was the main subject of the negotiations, the shocked and surprised tribesmen at the gathering were outraged. But it was Red Cloud who stood up and courageously denounced the government's deception. And it was Red Cloud who bolted the conference, taking with him many of the chiefs and shirtwearers who were rejuvenated by his example.

The short-range significance of Red Cloud's bold intervention cannot be underestimated. It had launched an organized opposition to the nation's expansionist policies in the West. In the months that followed, this new leader and his allies would make life so difficult for Carrington and the other soldiers who were trying to maintain a travel route for Montana gold seekers through the Powder River country that in the summer of 1868 the forts constructed to guard this trail would have to be abandoned. Also, largely because of Red Cloud's intervention, a large tract of land extending from the Missouri River to the Bighorn Mountains was set aside for the Sioux in the Treaty of Fort Laramie. Added to this treaty concession were other favorable treaty provisions, including a generous annuity. It was a good treaty for the Lakota Sioux; indeed, the only reason Red Cloud ultimately lost the peace was because the federal government reinterpreted many of the treaty's provisions until the domain of the Sioux had shrunk to six comparatively small reservations.

Some Native Americans have condemned Red Cloud for not taking up arms when it became evident that the treaty would not be honored the way Red Cloud understood it would be. His periodic reiteration that he would maintain the peace because he had given his word added to his loss of esteem. Yet it seems feasible, given the man's high intelligence, that his numerous trips to Washington made him realize the futility of warring against an opponent with such decided advantages. When Red Cloud signed the Treaty of Fort Laramie in 1868, the population of the United States was approaching 36 million, while there were probably fewer than 25,000 Lakota Sioux on the Northern Plains. Consequently, although Red Cloud did not seek martyrdom through hopeless military resistance, he did use his abilities as a negotiator to oppose every federal policy that he regarded as being against his people's best interest. His ability to stall, deviate from the subject, and filibuster often made him appear as an obstructionist to government negotiators, but it was through these tactics that he gained as much time for his people as possible. This strategy, moreover, was often accompanied by a successful appeal to friendly elements in the

East who would sometimes try to moderate the government's position on those issues considered crucial for the Sioux. In the end, though, Red Cloud's measures of confrontation short of war failed him as they failed his people.

Yet, even admitting that Red Cloud's strategy ultimately led to defeat, his efforts should not be demeaned. If he had not defiantly denounced the government's duplicity at Fort Laramie in 1866, the wave of white settlement might well have outflanked the Plains tribes in the West that year as it already had the tribes in the East. The hunting grounds of the Oglalas, Cheyennes, and Arapahoes in the Powder River country would have been lost, and the hunting grounds of the Hunkpapas and their Lakota allies in Montana would have been threatened sooner. Of course, another leader might have emerged to turn the tide, but would he have understood the white mind as well as Red Cloud did? In truth, a reasonable argument could be made that Red Cloud extended the Lakotas' traditional way of life by almost a decade because of his leadership in the Powder River campaign and his insistence that the Treaty of Fort Laramie guaranteed Sioux sovereignty over that vast tract of land that the Lakota Sioux occupied until their defeat in the Great Sioux War. In the long view of history, gaining a mere decade may seem minor, but to a people who revered their traditions, it was an important reprieve.

Although Red Cloud's reputation as a warrior and military leader seems well assured, his status as a spokesman for his people during the first four decades of reservation life is more controversial. Red Cloud, for example, did not join Crazy Horse and Sitting Bull in resisting the federal government during the Great Sioux War. He was often jealous of his major rivals. Although he helped end the months of conflict following the Battle of the Little Bighorn by escorting Crazy Horse to the Red Cloud Agency in the spring of 1877, he was conspicuous among those older Lakota chiefs who brought about the undoing of that proud and heroic warrior; his role in this tragic affair is probably the blackest mark against his name. But Red Cloud was involved in many rivalries, an indication that, although federal authorities believed he enjoyed clear-cut responsibilities as they did, his powers were both fluid and limited; indeed, under the Lakota political system tribal authority was customarily shared. As a consequence, rivalries among the Oglalas would continue after Crazy Horse's demise. Red Cloud's feud with the progressive-minded Young-Man-Afraid-of-His-Horses divided many Oglalas at Pine Ridge during the 1880s until the departure of McGillycuddy brought about their reconciliation.

Red Cloud could also be self-serving; he often equated his welfare and the welfare of his people as one and the same. On his first trip to Washington in 1870, he sulked until his delegation received seventeen horses, notwithstanding the more important issues in need of settlement. When Sioux sovereignty over the Black Hills was imperiled by discoveries of gold, Red Cloud seemed more interested in maintaining his advantages over Agent Saville than in this more serious threat. And during the Oglala Sioux's move to Pine Ridge in 1878, Red Cloud showed almost as much concern about the house the government promised to build him as about the conditions of this lonely new home where his people must locate.

Yet Red Cloud more than balanced these character flaws or questionable deeds by the leadership he provided during the often bleak reservation years. In the early 1870s he argued for an agency near Fort Laramie, a favorite trading center for his people for many years. Although that site, the Sod Agency, was not perfect, the second one, the Red Cloud Agency, was much better; under Red Cloud's authority it proved a comfortable winter sanctuary for many Lakotas who preferred to hunt in the unceded territory east of the Bighorns during the warmer months. During the federal government's drive to acquire the Black Hills in 1875, Red Cloud was able to disentangle himself from the Saville feud to stall the Black Hills cession until it was forced upon the Lakotas as a result of their defeat in the Great Sioux War. When that conflict ended, he effectively opposed Washington's plan to remove the Sioux to the banks of the Missouri or to Indian Territory in present-day Oklahoma; indeed, in the face of federal opposition, Red Cloud, on his own volition, ended his people's migration to the

Missouri about eighty miles short of their proposed reservation there. He struggled with Agent McGillycuddy during the 1880s to preserve such Sioux customs and traditions as the sun dance. And when Lakota sovereignty over half the Great Sioux Reservation was threatened by the Sioux bill of 1889, Red Cloud risked his much cherished special status with the U.S. government to oppose it. Finally, when it seemed as though the Ghost Dance movement would undo what little leverage remained to the Sioux, Red Cloud used the influence he still had left to discourage the movement's excesses.

The history of the Lakota people during the late nineteenth century cannot be fully told without focusing on Red Cloud's career. He was probably the most productive political leader of this great Indian confederation that had dominated the Northern Plains after reaching them by those "old trails" blazed from Minnesota. Among the great chiefs encountered in America's westward drive, Red Cloud was one of the most talented and one of the most tenacious; the relative dispatch by which he regained the respect he enjoyed before the Great Sioux War is a tribute to his leadership skills.

But his strength as a Sioux spokesman during the reservation years, curiously enough, was not as a cultural agent reconciling differences between his people and their new overlords. Nor was it as a stubborn obstructionist opposed to anything new. Rather it was as a man, forced by circumstances to fight a rearguard action, who contested every policy of the federal government to alter the Treaty of Fort Laramie under which his people had laid down their arms. Indeed, he resisted every governmental interpretation that would mean a loss of territory for his people. Without resorting to rebellious or self-destructive actions, he strove to preserve as much Sioux culture as he could. To a proud people his ability to articulate their most important anxieties and aspirations made him respected and honored even after he became too old to be their effective voice. Notwithstanding his shortcomings, the record he established by the end of his own difficult trail through life made him a warrior and statesman of great renown.

Sources

ALTHOUGH sources for Red Cloud's public role as a Lakota chief are fairly extensive, those that deal with his private life are limited and often contradictory. Nevertheless, the most valuable primary source for Red Cloud's private life is his still unpublished autobiography, titled "Red Cloud, Chief of the Sioux." This 135-page typed manuscript, compiled by Addison E. Sheldon, former superintendent of the State Historical Society of Nebraska in Lincoln, was ignored for a century until R. Eli Paul, senior research historian for the society, authenticated its legitimacy in "Recovering Red Cloud's Autobiography: The Strange Odyssey of a Chief's Personal Narrative," *Montana: The Magazine of Western History* 44 (Summer 1994): 2–17. Also useful as primary sources are the eighty-nine interviews conducted by Judge Eli S. Ricker during the first decade of this century. These are located at the State Historical Society of Nebraska, along with an unpublished analysis titled "The Interview as a Source of Indian History," by James C. Olson, another of the society's superintendents. Used for this study were interviews with such Lakota and white participants of Sioux history as Charles W. Allen, American Horse, Alexander Baxter, W. A. Birdsall, Louis Bordeaux, W. F. Clark, George W. Colhoff, William Garnett, Dr. William F. Girton, Joseph W. Horn Cloud, W. R. Jones, L. B. Lessert (Ben Claymore), George Little Wound, Peter McFarland, Magliore A. Mosseau, William Peano, Red Cloud, Clarence Three Stars, Dr. James R. Walker, and Philip F. Wells. Another valuable source at the Lincoln facility is Red Cloud's damage claim for property lost or destroyed as a result of Wounded Knee.

Sources for both Red Cloud's public and private life are also found in the South Dakota State Historical Society. Among the primary collections used were the Red Cloud Estate Papers and the papers of John R. Brennan, Charles P. Jordan, Vincent T. McGillycuddy, Doane Robinson, and Philip F. Wells. Important because they gave the names of Red Cloud's daughters were a letter from Mrs. John R. Brennan and a probate document from the mid-1940s, which again attempted to resolve, after seven decades, the still-controversial seizure of Red Cloud's horses by Colonel Ranald S. Mackenzie in 1876. Doane Robinson, "The Education of Red Cloud," a speculative account of a typical Sioux warrior's upbringing, is not only in the Robinson Papers, but also has been published in *Collections of the South Dakota Department of History* 12 (1924): 156–78.

Another important primary source is a May 13, 1908, letter from Red Cloud to Captain James H. Cook, provided by Palma E. Wilson, chief ranger of Agate Fossil Beds National Monument near Cook's ranch, in which Red Cloud reminisces about the "old trails" his people have taken from Minnesota to their final home on the Northern Plains. Also contributing to the debate over the origin of Red Cloud's name is a February 23, 1911, letter from George Bent to George E. Hyde from the Bent-Hyde Collection, Beinecke Rare Book and Manuscript Library, Yale University, provided by David Fridtjof Halaas, chief historian, Colorado Historical Society. Perused at the Denver Public Library, Western History Department, were the Indian Rights Association Papers, 1964–73, from the manuscript collection of the Historical Society of Pennsylvania, which were copied by the Microfilming Corporation of America, Glen Rock, New Jersey, in 1974.

Government documents consulted include Senate Executive Documents and House Executive Documents and the annual reports of the Board of Indian Commissioners,

Commissioner of Indian Affairs, Superintendent of Indian Affairs, Secretary of the Interior, and Secretary of War. Relevant to Red Cloud's controversies as a reservation leader for the Lakota Sioux are the *Report of the Special Commissioner Appointed to Investigate the Affairs of the Red Cloud Indian Agency, July, 1875* (Washington, D.C.: Government Printing Office, 1875), and James Mooney, *The Ghost-Dance Religion and the Sioux Outbreak of 1890*, 14th Annual Report of the Bureau of American Ethnology, 1892–93, pt. 2 (Washington, D.C.: Government Printing Office, 1896; reprint, Lincoln: University of Nebraska Press, 1991). Of the newspapers perused, the *New York Times* is an especially good source, not only for Red Cloud's eastern visits but also for his western enterprises as well. Although many newspapers in the upper states and territories were vitally concerned about the Sioux chief's future intentions, the *Omaha Weekly Herald* was probably the most influential news organ in that part of the West.

Of the secondary sources, James C. Olson, *Red Cloud and the Sioux Problem* (Lincoln: University of Nebraska Press, 1965), is the most valuable, although George E. Hyde, *Red Cloud's Folk: A History of the Oglala Sioux Indians* (Norman: University of Oklahoma Press, 1937), is essential for the years before the Little Bighorn. Olson concentrates on Red Cloud's role as an intermediary between the Lakota Sioux and the U.S. government, while Hyde focuses on the activities of Red Cloud's people, sometimes at the expense of personal information about Red Cloud himself. Designed for younger readers are Ed McGaa, *Red Cloud* (Minneapolis: Dillon Press, 1971), and Virginia Frances Voight, *Red Cloud, Sioux War Chief* (Champagne, Ill.: Garrard Publishing Co., 1975). The most recent publication of Red Cloud's life is Jerry Lazar, *Red Cloud: Sioux War Chief* (New York: Chelsea House Publishers, 1995), one of the volumes in the North American Indians of Achievement series edited by W. David Baird.

Helpful in understanding Crazy Horse, one of Red Cloud's

major rivals for leadership among the Lakota Sioux, are Mari Sandoz, *Crazy Horse: The Strange Man of the Oglalas* (New York: Alfred A. Knopf, 1942; reprint, Lincoln: University of Nebraska Press, 1992), and Alvin M. Josephy, Jr., "Crazy Horse, Patriot of the Plains," a chapter in his *The Patriot Chiefs: A Chronicle of American Indian Resistance* (New York: Viking Press, 1961). The career of Sitting Bull, who grew increasingly antagonistic toward Red Cloud, is carefully analyzed in Robert M. Utley, *The Lance and the Shield: The Life and Times of Sitting Bull* (New York: Henry Holt and Co., 1993). The leadership of Red Cloud's rival Spotted Tail is detailed in George E. Hyde, *Spotted Tail's Folk: A History of the Brulé Sioux* (Norman: University of Oklahoma Press, 1961). Also focusing on rivalries among Lakota leaders is George E. Hyde, *A Sioux Chronicle* (Norman: University of Oklahoma Press, 1956). Brief biographical sketches about important Lakota Sioux are provided by Virginia Driving Hawk Sneve, *They Led a Nation* (Sioux Falls, S.D.: Brevet Press, 1975). A comparative analysis of Comanche Chief Quanah Parker with Red Cloud, Geronimo, and Chief Joseph in William T. Hagan, *Quanah Parker, Comanche Chief* (Norman: University of Oklahoma Press, 1993), puts Red Cloud's leadership role into an especially broad perspective.

Among the more helpful books about the Lakota Sioux is Royal B. Hassrick, *The Sioux: Life and Customs of a Warrior Society* (Norman: University of Oklahoma Press, 1964). Providing an understanding of the soul of the Lakota peoples is John G. Neihardt, *Black Elk Speaks: Being the Life Story of a Holy Man of the Oglala Sioux* (Lincoln: University of Nebraska Press, 1961). Focusing on the Oglala Sioux and their political and social institutions is Catherine Price, *The Oglala People, 1841–1879: A Political History* (Lincoln: University of Nebraska Press, 1996). Limited chronologically but a good study of the southern Lakotas is E. P. Wilson, "The Story of the Oglala and Brule Sioux in the Pine Ridge Country of Northwest Nebraska in the Middle Seventies," *Nebraska History: A Quarterly Magazine* 21

(October–December 1940): 259–74. Books that concentrate on other branches of the Sioux Nation include Roy V. Meyer, *History of the Santee Sioux: United States Indian Policy on Trial* (Lincoln: University of Nebraska Press, 1967), and Herbert T. Hoover, *Yankton Sioux* (New York: Chelsea House Publishers, 1985).

Studies that deal with Sioux allies on the Great Plains include the classic George B. Grinnell, *The Fighting Cheyennes*, 2nd ed. (Norman: University of Oklahoma Press, 1956), and Virginia C. Trenholm, *The Arapahoes, Our People* (Norman: University of Oklahoma Press, 1970). Those that focus on Sioux rivals include Keith W. Alger, *The Crow and the Eagle: A Tribal History from Lewis and Clark to Custer* (Caldwell, Idaho: Caxton Printers, 1993); Frederick E. Hoxie, *The Crows* (New York: Chelsea House Publisher, 1989); and George E. Hyde, *Pawnee Indians*, 3rd ed. (Norman: University of Oklahoma Press, 1974). An especially helpful analysis of other tribes in the region is John C. Ewers, *Indians of the Upper Missouri* (Norman: University of Oklahoma Press, 1968). A comparative study involving the Pawnees with two tribes outside the Great Plains is Richard White, *The Roots of Dependency: Subsistence, Environment, and Social Change among Choctaws, Pawnees, and Navajos* (Lincoln: University of Nebraska Press, 1983). White's environmental approach in Indian studies is demonstrated by his collaboration with Richard Cronon in "Indians on the Land," *American Heritage* 37 (August–September 1986): 18–25.

A comprehensive and still helpful Native American study is Clark Wissler, *North American Indians of the Plains* (New York: American Museum of Natural History, 1934). Benefiting from more recent scholarship are Harold E. Driver, *Indians of North America*, rev. ed. (Chicago: University of Chicago Press, 1969), and Wilcomb E. Washburn, *The Indians in America* (New York: Harper & Row, Publishers, 1975). Dated but still valuable is Warren K. Moorehead, *The American Indian in the United States, 1850–1914* (Andover, Mass.: Andover Press, 1914). Masterful because of the way it handles Indian-white relations is Robert M. Utley, *The Indian Frontier of the American West, 1846–1890* (Albuquerque: University of New Mexico Press, 1984).

Among the more comprehensive accounts of the Sioux migration from Minnesota to the Northern Plains are George E. Hyde, *Red Cloud's Folk*, and Richard White, "The Winning of the West: The Expansion of the Western Sioux in the Eighteenth and Nineteenth Century," *Journal of American History* 65 (September 1978): 314–43. Especially valuable because of their demographic approach are Harry Anderson, "An Investigation of the Early Bands of the Saone Group of Teton Sioux," *Journal of the Washington Academy of Sciences* 46 (March 1956): 87–94; James H. Howard, *The Dakota or Sioux Indians: A Study of Human Ecology*, Anthropological Papers No. 2 (Vermillion: Dakota Museum, University of South Dakota, 1966; reprint, Lincoln: J. & L. Reprint Co., 1980); and Kingsley M. Bray, "Teton Sioux Population History, 1655–1881," *Nebraska History* 75 (Summer 1994): 165–88.

Studies of the warfare waged by Red Cloud against the U.S. government include Grace Raymond Hebard and E. A. Brininstool, *The Bozeman Trail* (Cleveland: Arthur H. Clark Co., 1922; reprint, Lincoln: University of Nebraska Press, 1990), which focuses on Red Cloud's successful effort to close the Bozeman Trail. Other accounts of Red Cloud's War include Dee Brown, *Fort Phil Kearny: An American Saga* (New York: Putnam, 1962); John D. McDermott, "Pride of Arrogance: The Short and Controversial Life of William Judd Fetterman," *Annals of Wyoming* 63 (Spring 1991): 42–53; Elbert D. Belish, "American Horse (Wasechun-Tashunka): The Man Who Killed Fetterman," *Annals of Wyoming* 63 (Spring 1991): 54–67; Jerry Keenan, *The Wagon Box Fight*, 2nd ed. (Sheridan: Fort Phil Kearny/Bozeman Trail Association, 1990); and Jerry Keenan, "The Wagon Box Fight: Its Meaning and Place in History," *Montana: The Magazine of Western History* 41 (Spring 1992): 69–72. Also helpful in understanding the various aspects of this war to control the Powder River are Edward J. Hawken, "The Military Problem on the Powder River Road, 1865–1868" (master's thesis, University of California, 1938), and chapter 4 of Ralph K. Andrist, *The Long Death: The Last Days of the Plains Indians* (New York: Collier Books, 1969). For information about the Medicine Lodge Conference, one of two prompted by Red Cloud's War, see Douglas C. Jones, *The Treaty of Medicine Lodge: The Story of the Great Treaty Council As Told by Eyewitnesses* (Norman: University of Oklahoma Press, 1966).

Good accounts of the Battle of the Little Bighorn include John S. Gray, *Centennial Campaign: The Sioux War of 1876* (Fort Collins, Colo.: Old Army Press, 1976; reprint, Norman: University of Oklahoma Press, 1988), and the more recent James Welch with Paul Stekler, *Killing Custer: The Battle of the Little Bighorn and the Fate of the Plains Indians* (New York: W. W. Norton Co., 1994). Provocative because of the new archaeological evidence provided is Richard Allan Fox, Jr., *Archaeology, History, and Custer's Last Battle: The Little Bighorn Reexamined* (Norman: University of Oklahoma Press, 1993). For insights into the various interpretations of the battle, see David Fridtjof Halaas, "Reflections of a Theme: Indians, Custer, and History," *Colorado Heritage*, Spring 1994, pp. 38–44. Helpful in viewing the Sioux conflict from the army's perspective is Paul T. Hedren, *Fort Laramie in 1876: Chronicle of a Frontier Post at War* (Lincoln: University of Nebraska Press, 1988), and William Waddell, "The Military Relations between the Sioux Indians and the United States Government in the Dakota Territory, 1860–1899" (master's thesis, University of South Dakota, 1931). Used for information about the important forts during the Sioux wars is Robert W. Frazier, *Forts of the West: Military Forts and Presidios and Posts Commonly Called Forts West of the Mississippi River to 1898* (Norman: University of Oklahoma Press, 1965). Essential because of their accounts of the other battles of the Great Sioux War are Jerome A. Greene, ed., *Battles and Skirmishes of the Great Sioux War, 1876–1877: The*

Military View (Norman: University of Oklahoma Press, 1993), and Jerome A. Greene, ed., *Lakota and Cheyenne: Indian View of the Great Sioux War, 1876–1877* (Norman: University of Oklahoma Press, 1994). Shedding light on Crazy Horse's death after the Great Sioux War is Stephen E. Ambrose, *Crazy Horse and Custer: The Parallel Lives of Two American Warriors* (Garden City, N.Y.: Doubleday and Co., 1975), an account especially critical of Red Cloud's role in the event. Other accounts relevant to Crazy Horse's demise and its aftermath are Paul L. Hedren, "The Crazy Horse Medal: An Enigma from the Great Sioux War," *Nebraska History* 75 (Summer 1994): 195–98, and Thomas R. Buecker and R. Eli Paul, eds., *Crazy Horse Surrender Ledger* (Lincoln: Nebraska State Historical Society, 1994).

Studies dealing with the army's involvement in campaigns against the Sioux and other Plains tribes during the late nineteenth century abound. Given its broad focus, Robert M. Utley, *Frontier Regulars: The United States Army and the Indian, 1866–1891* (New York: Macmillan, 1973), is a good place to start. Sources devoted to army officers who had personal encounters with Red Cloud include Martin F. Schmitt, ed., *General George Crook: His Autobiography* (Norman: University of Oklahoma Press, 1946); Michael D. Pierce, *The Most Promising Young Officer: A Life of Ranald Slidell Mackenzie* (Norman: University of Oklahoma Press, 1993); and Charles M. Robinson, *Bad Hand: A Biography of General Ranald S. Mackenzie* (Austin, Texas: State House Press, 1993). Helpful in understanding the breakdown of the 1866 Fort Laramie conference and the conflict that followed are these accounts by Colonel Henry B. Carrington's two wives: Margaret Irwin Carrington, *Ab-sa-ra-ka, Home of the Crows* (Philadelphia: J. B. Lippincott Co., 1869; reprint, Lincoln: University of Nebraska Press, 1983), and Frances C. Carrington, *Army Life on the Plains* (Philadelphia: J. B. Lippincott Co., 1910). For the career of a frontier soldier that extended from the Civil War through the mid-1880s, see Richard N. Ellis, *General Pope and U.S. Indian Policy* (Al-

buquerque: University of New Mexico Press, 1970). Works
on Custer are legion, with Robert M. Utley, *Cavalier in
Buckskin: George Armstrong Custer and the Western Military
Frontier* (Norman: University of Oklahoma Press, 1988),
evaluating many of the interpretations of that officer's controversial career. Perhaps the most imaginative Custer study
is Evan S. Connell, *Son of the Morning Star* (New York:
Harper-Collins/Perennial Library, 1985). Studies devoted to
those generals who probably played the most prominent or
successful role in dealing with the Sioux are Robert G. At-
hearn, *William Tecumseh Sherman and the Settlement of the
West* (Norman: University of Oklahoma Press, 1956); Paul
Andrew Hutton, *Phil Sheridan and His Army* (Lincoln: University of Nebraska Press, 1985); Virginia Weisal Johnson,
The Unregimented General: A Biography of Nelson A. Miles
(Boston: Houghton Mifflin Co., 1962); Robert Wooster,
Nelson A. Miles and the Twilight of the Frontier Army (Lincoln: University of Nebraska Press, 1993); and Jerome A.
Greene, *Yellowstone Command: Colonel Nelson A. Miles and
the Great Sioux War, 1876–1877* (Lincoln: University of Nebraska Press, 1991). Focusing on the caliber of the officers
and men of the frontier army during the late nineteenth
century are Paul Andrew Hutton, ed., *Soldiers West: Biographies from the Military Frontier* (Lincoln: University of
Nebraska Press, 1987); Richard N. Ellis, "The Humanitarian Soldiers," *Journal of Arizona History* 10 (Summer 1969):
53–66; and Richard N. Ellis, "The Humanitarian Generals,"
Western Historical Quarterly 3 (April 1972): 169–78.
Secondary accounts dealing with the Oglalas at the Red Cloud
Agency in Nebraska include Charles W. Allen, "Red Cloud
and the U.S. Flag—Story of an Eye Witness as Told by
Major Charles W. Allen," *Nebraska History: A Quarterly
Magazine* 21 (October–December 1940): 293–304; Thomas
R. Buecker, "The Crazy Horse Surrender Ledger: A New
Source for Red Cloud Agency History," *Nebraska History*
75 (Summer 1994): 191–94; and Henry G. Waltman, "The
Subsistence Policy with Special Reference to the Red Cloud

and Spotted Tail Agencies" (master's thesis, University of Nebraska, 1962). An interesting but biased source for Red Cloud's early years at Pine Ridge and his famous feud with Indian agent Valentine T. McGillycuddy is Julia B. McGillycuddy, *McGillycuddy: A Biography of Dr. Valentine T. McGillycuddy, Agent* (Palo Alto: Stanford University Press, 1941). Much more friendly to Red Cloud is James H. Cook, *Fifty Years on the Old Frontier as Cowboy, Hunter, Guide, Scout, and Ranchman* (Norman: University of Oklahoma Press, 1957). Two accounts that illuminate Red Cloud's Washington visits are Katherine C. Turner, *Red Men Calling on the Great White Father* (Norman: University of Oklahoma Press, 1951), and Herman J. Viola, *Diplomats in Buckskins: A History of Indian Delegations in Washington City* (Washington, D.C.: Smithsonian Institution Press, 1981). For insights into the western attitude toward Red Cloud and the Lakota Sioux during both the prereservation and reservation years, see Howard R. Lamar, *Dakota Territory, 1861–1889* (New Haven: Yale University Press, 1956); James C. Olson, *History of Nebraska* (Lincoln: University of Nebraska Press, 1955); and T. A. Larson, *History of Wyoming*, 2nd ed. (Lincoln: University of Nebraska Press, 1978). For the eastern attitude, see Francis Paul Prucha, *American Indian Policy in Crisis: Christian Reformers and the Indian, 1865–1900* (Norman: University of Oklahoma Press, 1976), and William Thomas Hagan, *The Indian Rights Association: The Herbert Welch Years, 1882–1904* (Tucson: University of Arizona Press, 1985). Comprehensive in its treatment of Indian policy is Francis Paul Prucha, *The Great Father: The United States Government and the American Indian*, 2 vols. (Lincoln: University of Nebraska Press, 1984). Significant for its focus on often controversial institutions that influenced reservation life during the late nineteenth century is William T. Hagan, *Indian Police and Judges: Experiments in Acculturation and Control* (New Haven: Yale University Press, 1966). Henry E. Fritz, *The Movement for Indian Assimilation, 1860–1890* (Philadelphia: University of Pennsylvania Press,

1963), remains a valuable account of the Indian assimilation movement and its reformers. Accounts of the years at Pine Ridge before the Battle of Wounded Knee Creek which deal with the Dawes Act and the Sioux bills of 1888 and 1889 are D. S. Otis, *The Dawes Act and the Allotment of Indian Lands* (Norman: University of Oklahoma Press, 1973), and Wilcomb E. Washburn, *The Assault on Indian Tribalism: The General Allotment Act Law (Dawes Act) of 1887*, ed. Harold M. Hyman (Philadelphia: J. B. Lippincott, 1975). For information on an organization anxious to defend Lakota land rights during the late nineteenth century, see Jo Lea Wetherilt, "In Defense of 'Poor Lo': National Indian Defense Association and *Council Fire's* Advocacy for Sioux Land Rights," *South Dakota History* 24 (Fall–Winter 1994): 153–73. A good source on the Ghost Dance movement and the Battle of Wounded Knee Creek is Robert M. Utley, *The Last Days of the Sioux Nation* (New Haven: Yale University Press, 1963). Raymond J. DeMallie, "The Lakota Ghost Dance: An Ethnohistorical Account," *Pacific Historical Review* 51 (November 1982): 385–406, is especially helpful in presenting the Indian perspective for these Ghost Dances. For further background on the religious beliefs of the Sioux, see James R. Walker, *Lakota Belief and Ritual*, ed. Raymond J. DeMallie and Elaine A. Jahner (Lincoln: University of Nebraska Press, 1991), and Raymond J. DeMallie, *Sioux Indian Religion: Tradition and Innovations* (Norman: University of Oklahoma Press, 1987). Essential in understanding the Battle of Wounded Knee Creek because of its personal testimony is Donald F. Danker, ed., "Wounded Knee Interviews of Eli S. Ricker," *Nebraska History* 62 (Summer 1981): 151–243. Richard E. Jensen, R. Eli Paul, and John E. Carter, *Eyewitness at Wounded Knee* (Lincoln: University of Nebraska Press, 1991), provides yet another element in understanding this tragedy through its photographs and relevant text. Other recent studies include Jerry Green, "The Medals of Wounded Knee," *Nebraska History* 75 (Summer 1994): 200–208, and R.

Eli Paul, "Wounded Knee and the 'Collector of Curios,'" *Nebraska History* 75 (Summer 1994): 209–15. For the aftermath of Wounded Knee, see R. Eli Paul, "Dakota Resources: The Investigation of Special Agent Cooper and Property Damage Claims in the Winter of 1890–91," *South Dakota History* 24 (Fall–Winter 1994): 212–35. The still pending legal settlement over the Black Hills is the focus of Edward Lazarus, *Black Hills/White Justice* (New York: HarperCollins, 1991). To get a lively overview of the legal settlement of Indian land disputes, see Patricia Nelson Limerick, *The Legacy of Conquest: The Unbroken Past of the American West* (New York: W. W. Norton, 1987).

Index

driven from, 21, 25, 27; guerrilla
warfare, 93; hunting, 146; Red Cloud's
leadership in, 104; Sioux council
(1870), 138; traders, 126; U.S. peace
efforts in, 108, 115; winter encampment
(1867), 102
Powder River Road. *See* Bozeman Trail
Powell (rancher murdered by Sioux), 148
Powell, James W., 100, 112, 113
Pratt, Richard Henry, 227–28, 253–55
Pratt commission, 253–54, 263
Pratte, Cabanne & Company, 57
Pretty Bear, 156
Pretty Owl (wife of Red Cloud), 43, 44,
280, 287, 294
Price, Catherine, 35, 213
Price, Hiram, 234, 235
Proctor, Redfield, 274
Progressives, 227, 249, 258, 261, 291, 293;
Ghost Dance, 267, 281
Protestants, 228, 242
Pueblo Indians, 16
Pueblo Revolt (1680), 16
Pugh, Robert O., 250, 270
Pumpkin Buttes, Wyo., 86

Quakers, 242

Radical Republicans, 109
Railroad, transcontinental, 78, 114, 115,
117–18, 143; defense of, 88, 107, 108, 109
Ranches, attacks on, 79, 81
Randall, Todd, 163–64, 165, 243
Raw Hide Buttes, 141, 142, 145
Raw Hide Creek, 147
Reconstruction Era, 109, 114, 117
Red Cloud, 4–5; abduction by Two
Strike, 280, 281, 282; agency location
controversy, 141, 142, 143, 147, 148,
152, 153; aggressiveness, 38; Allison
commission meetings, 187–95; appear-
ance and charisma, 49; arrest and fine
(1894), 295–96; arrest and incarceration
(1882), 235; Augur's opinion of, 138;

autobiography, 31–34, 37, 44, 47, 48,
69, 293; birth date and place, 30–33;
Black Hills issue, 160, 185, 187, 206,
286, 297–98, 303; Bozeman Trail issue,
96, 98, 117, 285; Bull Bear–Old Smoke
quarrel, 58–60, 292–93; burning of
closed forts, 120; Catholicism, 268;
census controversy, 156, 157, 159, 160;
chieftaincy, 48–49, 73, 76, 221, 230,
297; children, 44; cholera remedy,
63; Christian missionary controversy,
229; compensation for damages to
house, 286, 289; compensation for
horses taken, 256, 289, 290; Cook,
letter to, 3–4, 28; coups, 41, 42, 294;
Crazy Horse marriage ruse, 77; Crazy
Horse's surrender and death, 210–16,
302; Crook's removal from leadership,
208–209; Crow wars, 73, 77; cruelty
and vengefulness, 45–48, 293; Dawes
committee, 239, 240; death of, 298;
diplomacy, 289, 301; early combat
experiences, 40–43; early life, 36–37,
39; eastern visits, (1870) 128–38, 296,
298, (1872) 149–50, (1875) 162–69,
(1877) 219–20, (1881) 231–32, (1885)
243–44, (1889) 256–57, (1897) 296;
Edmunds commission, 237, 238, 239;
education and training, 38–39; family,
33, 34, 39–40; Fetterman Massacre, 99,
101, 104; flagpole incident, 159; Fort
Laramie meetings, (1866) 89–93, 300,
302, (1867) 103, 104, 115, 117, (1868)
118–24, (1870) 140–42, (1871) 143–44;
Fort Laramie Treaty (1868), 123, 124,
125, 133, 137, 138, 285, 289, 291, 304; Fort
Laramie visits (1869–72), 126, 139, 147;
Fort Phil Kearny fight, 102–103; Ghost
Dance crisis, 266–69, 272–75, 277,
280–84, 286, 289, 304; government's
disenchantment with, 255, 256, 259,
260, 271, 274, 283, 284, 287, 300;
government's respect for, 249–50,
286, 289; Grattan affair, 68; guns and

DATE DUE